SME
TO

G000166006

SMEATON'S TOWER

Christopher Severn

SEAFARER BOOKS

© Christopher Severn 2005

Published by:
Seafarer Books
102 Redwald Road
Rendlesham
Woodbridge
Suffolk IP12 2TE
www.seafarerbooks.com

ISBN 0 9542750 9 8

British Library Cataloguing in Publication Data
Severn, Christopher
  Smeaton's Tower
  1.Smeaton, John, 1724-1792 2.Eddystone Lighthouse (England)
  - History
  I.Title
  627 .9'22'0916336

ISBN-10: 0954275098

Typesetting and design by Julie Rainford
Cover design by Louis Mackay
Illustrations by Christopher Severn
Copies of engravings from Smeaton's *Narrative* reproduced by kind permission of
Plymouth City Museum and Art Gallery

Printed in Finland by WS Bookwell OY

To John Smeaton FRS and the men of the Eddystone
Service who built a lighthouse in stone, fourteen miles
out to sea upon the Eddystone reef

IN SALUTEM OMNIUM – EDISTONE RESURGIT

Contents

Foreword

As the tide around the Eddystone Rocks flows and ebbs, the present lighthouse stands like a great sentinel of the high seas, a reminder perhaps of a time long gone, when the importance of this beacon was known throughout the world. Four famous lighthouses have stood upon the Eddystone reef, shining their light across the turbulent waters, offering a guiding hand to the mariner. All have been the subject of fascination and intrigue for centuries, each one bringing to the annals of history its own unique story. Standing tall for all to see, these mighty structures pay tribute to the men who built them. One such master builder was Yorkshireman John Smeaton, who would create the blueprint for future stone-built, wave-washed lighthouses. His was the first, an architectural breakthrough and the supreme *pharos* that everyone else would copy.

It is therefore appropriate that the gifted author Christopher Severn has written his book on *Smeaton's Tower*, offering not only a full and electrifying account of the building of the lighthouse itself but also a splendid tale of daring and adventure. Through careful historical research Chris has produced a remarkable story, bringing to life the individuals who gave themselves to this great service. Indeed, through the author's own fantastic illustrations and lively text, the reader is taken on an incredible journey, like the crashing of the waves and movement of the great sea around the tower itself, where white water churns and falls about the reef in abundance.

Through his gripping book, we follow several strong individuals who were involved with the process of erecting a revolutionary new concept, a stone building attached like a great oak tree to a tiny rock far out at sea. With intense drama, the tale quickens, heroes and villains emerge, and the picture widens as a story within a story is played out – to the very end. Chris has seamlessly dovetailed together a timeline of events as the key players, Smeaton, Jessop, Hill, Colquhoun, Bowden and Trehearne increase the tempo of every scene. The tension heightens, building keenly to the very end, where finally the 'secret of the stones' is revealed.

Mike Palmer

Preface

John Smeaton (1724–1792) is known as the father of civil engineering for his pioneering work in the field, and the Eddystone Lighthouse is generally acknowledged to be his greatest achievement in a long and illustrious career.

This book tells the story of the building of the third Eddystone Lighthouse, on the infamous reef of red rocks, fourteen miles out to sea off Plymouth, during the years 1756 to 1759.

It is a story of heroism, daring and courage, telling of a truly remarkable feat of engineering in an age of sail and manpower. Until then, two earlier towers had stood upon the rock. Henry Winstanley's (first completed in 1698) was ingenious and daring, but within a few years it was swept away in one night in November 1703, along with the keepers and Winstanley himself. John Rudyerd's light withstood the test of time, but it too was destroyed almost overnight following a catastrophic fire in December 1755. The flames that ignited the lantern crawled down the pitched boards and devoured the timber structure, leaving nothing behind except the iron fixing straps, embedded in the rock.

Smeaton recognised many functional attributes in Rudyerd's design, but he soon came to the conclusion that his tower would be built in stone. Yet Rudyerd's had proved itself capable of withstanding the sea and the elements. It had lasted fifty years, and there were many who believed that 'only Wood shall last upon the Edystone', and that Smeaton's masonry tower would be 'overset' in the greatest of storms. Despite this, Smeaton strove to construct an edifice that would prove them wrong and last beyond the age he lived in:

> *My ideas of what its duration and continued existence ought to be, were not confined within the boundary of an Age or two, but extended themselves to look towards a possible Perpetuity.*

He realised his dream, for the tower still stands, re-erected on Plymouth Hoe by public subscription in the nineteenth century – but more than this, it would be the inspiration and design prototype for all the sea-girt, offshore lighthouses that followed.

John Smeaton left a double legacy – not only his lighthouse but also his book, published in 1791, *A Narrative of the Building and a Description of the Construction of the Edystone Lighthouse with Stone*. In the winter of 1783–84 Smeaton declined new commissions and began writing 'his works'. These he intended would 'do more towards the forming of Civil Engineers in the future generation'. He laboured on the book for many years, even saying that it caused him greater effort than the building of the house itself, but at last it was completed, a year before his death. It was a monumental work, unique in that the designer tells in his own words of how he made his building.

My story relies upon Smeaton's, and all the details of how the lighthouse was built, as well as many quotations, are taken directly from his journals and the *Narrative*. I have also incorporated some fictional characters and events that *might* have occurred at the time. These include the story of the fugitive and the mystery surrounding his disappearance upon the Eddystone. Among the fictional characters are:

John Trehearne – a fugitive who has deserted HMS *Dart* and who gains employment in the Eddystone service.

Robert Appleford – Trehearne's friend and fellow seaman, press-ganged into service aboard the *Dart*.

Alice Appleford – widow of Robert Appleford.

Squire Vasey and Mrs Vasey – Alice's parents.

Verity Vasey – Alice's younger sister.

Lieutenant Colquhoun – First Lieutenant of HMS *Dart*.

Midshipman Baines.

The captain and crew of the *Dart*.

Joshua Hawkins – a Cornish 'tinner' in the Eddystone service, William Hill's cousin.

Reverend Allsop – the new incumbent of Lostwithiel parish church.

The fictional characters bear no intended likeness to any person, living or dead.

There are also numerous historical characters who we know were part of the Eddystone story:

Henry Hall (also known as Richard Hall) was the 84-year-old light-keeper who discovered and fought the blaze in Rudyerd's lighthouse in the early hours of 2nd December 1755. He and his fellow keepers were rescued from a cave in the rock by a boat sent out from Cawsand. Hall died on 16th December 1755, and the lead that killed him is now in the collection of the National Museums of Scotland.

Thomas Strout and Roger Short were the other light-keepers on duty on the night of the fire.

Dr Edmund Spry treated Henry Hall's wounds at home in Stonehouse and performed the autopsy. Subsequently Dr Spry indulged in a series of experiments on animals to ascertain their resistance to ingested lead, and presented his findings to the Royal Society in the name of medical science.

John Bowden was one of the seamen in the Eddystone service, and Master of the *Weston*. Smeaton refers to him with gratitude for his seamanship and courage in saving the *Neptune* from shipwreck on the Cornish coast.

Josias Jessop (?1710–1761) was the Surveyor of the Eddystone Lighthouse, who became Smeaton's loyal assistant, colleague and friend during the rebuilding of the lighthouse.

William Jessop (1745–1814) was Josias's son, whom Smeaton later took on as his ward and apprentice, and who by 1792 had become an eminent engineer in his own right.

William Hill was a foreman in the Eddystone service, dismissed by Smeaton for his tendency to 'mutiny and combination'.

Thomas Richardson was a master mason from Plymouth and also a foreman in the Eddystone service.

Matthew Box was a moorstone mason and quarry owner at Constantine, in the county of Cornwall.

Walter and Peter Treleven were moorstone masons and quarry owners at Lanlivery, Cornwall.

William Tyrrell was a stonemason and foreman who came from Portland to supervise the finishing of the rough-hewn blocks of Portland stone used in the tower's internal construction.

Roger Cornthwaite was one of the stonemasons in the Eddystone service.

Samuel Medling was a seaman and Master of the *Assistant*.

Richard Edgcumbe, 1st Baron Edgcumbe (1680–1758), was succeeded by his son, Richard Edgcumbe, 2nd Baron (1716–1761).

HRH Prince Edward (1739–1767) was the son of Frederick, Prince of Wales (and younger brother of the future King George III). He became Duke of York in 1760. Smeaton presented the models and drawings of his lighthouse to the Prince at Mount Edgecumbe on 19th July 1759.

Sir Joshua Reynolds, RA (1723–1792) was a native of Plymouth (Plympton). His father was a close friend of the Mudges, and Joshua a school-fellow of John Mudge (below).

Benjamin Franklin (1706–1790), the American printer, scientist and statesman, achieved international fame as a result of his experiments with lightning in the early 1750s. Smeaton realised the significance of Franklin's discoveries, and his Eddystone Lighthouse was one of the first buildings in Britain to have a lightning conductor.

Benjamin Wilson was a friend of Smeaton's who had once helped him to make equipment for his electrical experiments. Smeaton described him later as an 'eminent painter in Great Queen Street'. He seemed to be the one person in London who knew of Smeaton's exact whereabouts in January 1757.

William Cookworthy (1705–1780) was a Quaker chemist with whom Smeaton lodged during his time in Plymouth. Cookworthy, a skilled mineralogist, discovered the use of Cornish china clay for the making of English porcelain and began to manufacture his 'Plymouth china' during the 1760s. Amongst his other accomplishments he is acknowledged by Smeaton for his help and guidance in the experiments to produce a 'water cement'. This was the highly effective 'Eddystone mortar', made of hydraulic lime and pozzolan, that was used in the construction to withstand the wash of the sea.

John Mudge, MD FRS (1721–1793) was a friend and contemporary of Smeaton, who shared his interest in the sciences and in the making of 'philosophical' instruments. Dr Mudge was a native of Plymouth, where his father the Reverend Zachariah was vicar of St Andrew's.

The Reverend Zachariah Mudge (1694–1769) accompanied Smeaton in a passage to the tower to give a hymn of praise for the completion of the work – *Laus Deo*. Zachariah Mudge was a lifelong friend of the Reverend Samuel Reynolds, father of the artist Sir Joshua Reynolds.

Robert Weston was the representative (and major shareholder) for the Eddystone Proprietors. Robert Weston was responsible for approaching the Royal Society in his search to find a man of 'natural genius' to build the new lighthouse.

George Parker, Earl of Macclesfield (?1697–1764) was President of the Royal Society at the time of Smeaton's appointment to rebuild the Eddystone Lighthouse.

Anne Jenkinson (died 1784), John Smeaton's wife, hailed from York. They married on 7th June 1756 and had three daughters, Hannah (born in 1757), Ann (1759) and Mary (1761).

After her mother's death Mary Smeaton and her sister Ann kept house for their father. Hannah had died in childhood. Mary was an accomplished artist. She also wrote memoirs describing her father and became the wife of Jeremiah Dixon, a local magistrate who served as Mayor of Leeds. Mary Dixon founded a free-school for girls at Staveley.

The first three keepers to serve in Smeaton's Eddystone Lighthouse were Henry Edwards, Henry Carter and John Hatherley, the last-named coming in to replace John Michell.

In the fictional story the fugitive John Trehearne and the seaman hero John Bowden are one and the same. Trehearne has concealed his identity to avoid detection and to put his past behind him. But events collude to reveal him to his pursuers, and following failed attempts, first to impress him, then to cause his death, they eventually seek him out in a desperate chase that ends in the tower itself. His extraordinary disappearance there takes him beyond his enemies' reach. The 'secret of the tower' is a fiction, but it is made possible by the tower's unique method of construction.

John Smeaton defended the men in the Eddystone service from the marauding naval press gangs. He acted to safeguard them wherever possible from undue peril and furnished them with a written contract of employment that included fair terms and conditions that recognised the dangers of the 'outwork' at sea. Perhaps he would have helped the fugitive to seek refuge and justice? It's just possible that he did. But my invention is only a small fragment of the story. All the rest is true.

Christopher Severn
February 2005

Spelling

In the following pages the spelling of some of the names, and of a few other words, follows Smeaton's eighteenth-century version – including Edystone (modern spelling is Eddystone), Edgecombe (Edgcumbe), Polparra (Polperro).

Acknowledgements

I would like to thank several people for their kind help with this book. First, Mike Palmer, whose book *Eddystone: The Finger of Light* I discovered on a visit to Plymouth, and then (following clues therein) whom I called upon unannounced to introduce myself and show him the beginnings of a manuscript. I thank him for his generous and unstinting advice and encouragement to me at all times.

I am indebted to Frans Nicholas, and Frans Nicholas Architects, for involving me in *Smeaton's Tower*, a project to conserve, reinstate, and re-present the building as it now stands upon the Hoe. I thank Frans for impressing upon me the importance of the time spent in research, to inform the conservation work. I soon realised that this was more than a famous lighthouse with a long working history. It was, I discovered, the prototype for all the wave-washed towers that followed. Mostly I thank him now for presenting me with his photographic record of Smeaton's *Narrative*. Those photos held in miniature the giant pages of Smeaton's 1791 original. I scanned each with a magnifying glass, searching for clues of the construction details and methods I needed to replicate in my drawings and specification. It was all here, but so was the epic story of the tower, the nights spent at sea 'lying on the oars', unable to land, the shipwrecks and press gangs, all summed up in Smeaton's own words 'to proceed until there is something to stop us'. Frans pointed out the unique significance of this work – a design prototype so thoroughly documented by its author. I am also grateful to Acanthus Holden Architects for their help and encouragement in the latter stages

Thanks are due to Nigel Overton, Maritime Officer, and to Nicola Moyle and staff at Plymouth City Museums and Art Gallery, for their assistance and for providing supporting material – including an important link with William Cookworthy. I also thank Eilis Scott and Andrew Gater of Plymouth City Council for their help.

The curator and staff of Armley Mills industrial museum in Leeds, and others in Leeds City Council, provided me with essential research material. I thank them, and also Bob Lawrence of the East Leeds History and Archaeology Society at East Leeds Heritage Centre, for further sources pertaining to Smeaton's life and works, and for local historical background material.

I would like to extend thanks to Patricia Eve of Seafarer Books, and to Hugh Brazier, Louis Mackay and Julie Rainford, who have made this book possible.

My thanks to my parents, William and Kathleen Evans, for everything. Finally – and most of all – my thanks to my wife Rosalind and to Katy and Sabrina for their patience, forbearance and kindness throughout.

1

Rudyerd's light: the catastrophe

Looking into THE LANTERN of a sea-swept lighthouse, at night

With every passing minute, the twenty-four candles that burn in their cups on the chandelier of the famous wooden lighthouse grow dimmer and dimmer. The tall lantern room appears to fill with luminous smog as wreaths of curling yellow smoke descend from top to bottom. From a seabird's view, circling high above the sea, the lantern now appears like a vessel filled with a glowing opaque gas. Inside, through the glass casements in each facet of the wooden lantern, the silhouette of a man can be seen. He stands within the octagon fumbling about in the smog. His arms gesture wildly and he throws his hands to his head – then, covering his face with a kerchief, he makes his way a few short steps to the door and breaks out onto the balcony. Instantly, a dull blast follows as the smouldering timbers of the cupola burst into flames, assisted by the cold night air.

It was two o'clock in the morning of 2nd December 1755 when the light-keeper on watch in the Edystone Lighthouse prepared to climb the ladder from the living room and enter the lantern to snuff the candles. This was Henry Hall's watch, and he went about his business in the usual way, as he had done for as many years as he cared to remember. At eighty-four years old he was the oldest and longest-serving light-keeper. Indeed he often mused on the remarks of his kin in Stonehouse, that *he* was around when Mr Rudyerd himself first exhibited a light in the wooden tower all those years ago, and he was certainly old enough to remember that dreadful night in November 1703 when the Great Tempest swept up the Channel from Biscay destroying countless great ships and buildings in one night, and took with it every single trace of the magnificent edifice built there just a few years before by Mr Henry Winstanley.

He had once seen Mr Winstanley in the dockyard admiring the magnificent craftsmanship in the great finials of ornamental ironwork for his new lighthouse, the first upon the Edystone. He was a fine, jovial gentleman, larger than life, and not the sort you might expect to be involved with maritime affairs. Henry had seen his lighthouse too, outward bound or returning home to Plymouth as a young seaman. But it wasn't there very long: the tempest took it away in one night – and with all hands. Henry crossed himself. The funny thing was, he could remember Winstanley, that day in the dockyard, saying that his greatest wish was to be within his building in the greatest of all storms – such a man he was! He was the bravest of men – why, had *he* not *himself* sailed out to the house with his men, in the onset of bad weather, only a few days before the end to direct the necessary repairs? There he would remain, as freshening gales blew up into in the greatest of all storms ever known on our coast.

Hall ruminated over the legend of the man and his crew who, along with the light-keepers, were all lost in the seas about the Edystone, and how his building was toppled by the mountainous seas and all was gone from there by daybreak. He still recalled how strange it had appeared afterward, a mere rock in the great expanse of the Channel, suddenly bereft of its magnificent crown. Yet it belied the great reef lying all about, on which so many ships had foundered.

Two o'clock – it was time to get on and trim the candles. He made his way up the ladder and pushed the trapdoor open above his head. Easing himself up through the hatch, Hall was suddenly aware that all was not well. He smelt the familiar but terrifying smell of tinder burning. Looking up, he could hardly make out the candles in the chandelier above him. Wisps of smoke wreathed down about his head and shoulders, almost to the floor, and the smog grew thicker and murkier above him so that it was impossible to see the cupola ceiling, and the lights were now so shrouded in smoke that they gave a strange milky glow that seemed to merge all into one.

'Oh, Lord God Almighty help us!' he said to himself.

Henry covered his face with a handkerchief and climbed up into the room. He made his way to the door to the balcony and, throwing it open, staggered outside. As he did so, he felt a great draught of cold air rush in, and a fireball immediately erupted behind him inside the cupola roof. He was thrown forward, almost tripping over the sill, and caught hold of the balcony railing outside.

The timber ceiling, which must have been smouldering for hours, starved of air, now suddenly ignited, and within minutes the fire seemed to take hold of the whole roof. Flames licked over the cupola and soon an intense heat was shattering some of the uppermost window panes, the new air feeding the hungry fire. He was suddenly terrified.

'Help below! We are on fire! For God's sake, awake!' Henry Hall was horrified at the speed and fury of the blaze and he made strenuous efforts to raise the alarm and get his companions to come to his aid. He leant out from the balcony stanchion and called down to the open port-lid of the bedroom, two floors below.

'Awake! Wake up, Thomas, Roger, Fire! We are on fire! Awake!'

He was met with voices from below.

'Awake? We are awake!'

There were bursts of raucous laughter as if this was the funniest thing.

'Oh, Lord God! The fools are drunk!' Hall muttered, and he leaned over the railing again as far as he was able, and put his hands to his mouth to hail them. 'Roger, Thomas, awake! Fire! Fire!'

By now the heat was so intense that it took all his strength and courage to step back inside the lantern room. The room was small – perhaps eight feet across from one side of the octagon to the other, but more than twice as high. He made his way around the trapdoor to a tub of water, grabbed the leather bucket kept there for such an emergency, plunged it into the water and stepped outside again to throw the water up onto the lead sheet cladding of the cupola.

Flames licked high into the chill night air, throwing an eerie glow onto the balcony and the ancient figure of Hall standing there. He called again for help below and heard the voice of Thomas Strout reply.

'Coming, Henry, coming!' There were further cries and whoops of laughter as another voice mimicked his, in a high-pitched squeak, 'Coming, Mr Hall, coming!'

Again and again the ancient keeper returned inside to the tub of water, filled his bucket, and attempted to quench the flames by repeatedly throwing the water up onto the lead cladding. The fire consumed the lantern interior, its light reflected in the old man's face. He was exhausted, but until the others came he would have to go on fighting the blaze. Without he shivered in the cold night air of mid-winter, but inside the lantern had become a crucible. He coughed smoke, and sweat beaded into rivulets that ran down the ancient leathery skin of his face and neck. He stripped his shirt, revealing a pale, almost skeletal figure – like a caricature in the broadsheets. Again he drew water from the tub and headed to the open door, his stooped frame silhouetted in the lantern doorway. It was a pathetic sight, a single old man fighting the forces of nature. By now he was so exhausted that he could hardly straighten himself to cast the water aloft – but sheer willpower and his determined constitution lent him the strength to continue. Half an hour had passed since Henry discovered the fire, and still he remained alone.

Henry alone fully appreciated their predicament. Flames licked upward, escaping from the confines of the lantern into the night sky, and were reflected in the turbulent seas of the reef some eighty feet below the balcony he stood on. In the light cast upon the tower, he saw the shape of its tapered circular column, all of wooden construction. Henry knew that the smooth outer cladding of vertical boards, caulked with oakum and covered in pitch, would be easily ignited from falling embers. The windows, hung with shutters (port-lids, he called them), were all closed except one, fitting flush with the surrounding walls and giving the effect of a neat, flush and simple design. It was a sound design to keep out the winter storms, he thought, but not this – not fire.

Unlike Winstanley's lighthouse, Mr Rudyerd's conical building was based on the smooth lines and materials of a ship. There were no projecting features or ornaments in the functional design that the seas might exert a destructive force upon. Rudyerd's design had proved itself more than capable of withstanding the heaviest seas. The smooth tapered column was capped by a circular balcony that ran around an octagonal timber-built lantern, giving the keepers external access to the lantern windows. But because the house was constructed in timber that was constantly washed by seas, it needed frequent and numerous repairs.

During the forty-nine years of its reign upon the Rock, many visits had been made by the surveyor and his men to cut away the rotted pieces of the main frame and scarf in new timbers in their place. Great timbers running from its base to the top of the column were jointed together in stages at the floors and in the lower base the whole was consolidated with solid courses of granite ballast laid between great baulks of laminated timbers. This gave it the necessary and sufficient dead weight to resist being over-toppled, a lesson that had been learned from Mr Winstanley's building. Now on the eve of its half-century, the tower had developed a distinct lean that gave it an odd, somewhat quirky appearance. One of the characteristics of the design was that the tower *moved* when it was struck by the largest waves. Mr Rudyerd had fixed the great timber frame by means of iron straps or 'branches' that were leaded into sockets cut in the rock. The continual action of the sea upon its sides rocked the frame, and the feet of the timber uprights (in their strap fixings) had become rounded against the hard rock bearing. In attempting to remedy this and to replace one of the excessively worn feet, a new upright had been scarfed into the base, but the great difficulty was to accurately fit and set the new timber within the existing framework. Consequently the replacement 'leg' could not be brought to level and the tower assumed its now familiar listing toward the western side. Yet it remained serviceable. Who would have thought it would prove so vulnerable to an element other than wind and water?

Night breezes coaxed the flames, and the lantern began to

resemble a great incandescent lamp, the wooden sashes leaking thick smoke through which the flames leapt skyward. The sound of breaking glass could now be heard at frequent intervals. Once again Henry appeared in the small doorway. Smoke escaped from under the door lintel into the night air as he prepared to throw another pail of water aloft onto the roof. Just as he did so he heard slurred voices, louder now, from the room below.

'What is it, Henry, what's the matter?

'Aye, on my oath,' added the second, and there was more laughter.

'Come quickly, my strength fails me, we are ablaze, the house is on fire!'

The head of Thomas Strout appeared in the manhole. Seeing the blaze sobered him at once. In an instant he was out onto the floor, on his hands and knees. For a second he stared upward in terror through the smoke, and raising his arm to protect his eyes he scrambled to the water butt. He pulled his nightshirt up to mask his face and snatched the second bucket from the wall hook. Throwing it in, he climbed up the side, and discovering that there was very little water remaining, he turned to Hall.

'The water is almost gone!'

It had been nearly three quarters of an hour since the fire was first discovered, and as Thomas panicked, Henry Hall mustered his remaining strength to throw more water aloft.

'Thomas! Fetch more buckets and ropes, we can draw water from the sea below whilst I ...'

As he spoke, pieces of burning timber and debris fell and shattered on the floor about them. The third keeper, looking up through the manhole, retreated back down into the room beneath at the sight of the falling timber and flung a gin bottle out of the window port. Sparks and flaming shards fell through into the room below and he set to extinguishing them by stamping wildly on the pieces. Casting around him he saw a kettle of water by the stove and taking this he tipped the water onto the smouldering fragments. A cloud of steam arose and merged into the smoke, now billowing downwards through the hole in the ceiling. Then a hot iron strap fell through, narrowly missing his face and hands.

'Lord God help us – are we to die here tonight?' he cried out loud.

Thomas shouted down for him to fetch the longest length of rope.

'Hurry, we need to draw more water from the sea below.'

Lifting the lantern from the ceiling, he made his way down the ladders through the bedroom and into the storeroom. He searched and cursed until at last he saw the rope hung behind some casks. Placing the coil of rope over his shoulder, he climbed back up through the floors until he reached the lantern steps. The sound of the roaring fire filled his ears and he could barely hear Thomas speak, as he reached down and took the rope from him.

'Thanks, Roger. God knows, I never wished for a storm before now, but I pray that He delivers one tonight!' As he spoke, the charred ceiling began to collapse. The fire had consumed the tinder-dry frame and ceiling, and intense heat was melting the leadwork above. Turning, he saw Henry make ready to heave more water up into the cupola. His face was upturned as he bent and swung the bucket aloft. In the same moment the timber ceiling gave way and a deluge of molten lead poured in. Thomas instinctively held the rope aloft and covered his head to protect himself. He was unharmed but Hall was spattered by the torrent of molten lead. It fell on his head, face and shoulders; burning the bare skin on his neck. As he looked up, breathing heavily, some lead plummeted into his open mouth. He gasped, choked, then fell to the floor clutching his chest.

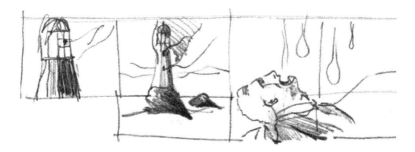

For an instant Thomas froze with fear, then, avoiding the burning debris and hot lead, he put his arms around Henry, raised his limp body, and lifted him onto the edge of the manhole. He was still conscious.

'I am burned, God Almighty, I've swallowed lead. It burns inside me, oh Jesus!' he moaned.

25

'Roger, help me to get him below. It's no use here, we cannot put the fire out – it has taken hold!'

Thomas Strout eased Henry down through the opening into the arms of the third keeper. Roger Short laid him down on the circular floor of the living room.

'Get below before we too are come to harm,' he called out.

Strout was already descending the ladder, closing the trap door behind him not a moment too soon. Debris and spatterings of viscous hot lead continued to drop onto the floor above them. He had had the presence of mind to bring with him one of the leather buckets containing the last of the water and he used it to dampen Hall's brow and to apply cooling rags to his burned skin. The sound of the fire raged overhead. They tended to the old man's wounds and tried their best to make him as comfortable as they possibly could. He gasped that he felt a violent pain in his chest and stomach and insisted that he had swallowed a quantity of lead.

'I feel it, the lead; it burns inside me.'

Strout lifted Hall's head and supported his neck to drink the gin.

'Here, drink this; it will ease your pain.' Thomas managed to get nearly a pint of gin down into the old man before he coughed violently and became unconscious.

The third keeper leaned out of a window, throwing open the port-lid, and looked up, craning his neck to see the balcony above. 'What shall we do, Thomas? The fire is beyond quenching, it roars above us.'

Thomas struggled to think, but outwardly calm he replied, 'We can stay here until the smoke forces us to go below. As long as we two stay alert we can shelter inside until morning.'

Henry Hall groaned, and coughed himself semi-conscious. Strout gestured to the bed blankets.

'Here, make him as comfortable as you can – we have a good supply of strong liquor. I have given him enough gin to float the lead back up, if it does lie in his belly! He is insensible.'

Roger Short held on dearly to this. There was still a ray of hope, even in their predicament.

'God willing, if the wind drops, then the sea breaking over the rock may yet put out the blaze.'

'It may yet,' Thomas reflected. He prayed under his breath for help from the Almighty. 'But since there's no more we can do up above, we may as well make ourselves as comfortable as we can. But we shall not sleep,' he warned.

Short went below for blankets, candles (there were plenty in the store) and some victuals. He also brought up the remainder of the gin. It was the beginning of a long, dark and terrifying ordeal until the dawn. Would someone come for them then? The thought preyed on both their minds through the hours of darkness. Smoke, falling embers and the thud of hot irons falling upon the floor over their heads forced them to retreat yet further, into the room below. A loud crash signalled the collapse of the chandelier onto the lantern floor. Roger jumped up from his makeshift bed and opened the nearest window. He pushed up the sash, wedged it open and took hold of the stay to throw open the wooden port. The iron stay burned his hand.

'God's teeth!' he cursed, picking up a blanket to wrap around his hand. The shutter had definitely jammed, and it took all his force to fling it open. Suddenly it released and flew back on its hinges. The momentum carried him forward through the opening, and he leant hard upon the sill. Acrid smoke and flames were all about him, the coating of tar pitch hissing and crackling in the heat. He let out a scream and instantly recoiled into the room. The flames had singed his face, eyebrows and beard. Thomas threw him one of the dampened cloths, which he caught and pressed to his face. Seeing the flames licking in at the porthole, he wrapped the blanket around his hand and arm once more, reached out for the stay, and pulled with all his might. The shutter swung around on its hinges and slammed shut.

The room grew noticeably warmer. The port-lids, made of two thicknesses of 'double planking' criss-crossed and clinked together, held firm, proving to be smoke- and fire-proof, and almost as sound as the walls they sealed against. The flames travelled downwards, creeping over the pitch-coat that was payed over the planking of the sea-washed tower. The whole house was turning into a giant torch, like a Roman candle at some great display of fireworks. The men within looked at each other in the dim light of their candles and knew they might not see daylight again.

'We had better get down to the store,' said Thomas Strout quietly.

'Aye,' agreed the other.

They gathered up their bedding and any items of use and took them below. The old man was lowered down through the manhole and laid in the cot bed. He groaned and cried out, but without waking. Roger nursed a gin bottle, carefully placing it in his coat pocket, and slowly descended the ladder before closing the hatch above him

The interior filled with smoke as the flames took an even greater hold and roared above them. The keepers lay terrified. They could do nothing now but retreat, whilst outside the flames crept slowly down the pitched wooden cladding. The tower burned in the night like the wick of a huge incandescent lamp. About six o'clock in the morning (although they had lost track of time, it still being very dark) they heard the terrible sound of crashing timbers as the upper structure collapsed onto the floor above them.

'Join me in a glass, Thomas. I wish to die dead drunk tonight, if it be God's will – and wake up sober in our Father's House.' The third and junior keeper was drunk. He sat down deliberately on the opposite cot and began to cry. Thomas Strout was tired and annoyed with him, but he tried not to show it, or his fear for their lives. He leaned over, laid a comforting hand on his shoulder and eased the flask from Roger's grip.

'No, not now. It won't come to that if we keep our heads and our resolve. Besides, we need all the gin to keep the old man out for the night. Perhaps none of this would have happened if we had answered his cries sooner, and for that I blame the strong liquor. We drank too much last night.'

Short breathed a deep sigh, to compose himself. 'Then, if we live, not a word of our night's drinking must get out. Henry need not know any of it. He spoke to me but there was no telling how much gin I had stowed.

'He knows it already,' Thomas replied dryly.

'They'll be looking for someone to blame for this. Oh! I know not the better alternative, whether to perish here, or be tried and hung for our drunken negligence at home.' The younger keeper broke down again and put his head in his hands. His shoulders gave great heaves as he sobbed aloud.

Strout was at the end of his patience and became suddenly fierce.

'Stop mewling, or I'll do the hanging for you!' – pointing to the main beam in the low ceiling above – 'and from that ceiling beam ere it gives way to the blaze above our heads! This is an act of God, we cannot be held accountable. God's will be done!'

This notion did something to alleviate the younger keeper's anxiety and he agreed that none of this was their fault.

'Amen – please let me drink to that, for I am afraid, more than ever in my life before!'

Strout gave in to his pleading and poured them both a full glass of gin. In an effort to make light of their circumstances, he gave a toast to all who had gone before on the Edystone.

'Three cheers for the Edystone Light – hip, hip, hooray – hip, hip, hooray – hip, hip, hooray – and long may she be remembered!'

Outside, the stricken tower burned incandescent, with flames leaping skyward. It was the early hours of the morning, and the midwinter dawn was still some hours away. The flames cast an eerie glow high above the Edystone Rocks. Another catastrophe was unfolding as it had done in the night of 26th November 1703, more than fifty years before. Then the first lighthouse – Mr Winstanley's – was destroyed by tempest. Now the second – Mr Rudyerd's – had succumbed in its turn to fire.

The news of the catastrophe reached Plymouth from Rame later that morning. From their vantage point on the Hoe, high up on the ramparts within the Citadel, the coastguard watch observed the lighthouse on fire.

The two men on watch trained their telescope onto the Edystone and the rescue taking place there. A column of smoke rose high into the sky above and was visible to the discerning naked eye.

'Aha,' one of the men exclaimed as he studied the view through the eyepiece. 'I see one of his Majesty's ships, looks like a sloop, and in full sail, Mr Daniels.' Into his line of sight sailed a sloop from Admiral West's fleet in the Sound. He motioned to the eyepiece for his colleague to view the developments.

The second watchman raised the telescope to his eye to view the vessel. He watched silently for a few moments and began to report quietly.

'I can see the contraption for fighting the fire, in the launch. They say 'tis one of those engines. Don't see how anything can stop the fire now, only the sea itself.'

The first watchman took a smaller spyglass from his pocket and opened it to look at the sloop; he had heard that the surveyor, Mr Jessop, had gone on board to take part in the rescue.

'Mr Jessop sails on board. He'll not be enjoying this trip.'

'Who's he?' asked Daniels without taking his eye from the telescope, which was set up on a wooden tripod behind the massive stone parapet of the fort. The other now leaned on the wall to steady his arm.

'Not heard of Josias Jessop, Surveyor for the Edystone Light, Mr Daniels?' He turned to look at the other man in mock surprise, and continued. 'I remember him when he was a shipwright in the dockyard. A quarterman he was. That was a few years back. He got appointed when the old surveyor passed on. He's been patching and mending the timbers for years since ... Worm gets in 'em so I'm told.' He paused and half closed his eyes to remember something of the details.

'He had a job of it I recall, to direct the repair work after the storm in '44. They said you could see right into one of lower rooms where the uprights had been torn away!' Mr Daniels was scanning the horizon and swung the telescope back to the lighthouse once again.

'I expect 'twill need a little more than a patch this time if that cloud is anything to go by. I can see nothing of the tower above the rock – and the lower part's lost in a thick smog.'

The sloop had sailed out of the Sound on the morning of 2nd December, and was making a swift passage to the Edystone Reef. Mr Jessop, the Surveyor for the Lighthouse, had been woken in the small hours. A naval messenger was sent by Admiral West to report to him the news from Rame, brought to Plymouth in the night. Dressing as quickly as he could, he had gone with the messenger straight to the King's Dockyard. All was in a state of action as the crew prepared to slip anchor and were busying themselves with raising the launch onto the main deck. On board was a mechanical pump that was driven by the new steam power. Jessop had studied it curiously during the short passage to the sloop, and had he not been so preoccupied with thoughts of the emergency he would have taken more interest in it, never having seen such a thing before.

On reaching the Edystone, the ship's crew set down the launch and a gallant attempt was made to fight the blaze. Mr Jessop watched the oarsmen in the launch steer their way into the channel known as the Gut, almost to be dashed upon the reef when a great wave lifted their boat onto the House Rock, until a second carried them off again. The launch was unscathed and the attempt to quench the sides continued until the jet of water suddenly stopped – the hosepipe becoming detached from the smoking fire engine. There was nothing more that could be done. Fortunately news reached them that the keepers were taken off and returned to shore on board a Cawsand fisherman. Despite hopes that a fresh wind from the sou'west would drive the seas higher and put out the blaze and perhaps save the lower part, Jessop saw how quickly and utterly all was lost. In just a few days, nothing remained standing and he could clearly see the iron 'branches' to which the wooden uprights had been secured. Bent and misshapen, these were all that remained of Rudyerd's magnificent lighthouse.

In the village of Stonehouse, Dr Spry was called again to the home of Henry Hall. He had attended the eighty-four-year-old since his rescue from the Edystone. He had dressed his extensive burns, but until now Hall had appeared remarkably well for his ordeal and seemed to be making an amazing recovery. He had certainly shown no ill effects that might confirm his claim that he had swallowed melted lead. It was now eleven days since the catastrophe, when Dr Spry arrived to find the man was suddenly grown worse. Approaching slowly up the village street on horseback, he stopped outside a picturesque (although shabby) thatched dwelling. He dismounted and knocked at the front door. An elderly woman opened the door. She was Richard Hall's daughter. She 'lived in' and kept the house, sharing it with a younger woman companion, who lodged there while Henry was away on the Edystone.

The village street was quiet and otherwise empty, so that prying neighbours, if they were inclined, might overhear their conversation.

'Good morning, ma'am.'

'Doctor, thank goodness you've come; my father has taken a turn for the worse, and calls for you!'

'Here I am! I am come to see what ails him and what can be done. He seemed so much recovered recently – I find it a pity to hear otherwise.' His tone was one of genuine surprise at Hall's sudden relapse.

'Do come in, Doctor.' She ushered the doctor inside.

As she followed him in a feeble voice was heard from upstairs.

'Who is it, Elizabeth?'

'The doctor is here, Father, come to see you!'

'I'll take you up, Doctor.' Elizabeth Hall was a portly woman with a pleasing face and ruddy complexion. She climbed the stairs, speaking in hushed tones, followed by the doctor.

'Mr Jessop came to see him yesterday, and Father would persist in telling him that his recovery depended on your relieving his stomach of the lead!'

Dr Spry, wishing to put her mind at rest on the subject, explained.

'That is something quite impossible, madam. It is incredible that *anyone*, let alone your father, at his advanced years, could possibly survive such a hurt.'

At the top of the stair landing he paused to consider the possibility of this happening and spoke in a hushed voice.

'The shock to the internal system would be so great, a man less than a quarter his age would be dead by now. He must be suffering a delusion.'

She led the doctor along the landing into the bedroom. Henry lay in the oak-framed bed in the centre of the room, which was simple and sparsely furnished. Steep sloping plaster ceilings followed the roof timbers and Dr Spry had to stoop to avoid the collar tie of an ancient crook frame that spanned across the middle of the room. The doctor opened his bag and carried out a close examination of his patient. There was no mistaking his sudden deterioration. He was drifting in and out of consciousness, and when lucid the ailing light-keeper pleaded with him to take the lead from his insides. Henry suddenly awoke, staring into the gloom above him.

'What time is it? I must go and snuff the candles and light new.'

Dr Spry took his arm to feel his pulse.

'There now, Henry, don't fret so. Has no one told you? The news in Plymouth is that the Edystone is no more!'

'Gone?' The old light-keeper gasped, suddenly recognising the doctor, and remembering where he was and what had happened. Tears began to roll down his scarred, hollow cheeks.

'Yes, completely destroyed. It is a great tragedy. The light is extinguished now,' Dr Spry reflected, solemnly although perhaps a little over-dramatically.

'As I will be, from the lead that lies inside me!' Hall whispered with irony. He eyed the doctor with a look of disgust and pointed an accusing finger to his chest.

Dr Spry carried on with his examination.

'Well, if that *is* the case, you are remarkable to have lived so long since your accident!

'I *am* remarkable, sir! I am eighty-four years of age. I might have reached an hundred had it not been for the other two! Are they apprehended?' He spoke of the other light-keepers, who had since disappeared. The talk in Stonehouse was that they had become *unhinged* following their ordeal in the tower.

Dr Spry continued with his examination.

'No,' he said, after a long silence, 'I am told that nothing has been seen or heard of them since they fled from Stonehouse Quay. The rumour is that they were turned quite mad by their experience.' He paused, then offered his own opinion, 'I expect they were afraid to answer for any consequences.'

Hall nodded, confirming the doctor's viewpoint and then struggled to speak.

'Conse ... quence of being dead drunk! They left me to it till it was too late!'

33

Dr Spry stopped what he was doing and looked at his patient thoughtfully, adopting a considered look and an 'I thought so' tone in his voice.

'Ah, I thought perhaps there was something in it.'

'Well at least I die with dignity, and my *mind*!' Henry Hall uttered. The doctor completed his examination in silence, and telling Hall that he would be along to see him again tomorrow he took his leave. Downstairs Dr Spry adopted an entirely different manner. He warned Elizabeth that her father might not last the night, and to prepare herself for his passing. He put his hand on her arm, as if to offer her some comfort, then he departed. She closed the door and heard the sound of the horse's hooves as he rode away.

Later that afternoon Dr Spry was called to return to the house. He arrived to find a small gathering directly in front of the cottage. The two women of the house now stood waiting outside. Henry had died. Amongst the small group stood Mr Jessop. Elizabeth Hall had sent word to him when Henry had grown worse. He secretly hoped that the doctor would not insist on him entering the house to witness his performance of an autopsy. They talked quietly in hushed tones.

'I offer my condolences, Mistress Hall. Your father was a good man. May his soul rest in peace,' said the doctor, then turned to Mr Jessop.

'Ah, Mr Jessop, very good of you to come. I quite understand that operations of this sort are not to your liking, but owing to the extraordinary circumstances of his case I think it best that I perform an autopsy on the body. As you represent the man's employers, will you inform them of our findings?' Seeing his look of anxiety, Dr Spry added, 'Don't worry. You need not attend me inside the house.'

There was a quiet and respectful hush amongst the small crowd that had gathered in the street about them, as Dr Spry entered the dwelling to perform his examination. When he emerged from the cottage a while later, he carried something in the palm of his hand and offered it forward discreetly to the kin and to Jessop for their inspection.

'Look at this,' he said quietly.

Josias Jessop took the object from Dr Spry and turned it in his hand.

'It looks like lead.'

'Indeed, that is exactly what it is,' Dr Spry replied. Then he turned to Elizabeth. 'Lord forgive me. I was mistaken in my diagnosis and your father spoke the truth, but I did not believe him. I thought it too incredible that a human being could live with such a mutilation to the internal system.'

Mistress Hall broke down in tears. She was comforted by her companion, wiped her eyes and stepped forward to examine the piece of lead. She steeled herself, taking a few short breaths, and asked the doctor what he had found.

'And this killed him?' She took the metal lump, which was solid and oval-shaped.

'Almost certainly,' he replied, 'I have taken it now from his stomach; it would have certainly poisoned him from lying there. And this would account for his rapid decline since appearing much better in the last day or so.' She returned the gruesome article to him and was led away by her companion to a neighbouring house, the relations and neighbours all following.

Jessop stayed awhile outside until the doctor had completed his work and the undertaker arrived to prepare the corpse for burial. The crowd melted away back into the straggling row of houses in the street. To pass the time of waiting, he closely inspected the piece of lead Dr Spry had handed to him. Turning it over, he noticed that the underside appeared to be moulded in shape to the surface of what he imagined to be the lining of Hall's stomach.

'I was quite astounded to discover it, and all the time he told me it was within him, I would not believe it!' Jessop looked up at the doctor who was now at his side, having completed the autopsy.

'It is certainly a very considerable size and weight,' Jessop remarked.

'Yes,' the doctor agreed. 'I have taken the opportunity to make a record of it for my report; it weighs seven ounces and five drachms to be exact.'

'God rest his soul.' Josias Jessop crossed himself. 'Still, he died in his own bed, not some watery place amid the flotsam of the light.'

'Tell me,' asked the doctor, 'is it true that nothing remains to be saved?'

'Indeed, I saw myself the reef both dark and picked clean of all, save the irons that held the tower fast.'

Dr Spry held out his hand and Jessop placed the dished lump of lead into his palm. The doctor looked hard at the metal.

'Fascinating! What little we understand of Nature,' said Spry.

2

Mr Smeaton expects visitors

Austhorpe Lodge, October 1792

'We are almost there, John.' Alice Trehearne placed her hand on his and then pointed out through the window. 'Look, there is the spire of Whitkirk.'

The mail coach trundled onward towards the family home of their friend, John Smeaton. He had sent word following his long illness of the previous winter that he was now recovered (as much as he could expect) and desired that they come and visit as soon as they were able. The letter had reached Breakstone Hall in the summer, but it was to be a while before they could leave their affairs at home. There was the harvest, then the apple picking and the cider pressing to organise before they could even consider travelling so far from home.

Soon after the lighting of the new Edystone light, thirty-three years ago, they had married and removed to her parents' estate on the edge of Dartmoor. She and John Trehearne had inherited the Hall upon her parents' death, when John became the new squire. In the years since the tower was completed and first lit, John and Alice had prospered.

They were blessed with three children, who now had children of their own. Their eldest son was proving an excellent farmer. His studies in the new methods of husbandry were proving of great benefit on the estate, and nowadays Squire Trehearne could afford to stand back and enjoy the things that delighted him most – like the cider making and the apple harvest. At this time of year, nothing pleased him more than to go down into the orchard, either very early or perhaps late in the evening, cupping his hand to lift an apple from the bough and then cutting it open to examine the fruit for its ripeness, just as old Squire Vasey did before. That is not to say he was not a busy man. As a Justice of the Peace he heard sessions regularly in Tavistock, and being a country gentleman and elder of his community, he was regularly called upon to advise on local matters or preside over events, as well as leading a still-busy social calendar. Alice had musical talents, and even now she would often be invited to play in the drawing rooms of the big houses around the moor. But, for all that this had brought him, he had never forgotten his days serving under John Smeaton in the Edystone service. He remembered how proud he had been when he rose from a plain seaman to become the Master of the *Weston*, the first of Mr Jessop's purpose-built yawls. Most of all, he would never forget his flight to freedom across the water, that rainy day in October thirty-three years before. He had re-lived it almost every day of his life since.

The coach wheels trundled onward through the fields of the South Riding. Though it was a fine autumn day in 1792, in his mind he was once more in the stern of the yawl, heading a course through the squalls and pursued by his enemy close behind. Alice's voice brought him swiftly back to the present.

'I think I see Austhorpe! Yes, look there it is, there is Mr Smeaton's observatory.'

John Trehearne smiled at his wife, and leant forward to see. There it was, the tall stone tower that Smeaton had built for himself and christened his 'sanctum'. It resembled the type of church tower that is square and has a castellated top. A small pyramidal roof, slated and lead-hipped, completed it, and its gilded wind-vane shone clearly in the sunlight.

'Perhaps he sees us approaching through his great telescope,' he laughed as he spoke.

'Oh, I doubt it, my dear. I should think that Mary will not countenance his climbing all the way up there as he used to.'

'It is my opinion that he built it to remind himself of the tower upon the Edystone. On our last visit he showed me inside. I count myself privileged – not even his dear wife Anne when she was alive was granted entry; I doubt not that Mary too is forbidden to go in. Even Waddington the blacksmith must call up to his master rather than climb the steps – as must any visitor, however important!'

'What is in it that he keeps so secret?' Alice was curious to know.

'All sorts of paraphernalia, but I doubt he'll allow you to see.' He laughed again.

Austhorpe Lodge lay ahead of them. The coach turned from the highway through the stone-pillared gateway, and they alighted in the courtyard, where Mary Smeaton and the rest of the household awaited them.

Mr Smeaton stepped out into the garden of his small country house, Austhorpe Lodge in the parish of Whitkirk, near the town of Leeds in the County of Yorkshire. The autumn frosts had come early this year. Today was a warm, fine day, though the garden already wore a rich mantle of autumn colours. He strolled slowly in the grounds, his frame stooped with age, and sat down at a table in a warm corner where a brick garden wall abutted the corner of the house. Opening the large, leather-bound book on the table before him, and with the aid of a magnifying glass, he studied the title page.

> The book depicts a lighthouse upon a rock. A strange, artificial-looking wave climbs up and seems to bend over the very top of the building. The wave more closely resembles a fountain, or *jet d'eau* (as Smeaton himself described it), than anything to be found at sea. It would appear that the artist who engraved the plate has deliberately adapted the great plume of surf to show more clearly the image of the lighthouse upon which it breaks. The book is entitled *A Narrative of the Building and a Description of the Construction of the Edystone Lighthouse with Stone*. The author is John Smeaton, and it was printed in London in 1791.

John Smeaton resided in the Lodge, having retired here to the place of his birth. His professional work engagements had continued to press upon him until his illness the previous year. He had led a remarkable life, distinguishing himself in the science of 'engineery'. But of all his achievements none was more renowned than the tower he had built on a sea-swept rocky outcrop off the coast of Devon – the one depicted here in the vignette. Smeaton's tower was the third Edystone lighthouse and the first to be built entirely in stone. The first of its kind. He perused the intricate detail of the drawing of the tower. It stood in the place where previously Mr Rudyerd's lighthouse had stood, until it was entirely consumed by fire – and his stood where Mr Winstanley's light had been swept away before that.

Smeaton's lighthouse was a technological marvel of the age, though once it had withstood the great storms that fell upon the coast in the winter of 1762 people soon forgot their fears 'that it would most certainly be overset'. He recalled how soon it was that they considered it unremarkable – it simply *was*. To celebrate and to record for posterity the building of the stone lighthouse, John Smeaton had busied himself in these latter years with writing the *Narrative*. This writing of the building of his most famous work had taken him seven years to complete. It was a task he found more difficult at times than the work of building the tower itself. The book, published in London in the previous year, told of how they had proceeded to complete the work in four seasons upon the dangerous reef. The old man continued his study of the intricate plates when his daughter approached.

'Are you sure you are warm enough?' she enquired, at the same time feeling his cheek with the back of her hand

'Yes of course, Mary lass, you worry too much. I am nine parts dead already and the tenth does not feel the cold. It's a glorious day and since I can no longer climb up into my sanctum, so happen I might enjoy these last warm days here, in the garden.' The elderly Smeaton did not take kindly to being fussed over and he usually said so, but he smiled at her. Today brought excitement and expectation; he was expecting guests, very dear friends, and they were due to arrive at any time. Mary understood, but she could not help showing her concern.

'Very well, I will sit with you a while. It was a terrible thing for me to find you after your seizure, collapsed out here and alone. You're still quite weak.'

'I know, I grow slow of mind and body. But nature must take its course, lass; the shadow must lengthen as the sun goes down.' He enjoyed the analogy and smiled again. He had not expected, even himself, that he would make such a complete recovery following his attack. It had left him partly paralysed, and he had fully expected to lose his powers of reasoning, but this was not the case. He praised the Almighty that his strength was sufficiently recovered, without lasting damage or loss of his faculties. Yet deep within he knew that he had but little time left. It made him inclined to be philosophical. He tried to concentrate once more and turned the pages. He was looking for something.

'It's no use, my eyes cannot see well enough. Can you read for me, Mary? Here, the Description of the Plates.'

Mary Smeaton sat down beside him and, taking the book, began to read aloud.

'Plate no. 8 entitled "South Elevation of the Stone Lighthouse completed upon the Edystone in 1759. Shewing a prospect of the nearest Land, as it appears from the Rock in a clear calm day."'

Old John Smeaton, seeing the fine rendering of the tower standing upon its rock, recalled in his mind's eye the events of another story, known only to him and his invited guests. Mary read aloud from the key describing the landing place at A, the channel known as the Gut at R, the steps cut into the rock at F, and the cavern at E, in the east side. He remembered vividly the dramatic outcome of a desperate chase to the lighthouse, which took place there all those years ago.

'How long is it since you last saw the Trehearnes, Father?'

'What? Well, tha knows it were a good while back.'

He pondered over the question, looking to the distant view

'Hmm. I think it is nearly seven years ago that they were here. Years ago I would stay with them when I worked on the harbour in St Ives. I did sometimes take the opportunity to visit the Edystone too.'

He looked up directly into Mary's face.

'And you will recall their visits to us here, when your mother was alive. This will be our last meeting, I think,' he added thoughtfully.

'Father, don't say so!' she exclaimed.

He smiled.

'Now, lass, don't take on! Knowing my time is at hand makes it all the more enjoyable. I have been most content these last few months to enjoy my family and home. Now I wish to meet with my friends to say goodbye. Besides, I want to show them my book. It will bring back our time together, and we have memories to rekindle. You may think my *Narrative* to be complete in every conceivable detail, but I can assure you that there remain some secrets, my dear, that I did not tell out in print.' He looked up at her knowingly. She knew that look – there was more in it than any words could say.

A maidservant entered the garden from the house and announced the arrival of his guests.

'Mr Smeaton, sir, the coach is here.'

'Go now, Elizabeth, prepare for our guests as I have instructed you. I am coming, tell them.'

Mary attended to the blanket on her father's lap; he waved his arm to dismiss her.

'Go on now, lass, I can manage well enough.'

Mary Smeaton emerged from the open front door of the stone porch and stepped forward to greet the Trehearnes. Enquiring after their health, she found them both well, although a little stiff and tired from the last stage of their long journey north. She escorted them through the house and into the garden, where John Smeaton awaited them. He rose slowly from his chair, smiled, and warmly greeted his guests by their first names, John and Alice.

'Dear friends, I cannot say how glad I am to see you both! I hope the journey was not too hard on you. Welcome to Austhorpe.'

Alice Trehearne took his hands in hers and smiled.

'We are both very well, John, but perhaps a little tired. The road to Leeds has more ruts and potholes than I remember – nothing I expect that a good engineer couldn't put right, but I daresay the parishes are too poor to mend them these days.' Mr Trehearne agreed.

'The wars in the Colonies with France take it all, my dear. Why, there's many a bridge or breakwater or drain that would be so much improved if only they had had the sterling to undertake Mr Smeaton's recommendations!'

The engineer smiled a wry smile. 'How true, by God – though never mind that, it makes me happy just to see you again, John. It's been too long since last we met.'

As he spoke, Alice thought how much older and how frail he looked, though he still took care in his dress. He wore a coat and long waistcoat of matching worsted cloth, dark blue in colour with a plain silk necktie, black breeches and white stockings and a periwig, giving him an old-fashioned appearance, that of a country gentleman of perhaps two or three decades before.

'Last time we met this book of mine was still in embryo, now here it is. It's taken all these latter years to finish, longer than building the light itself.'

'Has it really been seven years?' asked Trehearne in disbelief.

'Aye, it has. I think it were harder to write than our task to build.'

'It is well done, Mr Smeaton. I am sure the gentlemen in your profession will thank you for it, and I daresay some of us other folk too.' Alice teased him with the vitality and manner of the young girl he remembered calling at his lodging in Plymouth so long ago. He looked for Mary.

'Come, Mary lass, see to it that our guests are provided for! They have travelled far and are in need of revival. Will you take tea, or perhaps some beer, John?'

'I cannot think where that maid has gone! I will see she brings the refreshments directly.' Mary Smeaton got up and went back into the house, calling the maidservant to her. John Trehearne took Smeaton's hand in his own and placed the other on his shoulder.

'It's good to see you again, Master Smeaton! When Mary wrote and told us of your illness we were anxious for you, and forgive me, but none of us is getting any younger – I thought we might not meet again in this life.'

Smeaton looked grave and slowly nodded in affirmation.

'True, the shadows cast themselves increasingly long nowadays.' He gave Trehearne a knowing look, an expression of calm benevolence upon his face. 'And what of yourself – are you well?'

'Oh, I have some aches and ailments brought on with age, but my heart feels young again, to find you well and here in your dear Austhorpe – and so recovered!'

'I am grateful to the Lord for returning my faculties to me. But I am tired and slow; it takes a great deal of effort to write the simplest letter these days.' He took up the big leather-bound book and placed it in John Trehearne's hands.

'I hoped you would come, so that you should have this gift. I want you to keep it and remember the adventure we shared.'

Trehearne opened it at the plate showing the prospect of the lighthouse.

'It's magnificent! The house looks just as I remember it. And here's the *Weston* sailing into the Gut. She is drawn perfect in every detail!'

Mary rejoined them. The maid came after, carrying a silver tea service and tray, and waited upon them.

'Father's book has been well received in London and throughout the country,' she remarked proudly. The old man was appreciative of her support, but modestly less effusive.

'Ah yes, but as I was saying, John, I found it a task more arduous than the one we faced when we set out to build the house. My *Narrative* tells nothing of the adventure that led to your disappearance, sir.' Smeaton slowly lifted himself from the chair and beckoned John Trehearne to come with him to the tower across the garden.

'Will you come with me? I left Waddington at work on a piece and must go to him.'

They strolled across a wide lawn in the direction of the tower, which John Trehearne had recognised from the coach, solid and foursquare with rooms piled one above the other and a single stone stair leading up – his sanctum. No one else was permitted to enter, and the upper rooms – his model room, study and observatory – were filled with papers, models, tools and mechanical devices that he had invented as a means to pursue his work. A broom had never come near them. Trehearne had once seen some of his inventions, including the dismembered furniture that he had brought in from the house and adapted to his own use in their construction.

'Is your sanctum still as full of wondrous things as I remember?' he asked politely.

'Tha means is it still filled up with all the oddities my work has brought forth? Rubbish to everyone else hereabouts,' Smeaton remarked ironically. 'The answer is yes, but I cannot reach it nowadays. The steps, I am barred from climbing them.' He paused, then brightened, and added, 'Though I still have the workshop to hand.'

They approached the low door where Waddington was hard at work over the furnace, and entered.

'Mr Waddington, do you remember my friend John Trehearne?'

Waddington squinted and his eyes searched John's features, as though he were feeling the contours, then a look of recognition came.

'Nay, it's Mr Trehearne! Well! Tha's not been here in years, sir. Must be more than five, maybe ten?'

'Seven, Mr Waddington. But I see the years are treating you kindly, and still at your anvil?'

'Aye, that's right, sir, the work keeps me going – someone has to keep the shop.'

'Have your sons taken up the hammer?'

'Oh aye, but they are in the forge in the village, Mr Trehearne. There'll allus be Waddingtons hammerin' somewhere in Whitkirk. There's so much trade hereabouts these days, and Leeds grows like a mushroom. Factories and houses and workshops springing up out the ground. They all need ironwork. But the place is so changed. Still, we're all in work. Mr Smeaton keeps me goin at it!'

'Waddington is making up a new device, to assist me in my infirmity. I hope Mary will allow me to try it, so that I can regain some independence, and get back up to the observatory before I end my days.' He raised his stick aloft.

'Another queer-fangled thing as you have given me, though. I'm not certain what to make of it,' said Waddington. He turned about and produced the object in question, for his master's approval.

There was a moment's silence as the old man ran a critical eye over the work.

'Aye, that's well made – but what the devil's this? Lord knows what this part is supposed to be.'

'That's the frame that fits together,' Waddington began.

'Nay, I told thee I wanted it making like this,' he demonstrated the design principle with gesturing hands, 'to have such and such, d'ye see?'

Waddington raised his eyebrows to feign understanding, mumbled an apology and said he understood.

'Thou had best mak' another,' said Smeaton, and they left him to it. The sound of the hammer blows struck up once more, ringing out from the forge in a steady, slow rhythm.

As they strolled, John Smeaton raised his gaze and slowly craned his neck upward, pointing his stick to the battlemented spire above them. He had all his life, even during the busiest periods of his building career, made a keen study of astronomy. In the observatory, amidst the impressive array of telescopes, lay the papers he had written on the subject, including many he had contributed and presented to the Royal Society. The tower was built beside the ornamental pool in the courtyard. It stood on the site of his first workshop, where as a boy he had managed to construct a pump engine that successfully drained the pond, much to his father's displeasure.

'D'ye know my father was so angry he refused to let me continue with any more "experiments" as he called them for at least a month.'

'Did he forgive you?'

'Aye, of course he did. He could see I was caught up in mechanics, a new science that I had stumbled upon. Yet I knew in my heart that this was to be my destiny. The day I saw them build a new engine up at Temple Newsam, was like the mist lifting from the hills. It opened up a horizon beyond anything I had known before.'

'You have such a view from here, Mr Smeaton.' Alice had decided to join them; she raised her hand to shield her eyes from the golden sunlight and gazed toward the hills.

'Aye, you can see right across Pennines from up there.' He pointed to the mock battlements up above.

'Having you both here brings it all back to me,' Smeaton mused.

They walked through the grounds and talked in the sunlight, past the pond and down to the orchard. And in their minds, Trehearne and Smeaton were back on that solitary rock, fourteen miles out to sea. It all seemed like it happened only yesterday.

3

Thou art the man

London, January 1756

Mr Robert Weston strode purposefully across the new Westminster Bridge. The chill wind and slate-grey skies promised snow. He clutched tight the folio beneath his arm and headed on in the direction of the parliament buildings and the Abbey. Looking out across the great sweep of the river, he saw the new buildings and developments that had sprung up since the bridge was opened. So much was new to him, that it was reassuring to see in the far distance the great dome of St Paul's and, surrounding it, the spires of Mr Wren's city churches.

The bridge was thronged with traffic. A cacophony of sounds filled his ears, from the street hawkers' cries singing out in the crisp winter air, to the trundling of cartwheels as they rolled over granite setts in the carriageway. He paced in step with the stones in the pavement, and observed in passing how the long kerbstones were tied back with a dovetailed joint – his footfalls landing on each stone tie.

He walked on for almost half an hour until he approached a fine square in the new West End, but he was suddenly unsure of his way.

Was this Mayfair or Soho? He caught the attention of a passing gentleman.

'Sir, perhaps you can help me?' and he produced a notepaper with an address written on it. 'I am looking for the residence of Lord Macclesfield, I have the address here but I am not familiar with this part of town.' He unfolded the paper and handed it to the other man to read.

'Why yes, you're almost there. You see there is a square ahead? The house is in the centre of the terrace opposite; you will see it across the gardens.'

'Thank you, sir,' and with that Robert Weston touched his tricorn hat and made his way into the square, which was only recently finished, its centrepiece a formal garden with young trees in the lawns between walks of rolled hoggin. The broad paths formed a simple geometric pattern, and he thought it very pleasing to the eye. Here he stopped again to consult his notepaper.

Mr Robert Weston, Gentleman, held the greatest share in the ownership of the Edystone Lighthouse. Chosen by the other shareholders, his fellow 'Proprietors', to represent them in the business of its reinstatement, he had written to Lord Macclesfield, President of the Royal Society. He did so because he hoped the Society could help him find the 'proper person' to undertake the task of rebuilding the lighthouse, which had been so utterly destroyed by the fire in the month before Christmas. He paused long enough to fold the paper and tuck it into a breast pocket, then, taking up his folio under his arm, made his way across the square toward a doorway in the centre of an imposing façade in painted stucco with pilasters supporting a portico above. Weston passed beneath a wrought-iron lantern arch and climbed the Portland steps to the door; he rapped the knocker and stepped back to wait on the generous stone-flagged landing. His discerning eye took in the fine detail of the architecture until the door swung open. A manservant stood before him.

'Good day, sir,' he intoned as though asking a question and awaiting a reply.

'Good day, my name is Mr Robert Weston, here to see his Lordship. I believe he is expecting me.' The servant relaxed and opened the door a little wider. He stepped back and bowed his head.

'Yes, sir. Do come in. His Lordship awaits you in the library.'

Weston entered through the wide, arched portal and the door closed behind him. He found himself in a refined and fashionable interior. The only light came from the fanlight above the door behind him and the warm glow of a fire in the tiny fireplace alongside. His eyes adjusted to the dark, and as they climbed the wide staircase he heard voices. The elegant Portland stone cantilevered treads wound around in a semicircle to the landing, and light streamed down from an oval lantern high in the ceiling some three floors above onto wall niches containing figures from antiquity. The servant knocked at a door on the first-floor landing; a voice called 'enter', and he opened the door to admit Mr Weston.

'Mr Robert Weston, m'lud.' Lord Macclesfield arose from behind his desk and came forward, offering a hand.

'Good afternoon, sir. Cold today. Can I offer you something warming?' He gestured to a steaming jug of hot wine on a heating pan near the hearth.

'Thank you, my Lord. That would be most welcome,' Weston replied. 'We might have some snow, I shouldn't wonder.'

'Yes indeed – and I believe this to be the best remedy!' Lord Macclesfield poured two glasses of hot wine and handed one to

Weston. He took a slow draught from his glass, whilst eyeing him shrewdly, and then spoke.

'I understand from your letter that you represent the Proprietors of the Edystone Lighthouse, Mr Weston?'

This was Weston's cue. Producing from his folio a drawing of the former lighthouse, he placed it on the table before Lord Macclesfield.

'Yes, my Lord, I do. Thirty years ago the Westons purchased three-eighths of the shares in the lease from the former holders, and the executive part of these are now in my ownership. Following the fire, and since I have so considerable a share in my person, the whole body of the Proprietors have invested their trust and confidence in me, for our future undertaking.'

Lord Macclesfield sipped at his glass.

'Why, the loss of the lighthouse must weigh heavily upon you all – a great catastrophe! Our nation thrives upon seafaring trade, Mr Weston. Great opportunities are presenting themselves in India and Cathay.' Lord Macclesfield studied the drawing, contemplating the image of the wooden lighthouse as he spoke.

'We are taking great steps, with new scientific instruments to guide our mariners; but for all that, and notwithstanding such splendid skills as they have in following the stars, all comes to naught should our merchantmen founder on the homeward leg of their journey.' And he added pointedly, 'A cruel fate it must be, to be cast upon the teeth of the Edystone in sight of our shores!' Lord Macclesfield removed his wig and scratched his head in an almost comic fashion. He was completely absorbed in the seriousness of the danger to mariners. Then he looked up and fixed Robert Weston with a questioning look.

'Mr Weston, what will you and your partners do now?' he asked.

'We are obliged to rebuild in order to exhibit a light, my Lord. For many years we've enjoyed the fruits of commerce, since all shipping passing the House pays one penny in the ton on cargo. Although Mr Rudyerd's lighthouse required continual upkeep, it was a great asset to us.' Robert Weston paused and placed the greatest emphasis on his next words.

'Now we wish to raise another, so that a light can again be exhibited, and duties paid for the service to shipping.'

Lord Macclesfield was impressed. He considered Weston's words with eyebrows raised, and he nodded in affirmation.

'I commend your spirit, sir! My sentiments would be the same, but tell me – how can I be of service to you?'

'I consider this not a work to be advertised; nor put in the hands of a general undertaker in the building way. Neither would it be better for the ornaments to be derived from the five Orders.'

'Such as would be suited to a piece of architecture?' Lord Macclesfield prompted.

'Quite. It is a work of a very peculiar kind; and to reinstate it does not require a person who has merely been bred, or even rendered himself eminent, in this or that given profession.'

'As one might describe most of my fellows, I am afraid, Weston.'

But Robert Weston had more to say. He carried on forcefully, giving expression to his vision and insight.

'... but rather one who from natural genius has a turn for contrivance in the mechanical branches of science. I believed that I might find such a person within the Royal Society.'

Lord Macclesfield understood that Robert Weston was seeking a rather special kind of man, one who could rise above the conventions

51

of status and academic learning to bring his own genius to bear upon the challenge presented here. He listened with renewed interest while Weston continued to voice his thoughts and aspirations for the project. At length Lord Macclesfield spoke up.

'The Royal Society has instigated and promoted the greatest inventions of our times, and there are a great number of ingenious men within or connected to its ranks.'

He paused.

'Amongst them I hope to find a real artist,' Weston said, 'one whose genius can be brought to bear upon the task of rebuilding, making all possible improvements upon the former construction.'

There was silence. Had he asked for too much, thought Robert anxiously. Lord Macclesfield paced over to the window and then back to the fireplace, pausing awhile to consider. He frowned with concentration, and then gained himself a little more time to think by pouring another glass from the jug. He raised the jug and, looking at Weston, offered it to him, but Weston declined another glass.

'Hmm. This is a very particular brief you have presented me, sir. Here is a building to be reinstated, placed critically upon a single rock at sea, where both its forebears have perished. 'Tis a demanding circumstance to challenge the most original and inventive of minds!'

He returned to the window and gazed down into the square, sipping at the hot wine. Then it came to him and he drew a long deep breath. He turned, and Robert saw his Lordship's eyes twinkling as he spoke vigorously of the person he had in mind.

'Yet there is one of ours whom I can recommend, who I think will answer fully to the business! His name is John Smeaton. He first commended himself to the Society through the communication of several mechanical inventions and improvements. Having set up as a philosophical instrument-maker in Holborn, then finding this an unlikely source of a livelihood, he now engages himself in such branches of mechanics as you seem here to require.'

'Is he a Fellow?' Robert Weston asked.

'He is. And I believe I can vouch that he will not undertake your offer unless he himself believes he can carry it out successfully.' Robert Weston felt his spirits lifted and was keen to make contact with this person straight away.

'I am more than satisfied with your opinion, my Lord. How can I reach him?'

'Ah, there you have me. Finding him might prove difficult,' Lord Macclesfield remarked, in a cryptic manner.

'How so?' asked Weston.

Lord Macclesfield crossed the room, sat down at his desk and, taking his quill pen, began to write even as he spoke.

'Because he is, I believe, presently engaged somewhere in Scotland – or is it the north of England? I'm not sure as to where. But he has an acquaintance here in London, Mr Wilson the painter, who may well be able to help you find him. Wilson has rooms in Great Queen Street.' And with that he signed the paper, folded it and placed a dab of hot wax onto the end, to seal it. Handing it to Weston, he added, 'Here, take this to him as your introduction'.

Robert Weston was most grateful, and, expressing his gratitude, he offered his hand.

'Thank you, my Lord.'

They shook hands and Lord Macclesfield spoke again.

'I thank *you*, sir, for taking such an interest in our Society. I wish you well with your venture. Good day to you.'

Lord Macclesfield rolled the printed illustration of Rudyerd's light, and handed it to Weston.

'Here, don't forget this!'

He looked out of the window and watched as Robert Weston made his way across the square and a first scattering of snowflakes drifted across the windowpane, then he settled back in his chair next to the fireplace to finish his wine.

The snow had fallen heavily in Northumberland these past three weeks, and a continual frost had made it nearly impossible to make progress with the works to the New Mill. The country was in the grip of winter. John Smeaton had had no choice but to remain with the workmen lodging at the farmhouse, cut off from the rest of the world, at least until the weather improved. He had made the best of the situation by continuing as best he could to direct the efforts of the workmen in finishing the new sluice and the great waterwheel he had designed. Hardly any progress had been made since the beginning of

January when the freeze set in and put paid to laying any masonry. It was in the midst of this freezing inertia that a rider was spotted approaching over the moors. One of the workmen spied him crossing the bleak open landscape of the high fell.. His figure was dark against the whiteness of snow that lay on the hills and fells.

'Look, a rider comes yonder,' he cried, staring out into the whiteness. All eyes fixed upon him until eventually he arrived at the site. He passed by the millwheel scaffold, pulled up in front of them, dismounted and with hands fumbling from cold produced a letter from his saddlebag.

'Mr John Smeaton, Civil Engineer.'

'That's your man over there,' one of the workmen replied, pointing toward a man in his early thirties who stood talking to the blacksmith. They could see only his upper face, the rest of his person being wrapped in a greatcoat and muffler. He was tall, the thick muffler and greatcoat giving emphasis to his large frame, and he wore his hair in a pigtail beneath a broad tricorn hat. The rider trekked unsteadily across the frozen clay toward him.

'Sir, I bring a letter from London for you. I have carried it from York. The weather has been hard up here. Such cold I never felt.' He raised and delivered the sealed letter into Smeaton's outstretched palm.

'Tha's done well to reach us, rider. No one has passed this way during the best part of a fortnight. I thank thee, how much?'

'It is paid for from London – by express, sir.'

'Well – here's something for risking life and limb on the road. The drifts I'm told are all of six foot in places.'

'Aye, on the road sir, between the walls. I took to the open country to avoid such obstacles.'

'Good man – where there's a will there is a way.' Smeaton laid down the iron tongs upon the forge and, rummaging through his pockets, he eventually produced a purse to pay the weary messenger, and called out to his foreman.

'Mr Armstrong, show this man to the stables and see to it that he and his mare are fed and watered.' He pointed to a range of outbuildings. 'You can sleep as long as you like in the loft above the horses, though you'll have to put up with our commotion.'

The rider lifted his hat and thanked him for his generosity. Mr Armstrong led him and the mare away, leaving Smeaton standing in the middle of the workyard, his breath rising in the freezing air as he studied the handwriting.

'A second letter from Wilson,' he said to himself as he made his way toward the farmhouse. Inside, a wood fire was burning brightly in the ingle fireplace. Smeaton knocked the clods of frozen clay from his boots, and crossing the earthen floor he sat down heavily on a settle in the fireplace to read his letter. The mistress came in and brought him a pewter jug of warmed ale. He supped it and mused over this development. He had replied but recently to the first letter from Wilson, in which he had learnt of his name being put forward as a candidate to rebuild the Edystone Lighthouse. Now here was another.

I had but recently received a letter from Mr Wilson signifying that I was made choice of as a proper person to rebuild the Edystone Lighthouse.

... but as I had no doubt that its foundation part at least was built of stone, though its upper works had the appearance of timber, I could not readily conceive how it could be totally destroyed. I concluded therefore that the object was to repair or restore the Upper Works: and therefore I received the call without joy; concluding, as most public works were undertaken upon advertisements, the meaning was, that I should return to London to give my proposals along with other candidates.

I therefore returned my friend for answer, that I supposed it was meant that I should go back to town in order to form a scheme, which if it had the good luck to be thought preferable to that of others, I was to be employed in the Repair of the building ...

But this second letter was to dispel any doubts as to who should be appointed..

To this I received an answer from my friend even more laconic than before. That this was a <u>total</u> demolition, and that as Nathan said unto David 'Thou art the Man.'

As he sat in the ingle, John Smeaton could hardly believe what he read in the second letter. Once again he re-read the words and felt a great sensation of pure joy rise up within him. His eyes came again to the final extraordinary sentence, and the words that had been underlined by Wilson. He spoke them aloud.

'As Nathaniel sayeth unto David, Thou art the Man.'

'What was that again, sir?' Armstrong, having seen to the rider, had entered the room, closing the door behind him.

'I shall have to leave thee shortly, Mr Armstrong.'

'Is it bad news?' he asked, a concerned look on his face. Smeaton, seeing his anxious expression, was keen to allay his fears.

'No, be assured 'tis nothing of the kind,' he said quickly, 'but it is unexpected. Have you heard of the Edystone Lighthouse?'

'No, I can't say as I have, sir. Whereabouts is it?' Armstrong had little education but he was an intelligent man and had a great respect for the young engineer's learning. Smeaton gave him a brief description from the news he had received in Wilson's letters.

'It stood until recently upon a rock in the English Channel, off the coast of Devonshire. I read news of the fire there most recently, in a printed broadsheet. And when my friend Mr Wilson sent his first communication from London, I thought that my opinion was being sought for its *repair*. Now he tells me that the entire building is destroyed and I am chosen to replace it!'

'My congratulations, sir. I cannot think of anyone better for it. When must you start?' Armstrong enquired.

'I shall have to go straight away, as soon as I can. Will you be able to manage the works here?' He gave Mr Armstrong a look of concern.

'Don't you worry, Master, we shall cope,' Armstrong reassured him. 'I think everything is in hand and I doubt that we will be able to do much until the weather improves. Winter makes slow progress at the moment.' He looked out through the small glass panes of the window behind him. Already it was growing dark and the men were clearing away for the night.

'Very well, I will write to our employer to confirm your acting as my agent here until the mill is completed. Now I must first set down my reply and acceptance of this offer, to send with the messenger on his return to York.'

That evening Smeaton wrote at length to his friend in London. All the while his thoughts were turning to the printed image he had seen of the lighthouse standing on a single rock in the sea, and to the words set down in the letter from Wilson before him, that this was 'a total demolition' and that 'Thou art the man.'

4

The road to Plymouth

In those days it took at least five days to get from London to Plymouth, and this journey was no exception. The coach and horses made slow progress along the deeply rutted and waterlogged track that served as the road from London to Exeter. This was the London mail coach. John Smeaton was amongst the passengers on board; he was travelling to Plymouth.

To pass the time and alleviate his discomfort, he kept himself occupied for long periods in reading the notes and written accounts Robert Weston had sent him concerning the lighthouses built by his predecessors upon the Edystone Rock – though at that particular moment he amused himself with a pencil and sketchbook in which he drew designs for a coach of his own. He found the one he sat in so uncomfortable, that he decided he could certainly improve upon it if he were to produce his own carriage to take him about the country. So he determined to have one built as soon as funds permitted, to his own design and specification, that would serve him in his journeys by road in future.

Breaking off from his work, he looked out of the window as they lurched to yet another halt. He noticed welcome signs of spring in the surrounding countryside. In the hedgerows and along the roadside verges, swathes of early wild flowers were rocked by the March winds. Then the coach rolled forward again, ploughing its way through a large flock of sheep. They filled the wide trackway, ewes with their young lambs being driven to fresh spring pastures, the lambs bleating constantly. The coachman sounded his horn, sending the sheep scattering in every direction. The faces of passengers inside were pressed to the windows to look on the cause of the commotion.

Satisfied that all was well and having taken in the spectacle of the running sea of sheep, Smeaton closed the carriage window and leant back into his seat. He resumed his conversation with the clergyman sitting opposite him. The Reverend Allsop was the new incumbent of Lostwithiel, in the Duchy of Cornwall. He too was journeying to a new post and as the miles passed by they had discovered that they shared similar interests. Reverend Allsop was a keen amateur astronomer, who was most impressed to learn how Smeaton had made his telescope and ground the lens for it, and this helped to pass the time, but Smeaton found himself becoming impatient at the slowness and seemingly endless interruptions to their progress.

'Is there something amiss?' asked Allsop, who thought Smeaton was concerned at something he had seen outside.

'No, only my impatience at the loss of time that we must suffer, due to the badness of the road!' Smeaton replied abruptly. He took up his drawing materials and now tapped his pencil repeatedly on the sketchbook.

'Forgive my manner, Reverend, but the rural charms of the country wear thin after four days' travelling on the highway!' He made a grimace at the mention of 'highway', as if laughingly named. The Reverend, noting the heavy irony Smeaton placed upon it, made an inspired suggestion.

'Perhaps we might journey in a boat, upon your canals, in future. It would seem that inland navigations are the new thing.'

'Yes, there are a great many now being built. Mr Brindley has led the way for the rest of us to follow, but I fear that it may be some time before such a network exists, that could carry us from London to

Plymouth.' He spoke with an air of irritated resignation, as they jolted over a bump in the road.

'It would be a great deal smoother too!' the Reverend Allsop added, as he gripped his seat and reached for a strap hanging from the upholstered interior. He nursed a pain in his lower back that grew worse with each rut in the road. Smeaton saw his look of pain.

'Most certainly, we would now be gliding along like ducks on the millpond, yet making our destination sooner and without hindrance, I would wager,' he replied.

The Reverend Allsop regained his composure.

'Your business in Plymouth sounds most intriguing.' This energetic man of science had impressed the Reverend Allsop. 'May I enquire further as to the nature of your work?'

Smeaton told him more of the story of how he had been chosen by Robert Weston, and how he had come to London to learn more from him and to begin his proposed scheme.

'I have spent the last few weeks in London, developing my first sketches for a new lighthouse upon the Edystone rock. The former house was entirely consumed by fire in December of last year.'

'Edystone, eh? I think I might be able to see it from my new parish if I climb high enough. I am told that from the church spire in Lostwithiel you can see down to Fowey and all along the coast. I shall secretly set my telescope up there to follow your progress!' He considered this a short while, then added, 'It amazes me to think that men can build such things. You must have great resolve in your capabilities.'

'This is the first of its kind that I have undertaken.'

'And how did you come to do such work?'

'Machines have fascinated me ever since I were a lad in Whitkirk. After school I would spend hours in my workshop, where I taught myself to forge iron and make instruments – and I became utterly absorbed with "engines" and how things worked. My father hoped I would follow in his profession but I knew it had to be otherwise.'

'But "engines" and mechanical contraptions are not buildings,' interrupted Reverend Allsop, who struggled to see the connection.

'Quite. Though at first I trained in the law, my father eventually conceded that the law was not for me, and to be fair, he funded my training and enabled me to set up in the business of instrument-making in London.'

'Mechanical instruments such as telescopes?' prompted Reverend Allsop.

'Aye, but some were for experimental use in scientific applications. The best were a design for a new kind of pump using the natural phenomenon created by a vacuum. Then I made a mariner's compass with Mr Knight. We tried it in trials aboard HMS *Fortune*.'

'And you profited from these?'

'Enough to continue, but it was my experiments concerning the latent power of water that first brought me into the realm of building, namely watermills. I proved by my methods and calculation the superior power of a wheel that is powered by falling water, over that which is pushed by the stream beneath it.'

'I'm afraid your inventions are unknown to me. Speaking as a country parson I own that I am not well acquainted with science and mechanics.' The Reverend Allsop shrugged his shoulders in admission.

Smeaton was well used to a lack of knowledge outside his own small circle. Since his visit to the Low Countries to study the great dams and waterways, and his departure into this field, he now called himself a 'civil engineer'. He explained it to the Reverend.

'I consider myself a private artist, working for hire for those who are pleased to employ me and take my advice on any such scheme as they have need, involving the new science of *engineery*.'

Smeaton looked out of the coach window and noticed that they had, by now, left the sheep behind and were making a more steady progress. He thought he could just see the hills and tors of Dartmoor in the far distance.

'And how did you come to this scheme?' Reverend Allsop was curious to know more of the itinerant life of this 'engineer'.

'I was fortunate to be recommended to the Lighthouse proprietors. Being in Northumberland at the time, it came to me as a complete surprise. My friend Wilson, who is an eminent painter in town, wrote me that I had been chosen for it. I got myself to London by February's end and since then I have become acquainted with Mr Robert Weston, my client. He is one of the proprietor shareholders and acts as their representative.'

'The Lord has called you, I am certain of it. How else would this circumstance have come about? I will pray for you in your mission.' The Reverend Allsop did not believe in 'chance', seeing all happenings as resulting from the unseen hand of God, and he clearly saw this encounter as part of His great design.

Smeaton was conscious of the other passengers listening intently now to their conversation.

'Thank you, Reverend, that is a comfort to me. I am under no illusion as to the perils that the Edystone holds. Whilst I will do everything in my power to safeguard those in my company and to avoid unnecessary risk, I would that our Lord will guide me to a safe conclusion.'

'The Scriptures tell us of the man who builds his house upon rock. It has a firm foundation in faith.'

'Indeed, Reverend, I shall be giving my full attention to the firmness with which my design will conjoin with and stand upon *this* rock. Mr Weston has furnished me with plans and models of both former lighthouses and I have made a close inspection of them. Though both were created with great faith, I believe that their physical defect lay in the want of *weight*.'

'So as to resist the power of the seas striking upon its flanks?'

'Quite. For the first of these was swept from the place in one night, and I believe the latter – now destroyed by fire – would rock upon its heels like a drunken man from the repeated blows of the seas in a storm.'

'Then what is it you intend to do in such a precarious place?'

'My thoughts are to graft the building into the rock like the roots of our most ancient trees. An oak anchors itself deep into the earth by spreading its roots wide. To be sufficiently firm gives me to think that the new house must be built in stone. Such a structure would, I believe, endure and continue beyond the boundary of an age or two towards a possible perpetuity.'

The churchman was impressed by Smeaton's direct manner, his plain speech and his powers of analysis, but he paused to consider the metaphysical view.

'Yours is a noble concept, but I have in mind one of the Psalms, that I think we would do well to reflect upon. It brings a perspective upon such endeavours.' Reverend Allsop quoted from memory a passage from the Psalms.

'Except the Lord build the house, they labour in vain that build it.'

Smeaton smiled and agreed wholeheartedly. Afterwards they fell silent. The afternoon light faded, turning to gold with the onset of sunset. Occasionally the Reverend Allsop's words would return in Smeaton's thoughts until at last they approached Exeter, their stop for the night.

The coach left Exeter very early in the morning, on the last leg of the journey along the road to Plymouth. Upon its arrival in the city that afternoon, John Smeaton was only too pleased to step out from the confines of the coach. He wore his best silk shirt, with a long overcoat and a dark grey tricorn hat.

'I hope to make a good impression on the people of Plymouth,' he had told his travelling companions that morning. He knew that Mr Weston had sent word to the city authorities, that the engineer appointed to reinstate the Edystone Lighthouse would be arriving on the next mail coach from London. Even so, he was to be surprised by the interest his arrival had aroused.

He looked suitably imposing to the group of dignitaries gathered at the coaching inn to await his arrival. As he stepped down from the coach the little crowd took in every detail. They saw a tall, smartly dressed man now at the peak of his physical powers, aged thirty-one. Amongst the Plymothians stood Mr Jessop, Surveyor for the Edystone Lighthouse. Jessop watched with amusement as the Mayor introduced himself, and made the necessary introductions to others in the group. He invited Smeaton to join them for a supper in his honour, at his residence. Suitable lodgings were yet to be found, but in the meantime he would stay at the inn. Smeaton's baggage was already carried inside and he hardly had time to take his leave of Reverend Allsop and the other travellers, before being swept along by the Mayor and his entourage to the reception party.

5

Rendezvous at Polparra

The moon is full, and from high in the night sky it casts a pure white light down upon the headlands and coves of south-east Cornwall. In a small cove near to the fishing village of Polparra the sand lies blanched in its light, like a dish of milk placed between the headlands. The dark shoulders of the hills are silhouetted against the stars and the breaking surf. The breakers roll in and heave themselves onto the shingle banks with a thunderous booming, then rush foaming up the sands to the high-water mark. Suddenly from out of the surf a figure appears, staggering and falling two or three times before reaching the shoreline. Slow and exhausted, he lurches forward, his strength sapped by the soft shingle under his feet. He falls onto the shingle bank, makes a last great effort to get to his feet and then staggers up the beach to disappear into the shadow of the cliffs.

In a cavern, the exhausted swimmer fell face down and unconscious. He was unable to say how long he slept, but it was not long before he was woken by heavy footfalls crunching the shingle, and the sound of voices calling. One voice rang out and Trehearne snapped awake.

Though tired and confused, he recognised the voice of Midshipman Baines of HMS *Dart*. Chilled with cold and fear, he dragged himself forward to the mouth of the cave to see what was happening. He was too exhausted to run away from them. Instead he prayed for his life, that they would not discover him.

From the mouth of the cave he could see a ship's longboat pulled up onto the shingle and a train of men, sailors and locals, labouring in pairs to carry wooden chests from the boat up the shingle beach. The chests were small but obviously heavy, needing two men each to lift them onto the cart that had been driven down a track onto the shore. The midshipman strode up to the carter. From his hiding place, Trehearne could plainly hear their conversation.

'Where the devil have you been, Hill? We pay you to land goods and here we are doing it ourselves. I've a mind to see the Lieutenant revise our arrangement if you cannot prove reliable.'

'Couldn't be helped, Mr Baines. We had word from Polparra that a patrol of excise-men is on the coast path somewhere hereabouts. We came the long way round inland.'

Hill shrugged his shoulders in a matter-of-fact way, his manner sullen and contemptuous. The young midshipman's eyes bulged as he hissed out his words.

'By God, sir, we may be ambushed here. We must leave now.' And he made to turn about, so that Hill had to catch his arm.

'Ah, don't you worry about them. We passed 'em some way back. They were on their way back toward the village, they'll not be patrolling this stretch tonight.' Baines faced him and composed himself.

'Very well, in that case perhaps we can get on. I've had a devil of a time this night and I shan't sleep till morning. We must get back before we are missed and secure the launch.' Trehearne sensed from the midshipman's nervous demeanour that their preparations had not gone as expected.

'Where is the Lieutenant tonight? I'll wager he sleeps soundly in your stead,' Hill added dryly.

'I doubt it. He took a ball in the shoulder from our would-be pilot.' Trehearne strained hard to hear his words.

'There was a skirmish on deck. One of our landing party, your

Cornishman Robert Appleford, shot the Lieutenant. It was a mistake to press him into serving us, but tonight was our best chance to come ashore, being so near the coast, and he knows it here better than anyone else on board.'

'What have ye done with 'im?' Hill badgered the midshipman for more details.

'He is arrested and charged with the assault on the Lieutenant.'

'Will the man testify against 'ee and tell the ship's captain of our night's work?'

'He has no witness; the Captain will rely upon Lieutenant Colquhoun's account.'

'But will Colquhoun live, and am I to be paid?' demanded Hill.

'The surgeon operated immediately and said he should recover. Appleford is finished – one way or another we must see to it to protect ourselves.'

There was a coldness in his tone that sent an involuntary shiver up Trehearne's spine. He wondered what was to become of the shipmate he had left behind. Robert Appleford was a good man but now he was in serious trouble. Baines had regained his composure, and pointed to the boxes being shouldered up onto a cart at the top of the cove.

'And in those cases there is enough French gold to pay your account with interest.'

William Hill wanted to know more.

'And what of the others, the captain and the crew?'

'They'll not be any the wiser. Lieutenant Colquhoun accounted for the prize and a few cases shall not be missed. He has made out the account for the purser, to tally with the remainder left in the strong room.'

'Are there any who might talk – petition the Captain?'

'There was one, another Cornishman who fought alongside Appleford. Seeing the game was up he jumped over the side, but I doubt he lived to reach the shore. We are safe.'

William Hill was reassured and turned back to the night's work in hand.

'Right, let's get tonight's prize stowed away and well out of sight until all this dies down. I wish the Lieutenant a speedy recovery – tell him I look forward to calling on you to settle our account when you come into Plymouth next.'

The midshipman handed Hill a sealed paper.

'Very well, you have your instructions. See to it that they are carried out to the letter.'

'Aye aye, sir. God speed your safe return.'

Hill bowed and tipped his hat forward but the midshipman was already turning to call his men to him and make their way down to the longboat.

Midshipman Baines stepped into the stern of the launch and his crew slid the boat out into the water, heaved themselves in and, taking up the oars, rowed out of the cove. Trehearne watched them pull away into the rolling breakers. He rolled over and lay staring at the black rock overhang jutting out into the starry sky above. He wore a look of renewed determination on his face. He must go to Plymouth, he thought, find Alice Appleford and tell her everything that had come to pass.

He looked out again. The beach was deserted. With the immediate danger of discovery now passed, he made himself as comfortable as he could, wrapping himself in an old tarpaulin he found lying with some creels and pots nearby. He was exhausted, tired and hungry and longed for the respite of sleep, but sleep evaded him. Faint streaks of light appeared in the night sky to herald a new dawn. Then at last he slept, long and soundly until late in the afternoon. When he awoke he ached all over and could hardly move, but he forced himself to his feet and set off to find the nearest farm for food and shelter. He was 'handy', a skilled carpenter as well as a seaman; he could earn a living with his skills on a farm or in the town, and once he was recovered he would make his way to Plymouth. He would take a new name, find employment and seek out his friend's wife. He feared the worst for him, but she must be told the truth of what had happened last night.

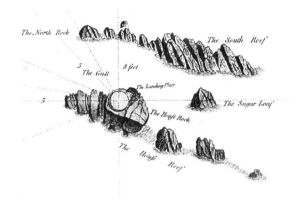

The North Rock The South Reef
5 8 feet
The Gull
The Landing Place
The Sugar Loaf
The House Rock
5
The House Reef

6

Nothing but WOOD
will last upon the Edystone

For the first few days after his arrival in Plymouth, Mr Smeaton stayed in temporary lodgings at the George Inn. The old coaching inn stood within a stone's throw of the harbour, its courtyard hemmed in by outbuildings and the ancient gabled façade leaning out upon half-timbered corbels over a flagged and cobbled lane. Mr Jessop came along the street below, weaving his way between the children and maids, gentlemen and sailors and the occasional coach or heavy cart that trundled along in the carriage way. He had been instructed by Mr Weston to visit Smeaton, and put himself at the engineer's disposal. And so, on the morning of 28th March 1756, Josias Jessop came to the medieval door of the inn and raised the iron ring to knock three times.

The innkeeper went about his business as usual that morning. He finished clearing away the remains of the breakfast served to a coach party who had left earlier. As he gathered up the platters, the sounds of a busy port mingling with the cries of street hawkers could be heard in the street outside. Carts trundled past and their iron-rimmed wheels grated on the granite road so that he did not hear the rapping of the iron ring on the inn door. The visitor waited patiently outside, staring at the oak-planked and studded door; eventually he reached again for the iron ring-knocker. After three louder knocks he stood back until a small square hinged port opened in the door and a face appeared behind the wrought-iron grill.

'Yes?'

Jessop was startled but soon recovered himself.

'Is Mr John Smeaton within?'

'Aye, he is. Just a moment, sir.'

The innkeeper's face disappeared as he closed the hatch, whereupon Jessop heard heavy bolts being slid back and then the door opened. A small portly man stood before him, framed within the ancient portal.

'Come in, sir. May I ask who calls?'

Mr Jessop stepped through, following the innkeeper, and entered the smoke room. Removing his hat, he appeared a hale and healthy Plymothian in late middle age. He was of medium height and strong build, and had the healthy, ruddy complexion of a man who spent a great deal of his time in the outdoors, and ate well.

'Tell him my name is Josias Jessop, Surveyor for the Proprietors of the Edystone.'

'Yes, Mr Jessop, wait here if you please,' and the innkeeper hurried away through a door into the hall. Jessop could hear his footfalls as he climbed the oak staircase.

He sat and looked around the dimly lit room. Seeing a model on the mantelshelf above the hearth, he picked it up and examined it carefully. It was a ship in a bottle. He sat in a chair beside the empty fireplace, holding the bottle to study the details of the little brig captured within. Hearing voices and approaching steps, he stood up as the door opened and John Smeaton entered the room.

'Mr John Smeaton?'

'Yes?' he replied.

'Josias Jessop at your service, sir.'

They shook hands and Jessop, finding the model still in his hand, excused himself and returned it to its stand on the mantel.

'Thou's a maker of models, Mr Jessop?' Smeaton asked the question with genuine interest.

'I am, sir. My son William never ceases from prompting me to build another; he has a keen mind and knows all the ships.'

'Capital. I myself believe that a "real" design ought to be the consequence of such models. I have an affinity for constructing them myself, where time allows, from my paper draughts. A solid object shows us what we cannot see on paper. I am certain we will have need of such models to execute our design for the new lighthouse.'

Mr Jessop went on to introduce himself, explain his position, and put himself at Smeaton's disposal in accordance with his instructions from London.

'As Surveyor for the Edystone Lighthouse, they have given me to provide you with whatever information or assistance you stand in need of.'

'Yes, Mr Weston told me to expect you. As it happens I do have need of something. I must find somewhere a little more permanent if I am to stay here the next three years.'

'I'll see what I can do, sir. I hear Mr Cookworthy, the Quaker chemist in Notte Street, is keen to find a tenant. He has a fine house and it's but a short walk from here.'

'That sounds perfect. See what you can do for me, Mr Jessop.'

'Very well, sir,' Jessop replied dutifully.

Smeaton turned to the business of the new lighthouse.

'Come. Let me tell you my thoughts concerning the scheme.'

They walked through the inn into the courtyard at the rear and sat in the spring sunshine on a bench in front of the coach house, sharing a jug of ale. The yard was bustling with activity, with grooms busy preparing the saddlery for a team of horses. Another coach was expected and the horses would need to be ready for a changeover.

These two men had been thrown together with a common purpose, but it would soon become apparent that each had independent, strong views about the project, and they were poles apart, in their character and background – and, most importantly, in their thinking. Smeaton lost no time in getting directly to the subject foremost in both their minds.

'I have in my interviews with Mr Weston come to see the former building as having served very well, and we are agreed that the new building will provide a similar accommodation.'

'Will it look like Mr Rudyerd's light?' Jessop's long experience of repairing the former tower put him in mind of its shortcomings, but it also made it difficult for him to conceive how it could be improved upon. He held Rudyerd's wooden tower in high regard. Had it not successfully withstood the most violent storms for approaching half a century? Smeaton was almost brusque in his matter-of-fact reply.

'It will have a similar form and conveniences, but as to the manner of building it, whether it be in wood or stone will be the subject of my further enquiry and report.'

Jessop was disturbed, but he warmed a little to Smeaton's acknowledgement of Mr Rudyerd's tower having served so well.

'Mr Rudyerd's design perfectly answered the end for which it was intended – the column, a cone unbroken by any projecting ornament. His principal aim seemed to me to have been *use* and *simplicity* – and it was directed in a masterly manner, don't you think, Jessop?'

'When I beheld the tower, I would marvel at its construction. The seams running from top to bottom, caulked with oakum the same as our ships, and the whole payed over with pitch. It was to me a wondrous piece of shipwrightry.'

'Quite so. I would I had seen it. So simple a figure must have been an agreeable engagement to the eye,' Smeaton mused, then he fixed the older man with a direct look and asked him, 'Did the house move?'

'Oh yes, 'twould rock like this in violent storms.' Jessop took up his tankard of ale and swung it from side to side, spilling a good deal of the contents onto the cobbled pavement.

'It was so like a ship in its motion that the trenchers would sometimes be thrown from the shelves in the upper rooms!'

Smeaton nodded his understanding and placed a hand to steady the table.

'Yes, I thought so! Mr Weston told me that fire notwithstanding, the light's safety and continuance in great measure depended upon the *elasticity* of the members, enabling it to give way to the violent shocks of the sea.'

Jessop was pleased to see that Smeaton had a good grasp of the former tower's ability to withstand the seas, and how it rolled like a

71

ship, thus absorbing the great impact. But it was just at this moment he said something that threw him completely.

'Now a construction in *stone* would not suffer any such agitation. D'you agree?'

Jessop was lost for words.

'I don't quite follow you, sir.'

'Stone, Mr Jessop! Stone, not wood, that is my meaning.'

'But how? The best-caulked oak is both durable and capable of absorbing the breaking of the waves. The house can bend like a reed and roll like a ship.'

'Nay, sir, the wooden house rocked from its want of *weight* as well as *strength*. I say to thee, Mr Jessop, that if something must give way, and if the building shall not give way to the sea, *then the sea must give way to the building.*'

Jessop was at first bemused and then perplexed. He fingered his hat, and then confronted Smeaton; he wore a puzzled, even angry look on his face.

'But if you intend to build in stone, how shall you fasten the *outside timbers*?'

'There are none,' came the reply in an instant. Jessop was astonished.

'No cladding? 'Tis not possible! Even if 'twere – I assure you that in my opinion – IT WILL NOT STAND!'

Jessop surprised even himself, as he spoke angrily the words that would echo in Plymouth society for the next three years, despite all John Smeaton's work to the contrary.

'Mr Smeaton, I have to say to you that nothing but WOOD will last upon the Edystone!'

There followed an awkward silence. They sat in an atmosphere of brooding contemplation. Smeaton took Jessop's outburst as a rebuff. Jessop truly believed Smeaton to be entirely without the necessary experience in the matter. At this moment the innkeeper returned with a fresh jug of ale. Seeing that things were amiss he left it on the end of the table.

'There you are, sirs, I expect you can do with some further refreshment.'

Smeaton took the jug and poured the ale into the tankards. They drank in silence until suddenly Jessop stood up to take his leave.

'Thank ye for the ale, but I cannot stay here a moment longer. I daresay you are a clever young man full of confidence and learning, and I don't wish to offend, but I speak my mind. You will see for yourself, out there on "the Stone". I have an older head on my shoulders – and, being a Cornishman, perhaps I am too traditional in my opinions. I speak as my heart tells me, sir. Good day to you.'

They shook hands, but as the surveyor made his way out through a passage into the street, Smeaton watched in dismay. What he thought had started so promisingly – had it now gone completely awry?

Nevertheless, Smeaton was keen to make a start and there was much to be done. First and foremost he had to find someone to take him out to 'the Stone', as Jessop called it. Despite making plain his objections to his ideas, Smeaton felt that he would be an indispensable asset to him if only he could be persuaded to open his mind. Jessop was highly respected and had for many years single-handedly taken charge of the former building. He determined to seek him out and try to make amends for this disastrous first encounter. On the following day Smeaton took himself down to the harbour and found Jessop on the deck of a small sloop in one of the docks. He observed him attending to the Edystone lighthouse boat at her mooring. Jessop looked up and saw him standing above him on the quayside.

'Good morning, Mr Smeaton,' he said without a trace of the anger he had shown the day before.

'Good morning. I was wondering if we might talk?'

Jessop secured a rope and gestured for Smeaton to come aboard.

'You will find the *Edystone Boat* is kept ready for your use. Though she has been idle since the fire, she is very seaworthy and shipshape – built especially for the Service by Mr Tolcher. She's only twelve tons burthen but a good sailer.'

'Excellent. I require the use of her immediately, for I am impatient to go off as soon as weather permits,' Smeaton announced.

Mr Jessop looked at the skies as if to reinforce his own thoughts.

'The wind is at north-west, which suits the passage out there, but I fear it blows too hard at the moment to land on the Stone. P'rhaps in a couple of days ...'

'Then perhaps tha can tell me where to get the tools and implements for making trials on the Rock.'

Mr Jessop finished up his work on the *Edystone Boat,* and then climbed up the ladder to join Smeaton on the stone quayside.

'I can take you to the King's Docks beyond Stonehouse. There you will find all manner of craftsmen and workshops for the making of anything you require.'

'I am very obliged to you, Mr Jessop.'

'Not at all, sir. It's my duty to provide you with every assistance.'

He took Smeaton with him in a cart to the dockyard, where they met with the naval artificers. It was precisely what the engineer was looking for. Nothing seemed beyond their capabilities, and he noticed how the naval men held his surveyor in great esteem. Smeaton gave them a detailed list of tools and specifications for what he needed making. It took up the remainder of the day, and Jessop found himself drawn irresistibly into the preparations, as the young engineer's guide. Despite himself, he found the excitement of a new venture and Smeaton's enthusiasm for the task an intoxicating mix. Without realising it, he was soon offering his own suggestions and was pleased that 'young' Smeaton listened attentively and consulted with him on almost every detail. But it would be a while before he could bring himself to believe in the engineer's radical proposals to build a tower in stone. He stubbornly refused to accept Smeaton's insistence upon such a heavy construction. The problems were enormous and he could not imagine how it could be done.

'The masonry would surely be spoilt by the violence of the seas there,' he thought to himself.

At the end of the day, Jessop invited the engineer to accompany him home to 'Mrs Jessop's' for supper. They lived close by, just outside Stonehouse, and it was 'no distance at all in the cart'. After a delicious meal of stew and dumplings, with baked apple pudding, Mr Jessop took out his pipe and sat with Smeaton by the hearth in the parlour. The room was cosy, lined with timber panelling painted in a flat aqua green. Jessop lit the wall sconces and drew shut the folding shutters from the window reveals.

Josias asked him if his son could join them. William, a boy of twelve years of age, had sat in silence at the table but Smeaton had drawn him in with his talk of models. After the meal they heard his footfalls as he ran upstairs and back down, more slowly now. The door opened and William entered, bearing a beautifully made model of a cutter. Smeaton was genuinely impressed, and asked if it were his. William nodded and pointed out the parts he had constructed.

'I think William has contracted my habit for making things,' said Josias. 'I did but help on the hull of this one.' William beamed as the engineer admired his work, then placed the model on the side mantel and sat quietly, running a finger along the lines of the boat as he listened to the conversation.

Smeaton took the opportunity of broaching the subject of the tower's construction once more, and hoped to gently persuade Jessop by means of a rational argument.

'Were it not for the moorstone ballast in the base, the old house would have been toppled long ago, Mr Jessop.'

'Aye, there we are of the same mind, sir. We shifted several rotten timbers in the south-west part in my time. 'Twas awkward, as the new could not easily be brought to an equal bearing, and afterward the whole building leaned over.'

'There, you see! Apart from the risk of a fire, a wooden structure requires constant attention.'

'Well, I agree, but I cannot for the life of me see how you can build as we do here on land, out there on a rock hardly bigger in its top surface than this here room!'

'Tha's right, it won't be easy, but I have given it great consideration in the couple of months since it first came to me to take on the task.'

'Well, Master Smeaton, you have youth and impetuousness, if I may say so, but I will not let it be said that I refused to listen to your proposals – even if I think badly of them!'

Smeaton saw his chance to convince the surveyor. He took up his folio of drawings.

'Here, let me show you how I propose to raise a building that is both durable and stable.'

Jessop cleared tankards and papers to one side and Smeaton unfurled his roll of drafts upon a wooden trestle that served as desk and tabletop. The drawings included a completed *fair Section* of the proposed new building.

75

'These are but the first draft and a work of the imagination, based on an imperfect knowledge. But they illustrate the fundamental principles upon which my proposals for a stone building are founded.'

Jessop took from his pocket, and placed precariously on the end of his nose, a pair of spectacles. He leaned over to study his drawings for the scheme.

'And this is to be built entirely in stone?'

'Yes, and see, I have kept strictly to the conical form but with an enlargement of the base. The rocking you described in the old house was, I believe, due to its narrowness. By enlarging the base and diminishing the waist and upper part, our column will have the greatest possible stability, to resist the action of the sea.'

Jessop asked more questions, testing the engineer's thinking on the design.

'Indeed, I can see that would be an improvement, but how do you suppose to fix the stones. The breaking seas around Edystone sometimes reach the lantern itself, and even higher again in a great gale! Will you use cramping?'

Smeaton dismissed this with a shake of his head and a wave of his hand.

'There'll be no need for it, not in the lower part, that which I call the "solid".' He was eager to explain his radical idea to lock all the stones together. 'I am thinking of forming the stones to fit together in the way of wooden dovetailing,' he locked his fingers together to convey his ideas, and went on, 'like wooden blocks shaped to tie together – or if you have been in London, you will see in the streets how the kerbs are fixed in this way.'

Jessop looked a little abashed as he replied with deference, 'I have never had the good fortune to be in the capital, Master Smeaton.'

'Well, no matter, let me illustrate, here.'

Smeaton took a pencil and proceeded to sketch what he had seen in London on the new Westminster Bridge – how the pavement's interlocking kerb was made up of dovetailed headers and stretchers in the manner of a carpentry joint. Then he produced from the drafts his rough plan of a stone course for the lighthouse 'solid'.

'If all our stone blocks inside and out are shaped into large dovetails so as to mutually lock together and make an entire course they will attain a greater firmness than any other fastening we could make by mechanical means.'

At last Smeaton believed that he was making an impression on Jessop. The old surveyor had listened quietly to the ideas put forward, and suddenly he began to make favourable observations in response to Smeaton's enthusiasm for the scheme. He quickly grasped the benefits this method would bring, if it worked.

'There's one thing – doing without cramps and stays in binding together the lower part will certainly make a great saving of time and money. And in my experience, time on the rock is the most precious thing of all.'

Jessop spoke the words slowly and with great authority – he was after all the expert in the matter. A good meal and his pipe had worked wonders. He was suddenly become helpful and full of practical suggestions. Smeaton was secretly delighted, and lost no time in making further headway.

'And speaking of time, I am impatient to set foot there and make a start, Mr Jessop. Can you see to it that we have enough men and tools ready, that will enable us to take a survey thereof?'

'Aye, Master, leave it with me.'

'When can we set sail?'

'As soon as Nature permits. We will have the swell of the spring tides to carry us high over the reef.'

Smeaton sensed that he had won him over.

'Good! Thank you for hearing me out. Perhaps you will send word to me when you think it looks favourable to go off.'

Jessop's rugged features lightened; he smiled and broke into a chuckle. It was as if the sun had come out from behind a heavy cloud.

'I shall, just as soon as the weather is for it. It's a bold plan, Master Smeaton. Who would have thought it? "The sea must give way to the building" – I like that, though no one in Plymouth will believe it, I promise thee.'

He took a lighted spill from the fire and pulled at his filled pipe until it glowed orange.

'Your proposals are sound even if they are radical – though there's no fool like an old fool – and half of me prefers to stick with what I know works. Yet here I am agreeing to the impossible! I wonder what William Cookworthy will make of you! He tells me you are welcome to lodge with him. He has a very fine house. We can call tomorrow, get you settled before we sail.

Although things did not go well with him and Mr Jessop at first, Smeaton soon found that they were in fact quite compatible, with each bringing to bear upon the tasks at hand their knowledge, skills and temperament. Now all their attention was focused upon making headway. It was the beginning of a great friendship. Jessop was solid and dependable and loyal. In those first few weeks he proved his worth in seeing to it that they reached the Rock at the earliest opportunity, but it was to prove harder than Smeaton had imagined to actually make progress. First they had to gain a foothold on the infamous House Rock.

7

Mapping the Rock

The 2nd of April being the first day there was any probability of landing on the rock, we set sail; it being at that time near the height of the Spring tides, the wind easterly and moderate. We got within a stone's cast of the rock, but could not attempt to land, as the sea broke upon the landing place. Though we could not land, yet as the tide was at its low ebb, I had a good view of the rock and an early opportunity of correcting many errors that I had been led into by the incorrectness of the several models and draughts which had come to my hands; and indeed I never should have had an adequate idea of this very turbulent place without seeing it ...

On the 5th of April we made our second voyage, the wind at N.W. and very moderate, so that though we went out of Sutton Pool at Plymouth before the water began to ebb, yet we did not arrive at the Edystone till it was nearly low water; and then I was rejoiced with setting my foot, for the first time upon the Edystone.

The Edystone Reef, 5th April 1756

With the Edystone Rock and its neighbouring Sugar Loaf rock in full view, the *Edystone Boat* approached the small channel known as the Gut that lay between. Mr Jessop expertly guided her in to the landing place and the hands jumped off to moor her tight to the fender piles, then they proceeded to disembark.

Smeaton stepped out onto the rock, followed by Jessop. Within a few minutes they had traversed and examined all the available surface area, and proceeded to examine the remaining evidence of the former lighthouse. This consisted of most of Rudyerd's iron 'branches' that were let into the rock and bedded with lead. These had provided the fixings for the timber uprights. They stuck up out of the rock, many of them bent or broken, and Smeaton laid hold of one. He carefully examined the crude attempts of his predecessor to cut steps into the rock that formed bearings for the uprights, all now gone.

'These have all the marks of hurry upon them,' he called out above the noise of the seas breaking around them.

'I expect there was but little time to do more than was needed,' Jessop said as one of the hands called them from below.

'Look, sirs, here are the stones!'

Both men made their way across the sloping top of the rock and down to join the others. They were peering into the waters heaving through the Gut. There they clearly saw a pile of granite blocks lying in the bottom. One of the seamen took soundings to ascertain the depth of water above them.

'Twelve feet of water on them, sir,' he announced.

'There lies the last of Mr Rudyerd's tower, gentlemen,' said Smeaton.

'By my reckoning they be piled more than two foot high down there,' added Jessop. These were the remnants of the granite courses that had given the tower enough weight to withstand the seas. Many had exploded in the intense heat of the fire.

''Tis the moorstone ballast from the interior. And look here!' Smeaton had found an ancient piece of chain. He turned and bent down to examine the traces of chain anchorages.

'This must belong to Mr Winstanley's earlier building. It looks as though the rock has been rent to the depth of the chain's embedding – it must have been torn up when the first house was overset in the Great Tempest.'

With little time to spare, they set to work. The artisans, taking up their picks and sharpened tools, set about cutting holes and chases in the rock to establish the workability of the surface. Smeaton orchestrated their efforts and got Jessop to keep time. After five minutes he measured the depth to which a hole could be punched out, using a hand drill known as a 'jumper'. The experiment proved that the gneiss rock could be worked by hand. Next he observed closely the arrangement of the iron branches.

'I think this the centre of Mr Rudyerd's building.' Smeaton motioned to a spot and took hold of one of the remaining iron stays; it rocked from side to side in his hand as he spoke.

'Each pair of irons held a leg of the frame, supported on the uncut rock.'

'Will we build in like manner, or d'you think we shall have to level the whole?' asked Jessop. He wondered how they would obtain a firm, level foundation for building in stone. 'We could blast away the crown with black powder and charges.'

'We could easily, Josias, but then we must make up the loss in more masonry, and this could never equal the strength of the natural rock.'

Jessop knew Smeaton to be right in this, but what were they to do? Seeing his doubtful look, Smeaton expanded on his line of thought.

'Nay, the footings shall be grafted into the rock itself like the roots of a great oak, as I showed you in my drawing. A stepped foundation will clasp the rock, like the oak tree's spreading bole. From that, and the weight of the stone column upon it, will come the strength to resist the force of the seas striking against the sides.'

'The footing will take a great deal of our time. I daresay we'll need to do more with this,' Jessop nodded his head at the rock summit, 'or it'll be turned over in the first winter gale.' He made a diving signal with his hand to emphasise the outcome.

Smeaton agreed, explaining his purpose in mapping the topography of the rock.

'I shall need to make several landings in the next few weeks. I have made an instrument that we can erect upon this point here to be the centre of the new building. It will allow me to measure vertically to the chosen points in any direction all around here, within a circle of 32 feet in diameter.'

'What then?' asked a bemused Mr Jessop.

'You remember my interest in models? I wish to model the very surface of the rock itself, and from this produce a *real* design without recourse to the imagination. A precise recording will save much work later in adapting stones to the rock.'

Smeaton took up a hammer and chisel and scribed a mark on the rock.

'I think this the centre of our predecessor's building, here! Set up the theodolite, centred on this point, Mr Jessop. I have it ready.

The Garden, Austhorpe, 1792

'Here it is, look, shown in Plate 7, 'the Elevation of the rock'. The elderly man turned the book around and showed the Trehearnes and Mary the intricate engraving of the rock as he found it. He pointed to his 'theodolite' set up as it was to survey the surface, and explained how he came to this.

> *The idea whereon it was contrived I took from LEON BAPTISTA ALBERTI's treatise of statues. Wherein placing a kind of dial upon the head of the statue, with an index or ruler, turning about on the center of the dial, and from this ruler letting fall perpendicular lines, the several parts of the instrument will shew the situation, distance from the center, and depression of any given point of a statue below the plane of the dial that the Artist is desirous of ascertaining for his guidance; which instrument he calls a 'Definitor'.*

'I see a description of it.' Mary Smeaton read aloud the passage he pointed out, to save his own eyes.

> *With this intent I brought with me from London, the plate and index of a large Theodolite, being a foot in diameter, and sufficient to shew the single minutes of the degrees of the circle. This plate I screwed firmly down upon the surface of a steady wooden three-legged stool, which when set level, would overtop every part of the rock. Being set up, it was so adapted to the rock, that the center was, as nearly as I could place it, perpendicularly over that hole in the rock, which I considered as having been the center of the late building. To the index of the Theodolite was screwed a ruler, 16 feet in length, commencing from the center. This ruler was preserved from bending by its own weight, in any material degree, by a rib raised upon its upper side and it could be brought justly horizontal by means of a pocket spirit-level being placed upon it.*

In an instant he recalled those early days on the rock, thirty-six years ago.

'All this took place before you joined us, John Trehearne.'

'Yes. I was not yet in Plymouth after my escape from the Navy. Though Plymouth was my destination, where I hoped to find the wife of Robert Appleford. I knew not then whether he was alive or dead.'

The Edystone Reef, 1756

They continued to take detailed recordings of the surface topography, using the theodolite to obtain hundreds of vertical measurements plotted accurately within the circumference of its beam. There were many more survey measurements needed for making an accurate representation of the rock, than Smeaton had at first anticipated, and on one landing their work was suddenly cut short by the sea's groundswell and rising tide. Jessop was ever vigilant to the sea.

'Time to get off, gentlemen!'

The boat's crew made ready to cast off and called to the others to come aboard.

'You see, Master Smeaton, how quickly the tide can catch us unawares,' Jessop said as he negotiated his way across the sloping top toward the mooring.

He heard Smeaton's voice behind him call out in reply, 'I see how dangerous our situation is, Josias! If our small boat be staved upon the rocks ... We must have another boat in attendance – I do not wish to increase the risk to our lives any further!'

The swell was making the Gut a very dangerous place for a boat to be in. Mr Jessop hoped to get out astern.

'Indeed, but we must hurry now or risk running the Gut. We can talk in the boat, sir.'

He called an order to the crew.

'Prepare to slip, and use the oars to go astern – there's shallow water ahead.'

They boarded as swiftly as possible and got under way. Rowing out astern, a wave swept through the narrow channel of the Gut and lifted them clear. Jessop gave the instruction to hoist sail.

'That's well done, now take her away clear of the rock and we can bend a sail for Plymouth.'

Austhorpe Lodge, 1792

The old man was, for a moment, lost in his memories of that spring in 1756, the sheer difficulty of getting on and off the rock where they were to build the proposed lighthouse. He told the story of it to his guests. Mary listened with a resigned expression. She was a dutiful daughter who loved her father dearly but there were times when he seemed to forget how often she had heard such accounts of his engineering exploits. The Edystone figured largely, but he often spoke too of his bridge at Hexham. The bridge had collapsed in a flood. At least the Edystone brought happy memories, she thought to herself.

'The elements plagued us constantly – even when conditions proved suitable to land and for our boat to lie alongside the House Rock, they could easily turn and make it impossible to stay.'

Trehearne recalled the danger vividly.

'There was many a time when we were carried and tossed like a leaf through the gap in the rocks.' He remembered how in high seas the yawl had flown through the lethal passage, carried on the back of a surging wave. Smeaton had had to devise some way of making it safer to reach the rock.

'I even considered building a timber breakwater across the gully to stop up the gap and to break the force of the seas. Then a simpler and more expedient approach came to me. I had seen the King's men o' war moored to transport buoys in the Hamoaze. If we also could moor a buoy with chains about fifty fathoms from the Gut, then by fixing a hawser between it and the landing place we could sail unhindered to the buoy.'

'We then were able to haul our boat back out against the wind and tides at our convenience, using the windlass aboard the *Neptune*,' Trehearne explained needlessly to Alice. She, like Mary, had lived with the story for more than thirty years.

'Mr Jessop added some suggestions of his own for its improvement, by fixing eye-bolts into the rocks on the east side of the Gut. These had cables attached to them when the wind was easterly and thus kept the boats from being blown onto the House Rock.'

John Smeaton described their final visit to the rock in that first season, shortly before his return to London.

May 15th in the year 1756. We landed on the rock at half past eleven in the morning and staid there till half past two in the afternoon. The wind being then Easterly and beginning to blow a little fresh, we found it proper to quit the place for fear of staving our vessel against the house rock ... there would have been much less danger, as she would have been far more manageable, had the proposed fender piles, or Mr Jessop's proposition been in use; for though we were six hands in the Edystone Boat, and used our utmost endeavours to prevent it; in coming out of the Gut the boat struck against the north rock and sprung a leak, though no considerable damage was done to her.

'But we got back somehow,' said Trehearne. 'I never have been so completely frightened as then – even if I could not show it.'

Smeaton let out a sigh.

'And it would not be the last time, eh, John Trehearne – or John Bowden, as we knew you in those days.'

8

A visit to Lanlivery

Some weeks earlier, on 14th April 1756, they had set out aboard the *Edystone Boat* for the Stone, but with winds becoming fresh and veering to the south-east out of the Sound, they made passage to Fowey instead. Smeaton wished to see the quarries of moorstone within reach of the coast. Lanlivery, a place about six miles from Fowey, was one such, where the stone was worked. Standing in the bows, his eyes rested on the town and river mouth ahead of them, as she sailed serenely up the tidal estuary to 'Foy'. The boat was soon approaching the harbour mouth, and he looked along the harbour walls to the shoreline, his hands clasped behind him. Mr Jessop joined him. They stood framed in a triangular space created by the deck, masts and shrouds, while the massive walls of the harbour came closer toward them.

'These walls are well built, Mr Jessop. It is a fine harbour, and yet I know nothing of it.'

Mr Jessop hung onto the shrouds.

'Aye, Mister Smeaton, many's the time freshening winds have sent us running for Fowey – and been glad to get in ahead of the storm.

There's deep water in the entrance and the harbour will take merchant vessels of almost any size, at any time of the tide.' He paused, then added solemnly, 'Many a ship has foundered 'pon the coast when its crew could, with better knowledge, have found shelter here.'

Jessop had greater experience of 'the Stone', including getting home safely from it, than probably anyone else living, with the exception of the local fishermen. He spoke his thoughts as they entered the harbour mouth.

'This place will serve us well. Plymouth Sound and Fowey Harbour lie nearly at a right angle from the Edystone.' Smeaton pointed out their positions, relative to the reef, on the folded chart in his hand.

Jessop nodded, and indicated with the line of his hand the courses to take, depending on the wind.

'Aye, that's right, sir. If it blows right ahead from the Sound, we set sail for Fowey – the wind will be upon our beam steering for Fowey. If it blows due north we run under the shelter of the 'Deadman' then turn into Fowey, but when it blows too far westward we can fetch Plymouth Sound with a single tack.'

'But on our last voyage, we could not so much as get within a league of the Rock!' Smeaton did nothing to hide his exasperation. Jessop wondered if he blamed him for his caution, but Smeaton was thinking only of the difficulties that had presented themselves when they were within a stone's throw of the place. Something would have to be done if they were to proceed.

'Seeing our Rock, calm and serene, yet unapproachable, confounds me! We have need of a vessel there to act as a station – within say a quarter of a mile – where the workmen can lodge and stow tools and materials. Then they can reach the work by rowing out in small boats, landing both themselves and the materials, except in the very worst weather.'

'That would make a great deal of difference.'

Jessop was a shipwright at heart and he instantly considered the kind of vessel he would like to build for this purpose.

'We should build a sloop of about fifty tons, Master, strong and sound, with a double skin. If the inner ceiling boards is caulked as well as the outside planking, 'twould remain watertight, even if she catches on the rocks.'

'And she could have two pumps, one for draining the hold within and another to clear the cavity between the plankings,' added Smeaton.

'Then she would be exceptionally fit for her purpose. Sloop-rigged, she would lie snug at her moorings and would be easily managed if she broke free in heavy weather.'

Smeaton aired an alternative, for he had been informed of the intention by Trinity House to commission a temporary lightship.

'There is another possibility, sound as this is; one that might save us the expense.' He went on to explain.

'There is at this moment a vessel being fitted out in the River Thames, intended to serve as a temporary floating light. She will lie all winter at her moorings. If near enough ...'

'She might also serve our purpose?' Jessop interrupted.

'Yes, my thoughts exactly – as well as housing the light, it might serve as our station and save our employers a great expense. We'll hang fire, Mr Jessop, put nowt into action until we know more.'

'Steady!' a crewman called out as the *Edystone Boat* inched up to the harbour wall. He cast a line to the harbour side, where another hitched the line to the rings, and they felt a gentle knock as the boat came up alongside. They disembarked and headed along the busy quay into the town.

That night they stayed in the relative comfort of one of the inns in the town. They rose early the next morning and saddled hired horses to ride to Lanlivery. When they got to the village they were directed by a man on the road to the house of Walter Treleven. Walter had as a young boy worked for his older brother Peter, who had been awarded the contract by Mr Rudyerd to prepare the stones for his lighthouse – the stones that now lay submerged in the Gut. They knocked at the door and waited. It was answered by Walter Treleven, a healthy-looking man in his sixties. He had very blue eyes and the leathery, dark skin of a man used to the outdoors and manual work. Smeaton introduced himself and explained his purpose for coming there.

'Aye, Mr Smeaton, my brother Peter can tell you more. He is still alive but he is quite infirm now at eighty years of age.'

Smeaton wanted to learn more of how the masonry in the lost lighthouse had been fixed, and he spoke to the two brothers.

'Were the stones inside the tower mortared?'

'No, sir, they were not. Although we neither of us actually visited the Stone to see them placed.' This was as Mr Jessop thought.

'None of the stones was above a ton in weight,' said Treleven. 'We prepared them with holes and chases so each could be cramped to its neighbour, and some – the stones nearest the outside – to those above and below as well.' Smeaton listened intently to what the old stonemason had to say on the subject.

'And to get a good fit and be certain of their going together well within the construction, the stones were all finished here at this place by ourselves and were tried together upon a flooring of boards – like a platform. We cut all the holes to let the cramps in from a pattern that Mr Rudyerd gave to us.'

'This is most interesting to hear, Mr Treleven. Now I would like to see your moorstone for myself. Can we get to the quarry from here?'

'Oh yes, sirs, if you go back toward the village and take the lane leading up onto the open moor. That will bring you to the stone quarries in about ten minutes at walking pace.'

They thanked him for his help, remounted and left on horseback in the direction of the quarry.

'These stones are much larger than those at Hingestone Downs,' commented Smeaton, clambering up onto the largest piece and proceeding to measure it. He called down to Jessop to take the ground measurement. The huge boulder of a stone appeared flawless. He clambered back down to tell Jessop,

'According to my rough calculation I believe it to contain no less than four hundred tons!'

'Remarkable, sir.'

Smeaton wondered if he meant the stone or his mathematics. Jessop had such a dry manner sometimes, he thought.

Walter Treleven had told them that from Lanlivery the stones were hauled along the road on wooden 'ploughs' to Par for shipping out. The largest stones would be around one and a half tons in weight, and these were the heaviest they could manage using the ploughs, which were crude sleighs pulled by teams of oxen. It was about three miles down to Par, but the road was very badly made.

It grew late and they decided it was time to begin their journey back to the coast, Smeaton took from his pocket a piece of Lanlivery granite that he had picked up during their tour of the quarries. He examined it and passed it over to Mr Jessop, riding alongside him.

'Treleven told me that this was the stone used in the pavements laid on the new Westminster Bridge. Do you remember my telling you how they were made stronger by the use of stone dovetails tying the kerbs to the pavement? How I got my idea for bonding our stonework from them?'

'Whoa, easy now!' He clung on to the horse as it negotiated a gully in the road, where the surface had been washed away. 'A pity they hadn't thought to use it nearer home!'

'Do you think it will serve us well enough?' asked Jessop, still looking at the stone sample, and oblivious to his companion's near-fall. He held it very close and studied its coarse grain, and the white spar pieces embedded into it, that the locals called 'dog's teeth'.

'Oh yes, perfectly well, I should say! Though I think it's softer than we saw at Hingestone Downs, all moorstone is equally imperishable to the weather, and this is easier to work with the pick. I should say it will suit us very well for the face work,' Smeaton concluded.

'But it's not the easiest of stones to get to Plymouth.' Jessop, as always, was pragmatic in considering the facts.

'We'll not find any nearer the sea than this, and if we *are* to build in stone then we shall need much more material than Mr Rudyerd did,' John Smeaton observed. Though granite was durable and impervious, it was also by nature difficult to work, heavy to transport and easily 'bruised'. For the quantity of stone needed, it would be better to use it sparingly. He considered it without doubt the only choice for the parts of the tower that would be exposed to the sea – the outside walls and the facing stones of the massive base he called the 'solid'. The stone used in the inner mass and internal floor vaults could be of another type, a limestone, its choice and characteristics being determined for a different purpose, easily workable, and readily available from a reliable source. In London, much use was being made of the white limestone from Portland Bill.

'I have in mind another stone for the inner work. I daresay I may have to look further afield, but "Portland" comes directly from the coast of Dorset.'

'I know it, Master. Commissioner Rodgers invited me on a tour around the King's Docks and I saw much Portland used there in the buildings and the quays. It looked an excellent stone to work.'

'Good – then we are of like mind on the subject. Once our survey work is complete and things are settled here I shall visit the Portland quarries.'

'When will that be?'

'Soon, I hope. I have an appointment this summer in London that I *must* keep if I am to be married.' Smeaton laughed.

'You are to marry? Is it true, sir?'

He assured Jessop it was.

'Why, Master Smeaton, this news deserves a wetting. Here, your health, sir!' Jessop produced from his waistcoat a small flask, unscrewed the cap and took a swig, then he offered it over. Smeaton took hold of it, and elaborated on his plans to marry Anne Jenkinson. He had proposed and was accepted, and they were to be wed in St George's Church in Hanover Square in June.

'So you see, I must not tarry too long here if I am to be at the church for the ceremony!'

'Indeed you shall not, sir. Wait till my wife hears of this! She will see to it that you are sent off in good time.' This man genuinely amazed Mr Jessop. Here he was, attempting the impossible (Jessop still had his reservations about building the tower of stone, but he was keeping them to himself), and here he was announcing his forthcoming marriage!

'And yet he seemed so sure in his purpose,' Josias thought to himself. He could not but admire his steadfastness.

On arriving back in Fowey they found the wind still a fresh south-westerly, and they sailed for Plymouth with the tide on the morning of Saturday 16th April. A few weeks later they learnt of another quarry where moorstone was worked, at Constantine, near Falmouth, and Smeaton recorded in his *Narrative* his meeting there with the owner and master stonemason, Mr Matthew Box.

He was at this time executing a Grave-stone, of the elevated kind, of which the pedestal of a column gives the idea; and in which he had formed the mouldings with so much delicacy and propriety, that I could not help considering Mr Box as a capital artist in that kind of material; and therefore felt a secret joy in meeting with such a person.

Such however is the nature of man, that he may be great in one branch of his profession and remain small in another: for on communicating the nature of my design to him, I quickly found, that (he considered) the forming and erecting of a well shaped Tomb-stone of Granite, as the greatest of all human performances and that having lived and been brought up in a retired part of the country, he had chiefly applied himself to the finishing of smaller works for the gentlemen of the county within a moderate distance from him. He seemed therefore rather frightened than pleased, when after I had explained a little of the nature and form of the work I should be likely to need, I mentioned the extensive order that I might possibly give for this article; for, to the execution of it he formed numerous difficulties, and did not know what to ask, either for his stone, his work, or the carriage down to Falmouth.

Having decided that moorstone should be used only for the outside of the lighthouse and that some other 'free working' stone should be used within, they favoured Portland. It could be supplied in larger and heavier sizes and would be easier to procure in the volumes that were required. Smeaton determined to visit Portland en route to London, before the wedding. In the meantime, he enlisted Jessop's help in the making of two models, one of the Rock in its existing state, and another of the completed tower. He would present these with his proposals for the scheme to the body of the Proprietors, and to the Elder Brethren of Trinity House, in London.

Mr Jessop volunteered the use of his small workshop in the cellar at home. It was where he made the models of sloops and men o' war for his son, William. They allowed William to join them for a while before his bedtime, as long as he behaved himself. The boy was fascinated by the small, intricate pieces all made in different woods – mahogany, cherry and lignum vitae among them. He was allowed to look but not to touch the miniature blocks of wood that were used to make each individual stone. He marvelled at the tiny pieces, the manholes and covers, ladders and shutters – even furniture. Josias had made three box beds with sliding doors and curved backs. William peeped in at them while his father put the finishing touches to the model of the Rock, measuring from Mr Smeaton's drawing with his compasses.

Smeaton was telling Jessop how he had brokered a deal and placed an order for the moorstone with both Walter Treleven and Matthew Box.

'Matthew Box is an odd fellow, Josias,' he said as he clamped two small pieces of the wooden base to dry together.

'Oh, why is that?'

'Well, at first I thought from his worrying and reluctant attitude that he no more wished to take such a large order for his stone, than to go to the moon.' He handed the piece to Josias. 'It's not as if we have called for the stones to be finished, being as moorstone is difficult to bring to a sharp arris and then easily snapped. I told him we only required rough-worked stone, to a size slightly larger all round, for finishing here by ourselves.'

'Has he refused you, Master?'

'No, luckily the opposite! He not only wants to supply the stone, but has offered it at a price lower than that of Mr Treleven in Lanlivery.'

' Well, I'll be! He must have learnt of Mr Treleven's offer! Will you take all from him now? His is the better in quality, there be no softness or spalling, and 'tis better coloured.'

'Nay, though what you say is true – I'd rather not put all our eggs in the one basket, if we are to have all the stone we need in time, this coming season.'

'I think we agreed a price of twenty-five shillings per ton, for stone from Mr Treleven,' said Jessop; 'at fourteen feet cubic measure, and he wanted four pence per foot for working of the beds.'

'Aye, and we undertaking the water carriage from Par.'

'What is Mr Box's offer?'

'Twenty shillings, laid down here in the yard, with seven pence per foot for working of the beds.'

'That's better indeed.'

'It is, but had I not gone to Walter Treleven in the first place, then we would not have terms so low from Mr Box. He sees that he has to agree with me or lose the whole order to his rival.'

'How will you choose?'

'The safe way is to order a quantity from both. I think we give forty tons to Walter Treleven and the remaining two hundred to Matthew Box, with a hundred tons delivered by him by Mayday, to match Treleven's date.'

Josias Jessop nodded in affirmation and let out a long breath.

'There, 'tis finished.' He stood up, putting a hand on William's shoulder. 'Time for you to go to bed! Come on, up we go. Mother will bring you a drink to bed.'

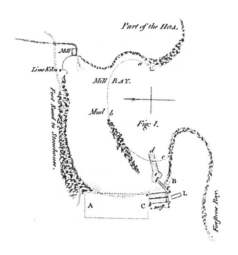

Part of the Hoa.

Mill

Lime Kiln

Mill BAY.

Mul b

Fig: 1.

Foot Road to Stonehouse.

A

C

B

L

Firestone Bay.

9

The fugitive

It was a warm spring day when John Trehearne entered the site of the workyard at Millbay. John Smeaton was continuing his visits to the Rock at every available opportunity. He aimed to complete his measuring work before his departure for London, but today he was at Millbay.

Smeaton had found a site for the workyard at Millbay, a muddy cove about a mile to the west of Plymouth, and lying just beyond the Hoe, on the road to Stonehouse. The bay looked out towards Drake's Island and was surrounded by open fields. The tenant, a Mr Delacumbe, had (with the requisite permission granted by Lord Edgecombe, his landlord) let a half-acre area of pasture for the workyard. A wooden fence was being erected around the perimeter to enclose it from the stock and make it secure on the three sides flanking the shoreline. In the bay, a channel was being dredged to allow the ships to reach the shore. A wooden jetty was being constructed out into the channel. This was for loading and unloading the stones that would be brought in by sea to the works, and later sent out as finished pieces for the building on the Rock. A pastoral scene

95

was suddenly transformed with the chaotic bustle of construction work, as the yard was laid out with new roads and tramways.

John Trehearne emerged along one newly cut track through the melee of workmen and carts. He was now recovered from his ordeal. He had made his way to friends in Cornwall, who gave him temporary work and lodging until he was ready to move on. He had heard of the new undertaking at Millbay and thought that here he might find employment as a seaman or shipwright. Here, he thought, he would be safe from the Navy press gangs, and from here he would find his friend's wife, and tell her what had happened to them that night on board HMS *Dart*.

News had quickly spread beyond Plymouth into the surrounding country, and across into east Cornwall, that men employed in the Edystone service would have inducements in their pay and working conditions far better and more preferable than any other common employment. People were talking about the man at the centre of this venture, who hailed from Yorkshire and who was come to build, so it was said, a lighthouse *entirely of stone*.

'Where can I find the man from the north country?' Trehearne called out to one of the men directing operations. He was in the midst of setting a timber pier truss, and he pointed Trehearne towards a makeshift timber cabin. Trehearne tipped his hat and passed on toward the cabin door. Trehearne knocked loud and heard a voice cry out to enter. Inside he found two men; one was John Smeaton and the other a Mr Harrison. The taller man gestured for him to sit while they pored over ledgers and account books. He had never heard such a strong Yorkshire accent as he did now. Smeaton was discussing the accounting procedures with Harrison, who was newly arrived from London to take up his post of Clerk to the Edystone Works. Trehearne took in the details of the room and the man before him.

John Smeaton wore a coat, waistcoat and breeches in a cloth of straw or buff colour. His grey tricorn hat lay on the trestle table, which served temporarily as a desk and drawing board. On the wall behind them Trehearne saw a poster which listed the terms and conditions of the workmen in the Edystone service. This was a 'Plan for carrying on the Works and Management of the Workmen'. John Smeaton had himself drawn up the document and presented it to the Proprietors. He intended to provide the best and most effective working conditions for the men, the consequences of which being that '*the work would of course be performed, not only as expeditiously as possible, but at an expense to the Proprietors, as low in regard to the value of daily labour as could possibly be expected upon the former establishment.*' This was to revolutionise the nature of the employment, and the effectiveness of the men employed in the Edystone service.

After a few minutes Smeaton broke off and, looking up, he gave Trehearne an intense look. Smeaton's shoulder-length hair was tied back, revealing a handsome face and strong features. He had an air of shrewdness and confidence, tempered with benevolence about him, and Trehearne felt here was a man he could trust.

'Good day, Mr ...'

'Bowden, sir, the name's John Bowden,' said Trehearne, bidding them both 'good day' and introducing himself as an artisan carpenter, skilled in shipwrightry and hailing from Polruan, near Fowey in the county of Cornwall. He had taken the name since coming to Plymouth, to lessen the risk of discovery. As a deserter he would have to answer to the Navy if they found him – but worse, he feared his enemies aboard HMS *Dart*.

'Ah yes,' Smeaton paused and looked him over with a steady gaze, 'we have visited Fowey only recently to observe for ourselves the working of moorstone there.'

Smeaton detected as he spoke that the man before him would be a valuable asset to their company, but something in his demeanour alerted him. What could it be? He surmised that John Bowden was not telling him everything. There was more to him than met the eye, he thought.

'Fowey is a fine harbour.'

'Yes, sir, it is,' replied Trehearne. 'I've sailed out of Fowey many times, in all kinds of craft. I grew up on the water and the fishing goes back a long way in my family. My father was master of a sloop, the *Foy Princess*.'

Smeaton bid Mr Harrison continue with the work of opening the ledgers. He stood up, then continued, 'So, Mr Bowden, thou's a sailor as well as a carpenter? Yes, happen we need someone of your abilities, now that the work is getting under way. You see for yourself how busy we are in making preparations.'

Smeaton pointed in the direction of the new quay. 'I like nothing better than to hear the ringing of hammers on iron,' he announced. He believed that he could make a fair judgement of a man's character in their first meeting, and he decided that this man, though he hid something, would serve him well.

Trehearne saw a model before them and found that there was truth in the rumours he had heard, that Mr Smeaton had every intention to build a lighthouse in the sea entirely in stone. Smeaton led him to the poster upon the wall.

'If thou's to join us then you will abide by and receive the benefit of the articles written here in the plan of work for the workmen.'

He elaborated on his method for organising his workforce.

'We are forming two companies, who will move between the work at sea – that I call the 'outwork' – and the preparatory work on land, here in the yard. The men have a weekly changeover, and I intend that the fewest possible operations remain to be done whilst on the rock, other than landing, raising and setting the stones.'

Trehearne listened attentively while Smeaton spoke of how he intended to devise the best possible mortar for this circumstance, one that would set in the worst sea – 'and become as firm as the stones themselves, making the whole a solid, impervious and therefore durable construction.'

'Tell me, John Bowden, can you read and write?'

Smeaton invited him to study the plan and to ask any further questions once he had done so.

'The rules and conditions apply to all who are employed in the Edystone service. If you are satisfied with these and willing to join us, I will send for Mr Jessop to sign you onto the books right away.'

Trehearne accepted and Jessop was sent for. As a shipwright/carpenter John Bowden was offered the same rate of pay as the masons: this was two shillings and six pence per day certain at sea, with a premium of nine pence per hour for every hour during that time spent on the Rock. For work ashore, the rate was twenty pence per day, with overtime at double the price per hour for the daily wage.

Smeaton congratulated him. 'Welcome to the Edystone service, Mr Bowden.' He took his hand and shook it firmly. 'But now if thou will excuse me, I have other business with Mr Harrison here.' Smeaton returned to his work with the clerk, leaving Jessop to introduce Bowden to the company.

'Come with me, Mr Bowden, I'll take you to your work,' said Jessop as they left the cabin and headed off through the workyard.

'You will be in the charge of William Hill,' he told him. They walked down toward the new pier where Hill's company were engaged, sinking wooden piles.

'Here is Hill's company, and Richardson's is the other over there. I dare say you will find there exists a friendly rivalry between the two, but we are all in the Service together.' As Jessop's words trailed away, a man turned about to face them. His was a dark face, lit only by his glaring eyes. He chewed a wad of tobacco in his mouth and sent forth a jet of brown juice onto the ground beside him.

'Extra pair of hands for you, Mr Hill.'

'Mr Jessop,' he signalled to the new man beside him, 'I could do with them right away. We've a devil of a job to get this jetty put in.'

'Well, Mr Hill, here's answer to your prayers, for John Bowden is come to start, and he is both a seaman and shipwright – it's your good luck to have him this day.'

Trehearne immediately recognised Hill as the man he had seen with Midshipman Baines that night he lay exhausted and near death on the beach. He was startled for an instant, but disguised any outward sign of his surprise.

HMS *Dart* arrived in the Royal Dockyard in Plymouth just a few days later, in May 1756. That morning Alice Appleford sat at her desk in the drawing room; the morning was fair and she decided she would walk to the obelisk on the Hoe to take in some fresh air as soon as her household tasks were completed. Perhaps there would be news of her husband today.

Alice was tall and dark. She had a look of determination, but this did not detract from her handsome appearance. She was the eldest daughter of Mr and Mrs Vasey. Her father was the squire residing at Breakstone Hall, and Vaseys had lived in that part of south Devon bordering on the edge of Dartmoor for generations. She expected a visit from them shortly. They were concerned for her, since Robert's disappearance and the news of his being taken by the press gang to serve aboard HMS *Dart*.

Her younger sister, Verity, could still not believe such a thing could happen to a gentleman. Verity lived with her parents at home, she was sixteen and bored with life at the Hall, and so took every opportunity to come and stay with Alice in her smart town residence. This crisis was a good reason and Alice enjoyed her company – seeing Verity was a welcome distraction to her. Verity was full of life and enjoyed meeting the society in Plymouth. Alice had taken her to the Assembly Rooms and she had noticed how Verity turned the heads of the young officers there, with her striking russet hair and winning ways. She was already a beauty, an elegant young woman, brimming with a confidence that could be described as precocious. Alice was thinking of her as she wrote in her diary. It would soon be time for her arrival.

Outside, the sun shone brightly upon the elegant stuccoed façades of the terrace. Beyond the streets she could see the green fringe of the Hoe and beyond that Drake's Island and the wooded slopes of Mount Edgecombe Park far, far away, merging with the Sound. The sea beyond was a deep blue band. She was about to rise and make her way out into the warm sunshine when she noticed a party of naval officers in the street below. They stopped outside the house and then she heard the knocking at the door. Her maid answered it. Alice heard their voices and the sound of hurried steps coming up the stairs to fetch the mistress. She suddenly felt a cold dread as the maid knocked and entered the study. Her face looked anxious.

'There's a Lieutenant Colquhoun downstairs, ma'am.'

'What is it he wants, Mary?' Alice asked, trying not to show her fear.

'He says he has come from the *Dart*. He has news of Mr Appleford.' She spoke with a quiet concern that made Alice feel sick in the pit of her stomach. Feeling herself becoming faint, she fought to overcome her fear. No longer aware of the beautiful day outside, Alice stood up, closed the diary and replaced it in her bureau.

'Tell them I will receive them shortly, Mary.' Alice steadied herself and smoothed her dress before Mary returned with the officer leading the party. Alice introduced herself and invited them to sit. She sat opposite and prepared herself for news of her husband.

'Sadly I am the bringer of bad news. I am sent by the Captain, madam, to inform you of your husband's death.'

She sat motionless as Lieutenant Colquhoun prepared himself to describe how the events of one night had resulted in the trial and punishment of her husband, and his subsequent death and burial at sea. Then he cleared his throat to speak.

'Madam, I regret the circumstances of my visit, but I must also tell you with regret that your husband did not die honourably.'

Alice's face blanched, as if she were drained of all vitality. She was unable to speak. He continued.

'I regret your husband was caught in the act of deserting the ship, and resisted arrest. We were to find that he had stolen a large sum of gold that was aboard the ship – a French prize. When the alarm was sounded, he drew his pistol and shot an officer in the ship's company. The offence called for a severe punishment from which, I regret to say, he did not recover.'

Alice was devastated by the news of Robert's death and appalled at the circumstances. She did not for a minute believe the accusations brought against him and was filled with the mixed emotions of anger, sadness and longing – longing for her husband's return, despite all she had just been told. She felt sick with grief and fury. As if it was not enough to learn that her husband was dead, he had died a humiliating death, convicted of thieving and attempted murder, as a common criminal.

But despite the inner turmoil that was tearing at her, she kept up a façade of decorum, and listened in silence while the Lieutenant coolly described his version of the events. She fixed her eyes on his cold stare and pallid face, and the correctness of his manner.

'The evidence was overwhelming. The Captain had no other choice but to sentence him to a punishment in keeping with the seriousness of his offence.'

Alice was close to tears but she wanted to know more.

'How did he come to shoot a man; surely he was provoked in this?'

'The pistol was his own. He produced it during his arrest to escape capture. He aimed and shot to kill.' The Lieutenant spoke slowly and quietly, so that she hung on every word.

'But it is not like him, he was most gentle and kind. I cannot believe that he would do such a thing unless his own life depended on it!' Alice could contain herself no longer and made it plain that although Robert was pressed into the Service, and the Navy was not his chosen career, he would not disown his family honour without good reason. Colquhoun felt uncomfortable, seeing too plainly that here was an intelligent woman and that she was deeply suspicious of his account.

'I am sorry to have to tell you the worst,' he insisted. 'Perhaps your husband acted out of character, for I own everything I have told you is the truth, as you will read it in the captain's log.'

'Sir, my husband served on your ship amongst the rank and file but I assure you that he was no common tar; he was a gentleman. His family are well respected in Cornwall and with connections in Bath and Somerset. The Navy took him and the Navy have killed him.'

Her eyes flashed with anger and contempt. 'And why is it that the Captain has not come, but sends his subordinate?' Alice was in full flight. Colquhoun's face twisted with a look of annoyance and dislike at this treatment. It was an unpleasant duty; he determined not to let her get the better of him.

'The Captain regrets his not being here to convey the news himself, as he is presently detained with the commissioner. However, you may have full redress to him with any grievance, whilst we remain in Plymouth. I will convey your sentiments to him.'

'You needn't, sir. I think since he is unhurried to call upon me with a duty I would expect, then I shall instead make my own acquaintance with Commissioner Rodgers to petition him in this matter. I wish to know why my husband was made to suffer trial and punishment at sea, when it could have been conducted here in Plymouth.'

Rattled by her persistence in finding out the truth and in making Appleford's death a public investigation, he sought to control the situation. He stood up before her, with his back to the fireplace.

'Life at sea is hard and discipline must be maintained at all times. Under the Articles of War this was an act of treason.'

'But the manner by which he was tried appals me! He had no means of redress. He was a good man, of good birth and with all good prospects until the day he went into Stonehouse and met with your recruiting party.'

The Lieutenant had heard enough. It wasn't his fault that the man had died; other men lived beyond a flogging, he thought to himself.

'I beg you; it was not our intention to take his life, but he committed a mutinous act for which he paid the full price.'

He signalled to one of his deputation to bring forward and present Alice with her late husband's effects. Amongst the items laid before her was the box containing his pistols. They bowed and took their leave of her. Mary followed them downstairs and showed them to the door. She slammed it shut behind them.

In the weeks that followed Alice grieved for her lost husband, but she determined to do everything she could to resolve her nagging doubt, and clear her husband's name. When Verity arrived they talked of little else, although Verity did her best to relieve her sister's mood and to interest her in society events in the town. At last the day came when Verity was to return home to their parents. She pleaded with Alice to accompany her, but Alice would not leave. She needed to know more, but who would tell her the truth? The following days seemed empty to her; she felt in the depths of despair.

It was at this point that she received a visit from a stranger who said he knew her husband. The stranger introduced himself as John

Bowden, but out of earshot of the servants he told her his real name.

'You see I must of necessity take such precautions. I am a fugitive – I will hang if my enemies discover me. I have gained employment in the Edystone service at the works in Millbay, but I am only recently arrived here and this is the first opportunity I have had to find you.'

Alice was wary of their being overheard even here within the household, and she beckoned him to follow her into a small reception room on the first floor, where she closed the door behind him.

'I had your address from an acquaintance of your husband known to me as Mr Sheldrake. I called on him earlier today. I have not been into the town before now for fear of someone recognising me, and then there are the press gangs, of course.'

'Tell me everything that happened that night,' Alice begged.

'We were making for Plymouth and our course ran very close to the coast, passing well clear inside the Edystone because of the loss of the light. Being so close presented an opportunity to the smugglers to land some of the prize gold that they had stolen.'

John Trehearne began to tell her the events of that night, and then saw how upset she became.

' I came here tonight hoping to learn news of Robert's whereabouts and welfare, but I see in your face that something terrible has happened.'

Alice broke into tears when she told him what had happened to Robert, and how the Lieutenant's lies led to his being flogged to death on board HMS *Dart*.

' I am truly sorry to learn of it, ma'am. He was a good man and a friend. I wish that it could have been otherwise, but I tell you – your husband did not die a dishonourable death. I know the truth.'

Alice fought back the rush of emotion. 'Please, Mr Trehearne, I beg you tell me all.'

She listened in silence while he told her his account from the beginning.

'We boarded a French merchantman – the *Liberté* – and in the action that followed, Robert your husband distinguished himself. He was in the vanguard that swept onto the deck of the enemy ship as we came alongside. Our boarding party soon gained the upper hand.

With the French subdued, we put them down into the water in their launch to make for the French coast.

'Ours poured onto the stricken ship to remove as much of her cargo and any loose valuables as was possible, before the sea claimed her. It was then that the gold bullion was discovered and First Lieutenant Colquhoun took charge of its removal. That evening there were great celebrations as we made course for Plymouth. The ship's rules and regulations were relaxed and the men enjoyed grog. A fiddler played well into the night and the men were happy, knowing that on their return to shore they would receive their pay and surely a little more besides. The Captain was hard but fair in sharing the spoils and we each hoped for some extra reward.

'Midshipman Baines woke Robert in the early hours. He was taken up on deck, where the Lieutenant attended a small party. I awoke and followed, and hid on the main deck. They were lowering the launch and I heard Colquhoun's order to Robert to pilot them ashore. This wasn't the first time. Smuggling took place regularly off this coast, under orders from the Lieutenant. The men involved were bound to silence or would suffer the consequences. Below decks we all knew what was going on. But this time it was more serious. They were stealing a portion of the French prize from the Captain, and his Majesty the King, and they could hang for it.

'From my hiding place I saw what happened next. Robert refused to join them and the Lieutenant flew into a rage. He ordered the men to take him by force. There was a moment's hesitation, just long enough to allow Robert to draw a pistol. He was outnumbered but had the advantage of holding Lieutenant Colquhoun at gunpoint. That moment seemed an age. I looked about me and took hold of an oar. I stood up and rushed the nearest of them. Before he had time to move, I rammed the butt end into him and brought the blade of the oar in an arc above me, crashing down upon the rest. They scattered but soon regained their resolve and pulled knives from their belts. As they dashed forward, Lieutenant Colquhoun drew his sword and cut Robert with a slash across his chest and forearm. I saw him fall backwards, and as he fell, he took aim and discharged the pistol, shooting Colquhoun in the shoulder. The ball passed right through and he dropped like a stone to the deck.

© Plymouth City Museum and Art Gallery

A

NARRATIVE OF THE BUILDING

AND

A DESCRIPTION of the CONSTRUCTION

OF THE

EDYSTONE LIGHTHOUSE

WITH STONE:

TO WHICH IS SUBJOINED,

AN APPENDIX, giving some Account of the LIGHTHOUSE on the SPURN POINT,

BUILT UPON A SAND.

By JOHN SMEATON, *CIVIL ENGINEER*, F.R.S.

The MORNING after A STORM at S.W.

See §. q. n. v. 90. and Technical References.

LONDON:

PRINTED FOR THE AUTHOR, BY H. HUGHS:

SOLD BY G. NICOL,

BOOKSELLER TO HIS MAJESTY, PALL-MALL. 1791.

© Plymouth City Museum and Art Gallery

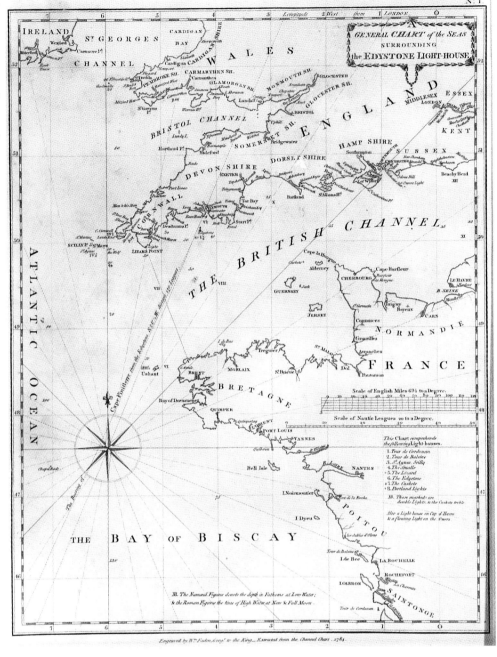

1.   (Previous page) The title page of Smeaton's own account of his project. *The wonderful rising of the water … so far from being exaggerated is much reduced in both height and bulk, in order that the building therein may present itself.*

2.   (Above) Eighteenth-century chart showing the Eddystone Rocks in relation to the Western Atlantic.

© Plymouth City Museum and Art Gallery

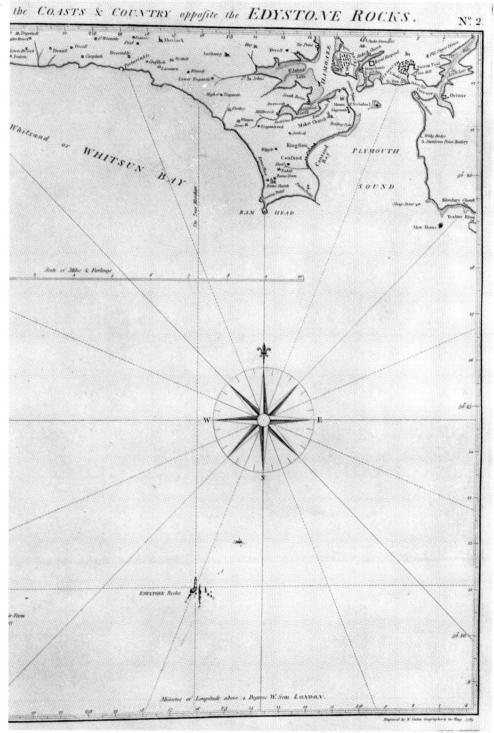

3.   Map showing the Eddystone rocks' position fourteen miles SSW of Plymouth.

© Plymouth City Museum and Art Gallery

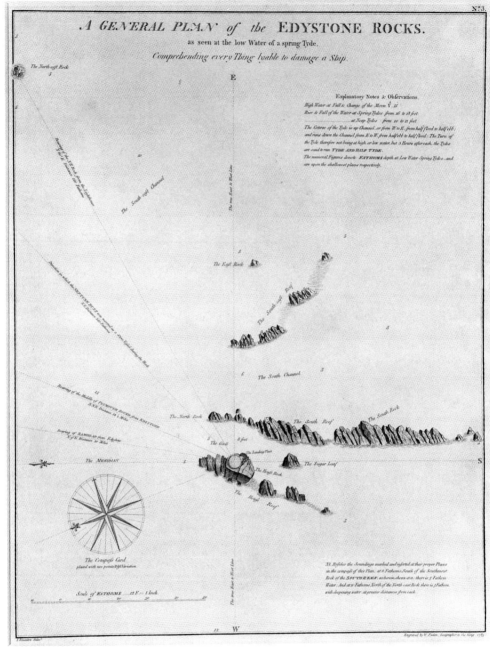

4.   Detailed plan of the rocks – *comprehending every Thing lyable to damage a Ship.*

© Plymouth City Museum and Art Gallery

Scale 1 Inch = 6 Feet.

South ELEVATION *of the* ORIGINAL LIGHTHOUSE,
Built upon the EDYSTONE ROCK, *according to the first Design of* M.ʳ WINSTANLEY.
Taken from a Perspective Print, drawn at the Rock, by Jaaziell Johnston. *Painter.* ── *Engraved by* Hen. Roberts. *1761.*

5. Winstanley's original wooden lighthouse, completed in 1698.

© Plymouth City Museum and Art Gallery

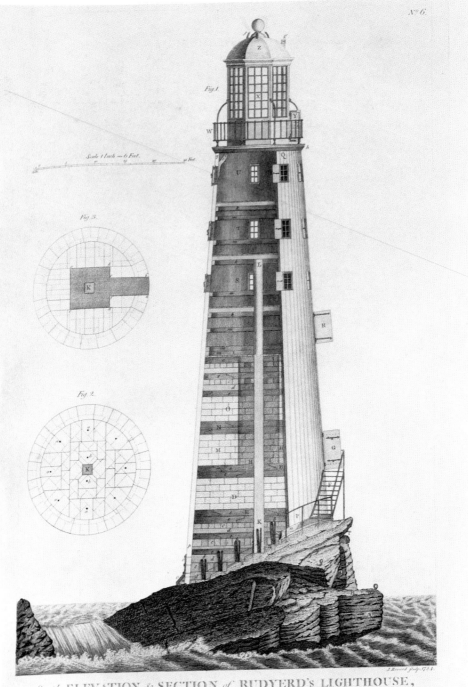

South ELEVATION & SECTION *of* RUDYERD's LIGHTHOUSE,

Completed in 1709, represented as it stood previous to its demolition by Fire, in the Year 1755.

6.   Rudyerd's wooden lighthouse, destroyed by fire in December 1755.

© Plymouth City Museum and Art Gallery

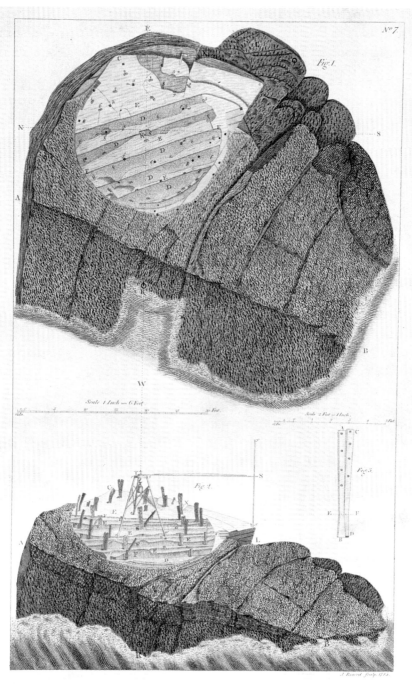

PLAN *and perspective* ELEVATION *of the* EDYSTONE ROCK,

Seen from the West. Taken from the Model thereof mentioned Sect. 105.

7. The Eddystone Rock as it was found by Smeaton on his first visit, showing the remains of Rudyerd's lighthouse.

© Plymouth City Museum and Art Gallery

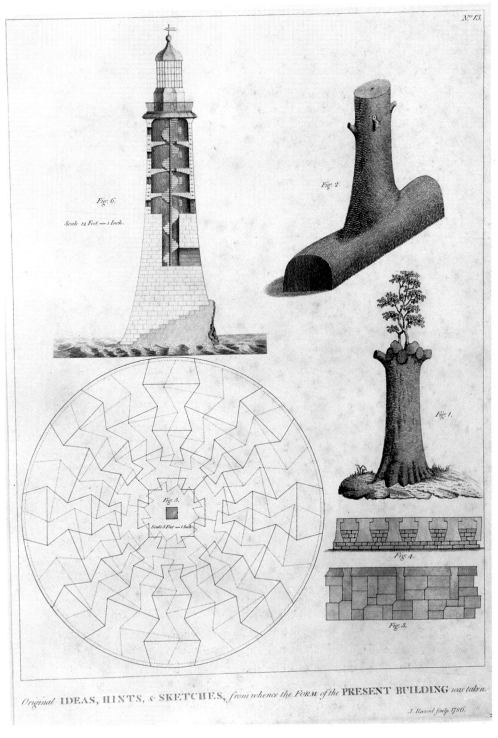

Original IDEAS, HINTS, & SKETCHES, *from whence the* FORM *of the* PRESENT BUILDING *was taken.*

J. Record sculp 1786.

8. One of Smeaton's plates showing an early design with a full spiral staircase and some of the ideas that inspired him — the oak tree anchored by its roots, and the dovetail pattern of paving stones in London's streets.

'Two of the men fell upon Robert and the rest, under orders from Baines, came at me. I had no choice but to throw the oar into them and run for the side. Leaping onto the gunwale, I threw myself as far forward as I could and plunged into the icy seas below. I am a good swimmer but it took all my strength and will to reach the shore. I came ashore exhausted and near death from the cold, but I was able to haul myself up the beach and into a small cave in the cliff. Here I remained till I was recovered sufficient to walk to the town of Looe. There I gained employment and came from thence to Plymouth as soon as I was recovered.'

He fell silent, watching Alice for her reaction.

'Thank you, Mr Trehearne. I am indebted to you for telling me the truth. It consoles me to learn that my husband was innocent, but my grief is fuelled by anger. Anger of his treatment and the lies that led to his unjust punishment at the hands of that horrible man, the same officer who came here to see me and who blatantly concealed the truth of it for his own sake.'

Through her tears, Alice's eyes blazed in the candlelight. She felt that she must do something to clear her husband's name. 'I am resolved to petition the Admiralty concerning my husband's fate, and present evidence to them that will shed light on Lieutenant Colquhoun's cowardly conduct.'

'I have carried the complete episode in my mind,' said Trehearne, 'and spoken of it to no one until now – in fact I have made an art of concealment, for my own preservation.' He felt a burden lifting from his shoulders; he was glad to share the truth with Alice, and know that it gave her solace. They slipped quietly downstairs and she bade him goodnight. He took her hand, then turned and went out into the night.

Afterward she sat awhile, staring into the dying coals in the fire and pondering over the whirlwind events and news brought to her by this man. She felt she trusted him and shared a bond in their knowledge of the truth about the events surrounding Robert's death. She could not help but admire the courage he had shown in his willingness to risk his own safety to clear her dead husband's name. In the next few weeks he visited her frequently and their friendship grew. Then she received a reply to her letter from Commissioner

Rodgers. The Board were sympathetic toward her, but upheld the actions of the Captain in suppressing mutinous actions, and administering a suitable punishment forthwith. He ended that they considered naval discipline to be paramount on board a ship of the line in his Majesty's fleet.

Alice knew that she might never be able to prove her husband's innocence. Her only consolation was that in meeting John Trehearne she knew the truth of it, and she was not alone.

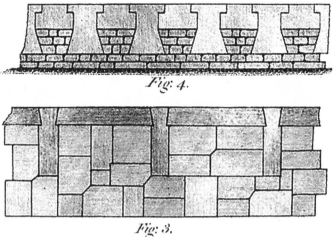

Fig: 4.

Fig: 3.

10

London

Alice first met John Trehearne on 5th July 1756. That same day, a newly wed John Smeaton stepped aboard a vessel that was being fitted out in the River Thames. The *Neptune Buss* was originally commissioned as one of a fleet of ships for the herring fishery. Now purchased by the Corporation of Trinity House in Deptford, she was being converted at the Corporation's expense for the purpose of a floating light, to make safe the Edystone Reef. John Smeaton had left behind him the preparations in Plymouth, which included plans for improving the landing stage in the Gut. On Mr Jessop's advice they had decided to abandon the idea of building the timber breakwater that Smeaton had proposed to tame the seas around the landing place. Instead Jessop made headway with preparations for placing chain moorings and a transport buoy to which their vessels could be secured safely on the reef.

Smeaton had arrived in London on Friday 21st May. On the journey from Plymouth he had visited the quarries on the Isle of Portland, and had successfully concluded the search for a suitable stone to build the inner solid of the lighthouse. Portland was readily

available and could be got to Plymouth by sea at a reasonable cost
and in sufficient quantity for their needs.

Since arriving in London, he had married Anne Jenkinson, a native
of York, at St George's Church, Hanover Square, on the 6th June. The
wedding had been a joyous occasion and the weather most
favourable, but there was little time for the wedded couple to enjoy
solely in each other's company. The very next day Robert Weston
came to the house to view the painstakingly completed models of the
rock and the lighthouse, showing the proposed construction in stone.
These illustrated Smeaton's idea for adapting the existing rough-hewn
steps to a more regular shape, with steps to fit the stone foundations.
Each level would have pockets cut in from above in order to receive
the dovetail shapes of the lowest foundation stones. He demonstrated
the principle to Weston, by picking up his model of the house and
placing it carefully into the socket sunk in the model rock. It fitted
perfectly to the circular footprint of the base of the column.

'See here: to make the foundation last, every outside piece of stone
is to fit a socket in the rock, guarded by a border at least three inches
higher than the bed joint. We intend to cut the rock as little as we can
help, and knowing fully the nature of it, we can humour its
irregularities'.

Smeaton went on to describe why he had invested such effort in
replicating the form of the rock.

'My intention is to cut in the rock such a figure as will suit the
building.'

'And how will you do it?' Weston asked him. 'The model is
beautiful in its intricacy, but surely, shaping the rock to your design is
a great labour in itself, made much worse by the wash of the tide?'

'Indeed, but there is no avoiding it. It entails blood and sweat and hard graft, but I would not ask your approval, nor the men to undertake such a task, if I did not believe it can be done.' Smeaton took from his pocket a sample of the red rock that he had brought back with him. 'We have in our earliest landings cut chases and drilled holes into the rock with hand tools, that prove it to be workable.'

Weston realised the enormity of the work that was involved just in preparing the rock itself, before a single stone could be laid. Seeing his expression, Smeaton explained his reasons for not blasting the rock down to a level formation, just as he had with Jessop, but there was no denying that his decision to cut the rock without the use of gunpowder entailed a mammoth task ahead.

Had it been practicable to have cut the rock down to the level of the lowest part of the intended base of the building, little previous contrivance or consideration, would have been wanted for the purpose; but besides that this would have been more than the work of a full season; the space which had been previously occupied by the rock so cut down must have been made good by fresh matter.

'Were we simply to blast away the rock as Mr Jessop suggested, we should lose the very "holdfast" and buttress that the rock affords for our security; especially against the great sou'westerly seas.'

At Wapping steps they hailed one of the many boatmen who plied to and fro across the Thames. He rowed them out into the mainstream. Scores of small craft sailed up and down the wharves, where the great merchantmen were berthed, all crammed together.

At Deptford two new men o' war were nearing completion, decked in flags in the naval dry dock, then ahead of them in mid-river came ships of the East India Company at their moorings between Greenwich and Blackwall Reach. Ghost ships strung out in long lines, stripped of sailcloth and rigging, some without their masts and shrouds. Their cargoes would have been swiftly transferred to the great East India warehouses and now they lay deserted, awaiting the necessary refit before embarking again on a new voyage.

The taxi carried them downriver to Blackwall, where the *Neptune*

Buss was undergoing some last-minute adaptations before she sailed for Plymouth. She was moored in the river and they recognised her by the lantern on her mainmast. The boatman brought them alongside.

Once aboard, they made their acquaintance with the master, who took them on a short tour of the vessel, pointing out the improvements that were being made. Carpenters were busy completing the alterations to her deck and sides. Mr Weston, who was not an experienced mariner (although he had made the sea-going voyage to Plymouth and accompanied Mr Jessop on visits to the former lighthouse), listened attentively.

'She has her deck and sides raised some four streakes, fitted flush fore and aft, so heavy seas can wash over her but she stays dry within.' The master pointed into the hold. 'That fir timber ballast will keep her buoyant even if she's holed beneath the water.'

He opened the hatch and beckoned them to follow him below, talking all the while as he disappeared below the deck. 'Even so there remains a spacious accommodation. Come and see'. They joined him in the living quarters below and found her both 'roomy and well equipped'.

'What is her burthen?' Smeaton enquired.

'She is about eighty tons, sir.'

The master begged them to excuse him. 'I have a score of things to attend to, if we are to be ready to sail in three days' time.'

Out of earshot of their guide, Smeaton confided in Robert Weston.

'I hope they place her within a league of the House Rock where we can make use of her as a store vessel; she's room enough for the keepers and the Edystone workers to live happily side by side. And I calculate that 'twould save you no less than £500.'

'How is that, Smeaton?'

'Mr Jessop and I hold that this is the sum necessary in fitting out a similar vessel for our own use. If we are to expedite the work and take no longer than my forebear Mr Rudyerd did to complete the wooden house, we will need a secure vessel stationed at sea. And she must be held fast with strong chain moorings to keep her from harm upon the reef.'

Smeaton was keen to drive home their need of a floating workstation. Weston thought it over in silence as they made their way

112

back up on deck, where a new windlass took Smeaton's eye.

'You see, Mr Weston, how excellent the new equipment is. This is a fine windlass, give praise where it is due; the brethren of Trinity House have done themselves credit.'

Robert Weston blinked in the strong sunlight as he emerged from the dark cabin into the afternoon light. He focused on the windlass, still thinking about Smeaton's idea to share the *Neptune* with the light-keepers.

'I agree with you wholeheartedly, but I cannot influence the Elder Brethren of the Corporation to what might be considered our own self-interest. They are the proper judges of where the floating light should be moored.'

'Very well, we might find something else to suit our purpose if this is not available to us,' Smeaton said as he climbed up onto the deck.

'Have you any news from Plymouth?' asked Weston.

'I am keen to return there and make a start. Mr Jessop has sent regular reports of the preparations at Millbay. He has put in hand fitting out a sloop to join the *Edystone Boat* in our service, and he has purchased a large yawl from the sale of the *Sea-Horse*.'

The tide had turned on the river. In a gap at the ship's side, they saw below them the brown eddies flowing upstream. The flow of the great Thames was stemmed and for a while turned back upon itself. It was time to leave. They descended into the water ferry attending them, to return to the city. Once they were settled in the boat, the boatman cast off, rowing swiftly with the incoming tide back upriver.

Robert Weston gazed across to Greenwich. They came around the great bend where the East Indiamen lay at their moorings. He spoke his thoughts.

'Smeaton, can you present your scheme to the Proprietors in a week's time? I can muster the greater part of them by then.'

Smeaton fixed him with a steady eye and smiled. 'Indeed I can, sir. I have completed the drafts and models and was hoping to present them to yourselves and the Elders as soon as possible. I really must return to Plymouth soon if we are to progress the work upon the rock in this season. For that I need your final approval of the scheme I am proposing.'

Put ashore, the two men walked a short distance together from

Billingsgate to St Paul's, and then parted. They agreed to meet again on Tuesday 13th July with the body of the Proprietors, at the lawyer's office in nearby Ludgate.

Smeaton walked northward toward Clerkenwell. On the way, he passed by a shop window and something caught his eye. It was a delicately painted 'Chinese fan', brought here no doubt by one of the Indiamen he had seen moored in the docks.

'It would make a delightful gift for Anne,' he thought to himself. He went inside and later told her how he had come by it, as if on purpose. She kissed him. She was very happy, though she knew that he would soon be leaving her to continue his work in Plymouth. They agreed to make the most of the short time remaining to them. That evening she carried the fan with her as they walked in the hot midsummer night toward the theatre in Drury Lane. He was not particularly fond of plays, but Mr Garrick's production in the Playhouse was the talk of the town and Anne talked of little else, but to see it.

The days passed quickly. On the evening of the 13th Mr Weston gathered the Proprietors at Ludgate for a presentation of the proposals by Mr Smeaton. There was an air of expectancy as Smeaton arrived and was ushered into the waiting room. He heard the voices of his audience gathered there awaiting him. Without any further delay, he entered the room. Robert Weston made him welcome and then formally introduced Smeaton to the individual owners, who each held a share in the Edystone Lighthouse. He had a number of models and drawings with him. These held their attention, and following a short introduction from Robert Weston he proceeded with an explanation of his design. Smeaton observed how curious they were to see the models of the new design. He presented before them his first model, showing the existing rock and remnants of Rudyerd's light.

It soon became apparent that many of the Proprietors had never actually seen an accurate representation of the house. Their spokesman begged his patience.

'I think I should tell you, Mr Smeaton, that the majority of the owners here tonight have never yet set foot on the Edystone, nor ever been in the vicinity, and have only known it from artists' representations of the former lighthouse.'

The owners gathered round the model of the rock. They marvelled at the intricacy of its detail and were very curious to know the purpose of the forest of small metal branches that stood up out of the surface. Smeaton described how Mr Rudyerd had let these into the rock and fixed them with hot lead so that the upright timbers at the base of the timber column could be secured. After a lengthy description of the former lighthouse constructed by Mr Rudyerd in 1703, and sensing that they were satisfied and the ground was prepared, he produced his second model. It showed the rock, and now, set upon it, the entire proposed house, including the lantern – the third Edystone Lighthouse.

Robert Weston unfurled Smeaton's drawing and fixed it to the wall behind them. The fine lines looked spidery in the flickering candlelight he held aloft. The drawing, entitled 'a Fair Section through the proposed Lighthouse', was drawn to the same scale as the model before them, and showed the interior cut through, with the order of rooms shown one above the other. A great stone spiral staircase passed up through the centre from the entrance passage, through the rooms up to the lantern interior. A flurry of questions followed, directed toward Mr Smeaton, and Smeaton, now well versed in the scheme, was able to answer these fully.

Then came the question he knew would sometime be put to him.

'We understand, Mr Smeaton, that it is the popular opinion held in the vicinity of Plymouth that nothing but wood can last upon the Edystone. How do you propose to convince us otherwise, proving that your methods and materials will indeed last?'

'Let me show you how!'

He carefully took hold of the solid maquette of the lighthouse and lifted it away from the rock. It revealed a socket cut into the rock and the imprint of the tower base and foundation. Turning the lighthouse base toward the audience he pointed to the pattern of dovetailing in each step or course of the foundation and told them how this would marry the great mass of the stone column to the rock itself, and that this intricate joint would have the effect of rooting the building into the rock below the surface.

'The whole column will resist the sea, just as an ancient oak tree resists the winds that tear at its spreading canopy, by being set firm into the rock itself.'

There was a spontaneous applause; the Proprietors agreed they were unanimous in their approval of the design and desired that Mr Smeaton should show his drafts and models, and explain his scheme, to the Lords Commissioners of the Admiralty, and to the Corporation of the Trinity House. A second meeting was to take place in the next few days, before Mr Smeaton's departure for Plymouth. Tonight had been a resounding success, and afterward Robert Weston congratulated him; he had gained the unanimous backing of the Proprietors, who gave him full powers to run the project as he saw fit.

The *Neptune Buss* slipped her moorings in the Thames and sailed for Plymouth on the morning tide of 8th July. Smeaton left for Plymouth on the 19th, without the opportunity of presenting his design to the Elder Brethren of Trinity House. This was disappointing because he believed that their support for the scheme would help '*to dispel the opinion of those who by way of security to their own, generally fall in with the popular opinion; which was that nothing but WOOD could possibly stand upon the Edystone.*'

The morning of 19th July dawned fine and clear. Smeaton rose early to pack the remainder of his luggage, including the models, which were carefully placed in wooden crates for the journey. The coach stood in the mews outside and during the morning a steady stream of trunks, boxes, baskets and crates were carried down through the house and across the small garden to be loaded into it by the footmen. Smeaton looked on with satisfaction at his new coach. He had had it built to his own design, to improve his comfort on the long journey ahead of him. Lastly he checked the loaded pistols, kept inside the benches as a deterrent to any would-be highwaymen, should they be met with on the lonely road.

At breakfast Anne did not say much, but he could sense her mood. She was concerned for his safety, and she resented his leaving her so soon. Would her marriage always be like this, filled with interruptions and long absences, she thought to herself. They ate together in silence. Smeaton for his part was thankful that she did not enquire of him about his business. He preferred the silence and was quite relieved not to have to tell her the exact nature of his work. 'It would do no good,' he thought, 'she would only have greater cause for concern.' He himself was frightened to think of the endless possibilities for disaster that lay ahead, and preferred to put such thoughts aside.

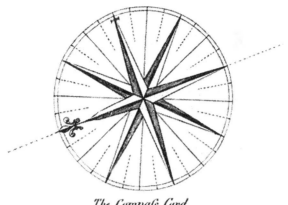

The Compaſs Card
placed with two points Weſt Variation.

11

A maiden voyage

John Smeaton returned to Plymouth on Friday 23rd July 1756. During his absence in London the weather had not been favourable, but Mr Jessop had made good use of his time ashore, completing the repairs and re-fitting of the *Edystone Boat*, the attendant vessel *Hancock's Sloop*, and a large yawl he had purchased, known as the *Great Yawl*. By Sunday their prospects improved. The weather was fine but with little wind, and since the ground cables for the sloop were not yet ready, Smeaton determined that they should try rowing out in the new yawl *'with the aid of such breezes as might happen'*.

There was an air of optimism for the yawl's maiden voyage to the Rock. The oarsmen picked up the stroke and rowed out across the fourteen miles. The sloop was directed to follow them, but she made no headway in the calm seas and remained in the Sound (where they met her on their return later that afternoon). Smeaton sat happily in the bows, reflecting upon the light and airy mood of high summer, writing down his thoughts later that evening in his journal.

At last the season's outwork began, and the companies, led by the foremen William Hill and Thomas Richardson, soon began to make an impression in the shaping and cutting of the foundation. Following a weekly timetable in which each company took its turn to cut and hew the surface, they made steady progress. They were served by *Hancock's Sloop*. As yet there was no proper store vessel and they had to ferry materials and sharpened tools between the shore and the rock as best they could. They anchored the sloop in safer waters, about a hundred fathoms north of the Gut, where the soundings were even and the seabed less irregular.

John Trehearne, for his part, was happy to have found himself in a regular employment where he was, he thought, safe from discovery by the Navy. As 'John Bowden' he worked well with the men and quickly became a trusted and valuable member of Hill's company. He worked as a carpenter, and doubled as one of three attending seamen who would crew the sloop and the yawl. His seamanship and maritime skills were obvious and soon recognised by the hands. They valued the protection afforded by such seamen in landing, supplying and taking them off the reef, depending on the tides and winds. It was always a precarious operation, demanding the utmost of the companies, but morale was high and between them they had landed and worked every tide since they began.

At this time of year the prevailing winds along this part of the coast blow, in fine weather, from the north, or from land to sea toward the evening, and turn around to blow from southerly points in the early hours following sunrise. The *Edystone Boat* took full advantage of this pattern, making a regular trip every twenty-four hours. Departing in the evening from Millbay, she would return from the Edystone by mid-morning of the following day. This pattern allowed the work to continue without interruption throughout the first two weeks in August, until the 15th, when rough weather forced Richardson and his seamen to slip the bridle cable and make for Cawsand Bay. Hill's company had had the best of it and were all pleased to have spent so much time during their week away actually working on the Rock. It had gone so well for them that they had each earned more in a single week than at any time since joining the Service.

But despite their high spirits and good morale, there soon developed a growing tension between Hill and some of the men.

Trehearne himself noticed Hill's increasing impatience with them. He disliked William Hill but he was careful to keep his opinion to himself. The last thing he needed was to draw attention to himself and his background. He remained a fugitive, and if Hill learnt of it, he was the sort to exploit a weakness. Hill was resentful that the men beneath him, including 'John Bowden', were earning so much double pay and overtime as set out in the plan drawn up by Smeaton for time spent working on the Rock. He would provoke disputes, and chose to favour some above the others to gain their loyalty and allegiance. Trehearne saw it was his intent to disrupt the workings of the company, so that he might abuse his power with harsh discipline and bullying, whilst appearing to keep order amongst the unruly ranks.

The floating light arrived from Plymouth on the evening of Friday 13th August. The Corporation of Trinity House, having encountered difficulties in the leasing of the *Neptune Buss*, had commissioned another vessel to serve as a floating light in her place. The *Buss* now lay idle in Stonehouse Creek, since her arrival from London almost a month ago. Josias Jessop and John Bowden, standing together on the deck of *Hancock's Sloop*, watched as the new vessel sailed past them. To Jessop's dismay she continued onward for some distance until eventually she laid down her moorings about two miles west by north of the House Rock. It was in a location too far away to be of any use to them in their operations. A light was exhibited from her that same evening. As twilight deepened into full darkness Jessop came back up on deck to observe the efficacy of the light. He found John Bowden taking the first watch.

'That's of little use to us,' Jessop remarked as they watched the dim glow of the light in the evening sky. The lantern, held aloft on the ship's mast, was barely discernible. 'If we can hardly see it here, then tell me how mariners will, and know the exact position of the reef?'

'P'rhaps they think it too risky to moor her any closer and have placed her deliberately ahead of the reef as an early warning to incoming shipping,' Bowden replied.

'Oh, I expect you are right. Fog-bound voyagers, probably out in their reckonings coming into the channel, will be glad of meeting the light early, before they are come to harm.' Mr Jessop was tired and ready to turn in. They would be up early to meet Smeaton, who was due to arrive in the morning on the next tide with Mr Richardson's company. He turned to John to bid him goodnight.

'Well, I'll say goodnight, Mr Bowden. Mr Smeaton will be with us tomorrow and will decide matters. We thought to share the lightship as a transport station but she's of no use to us out there, and we need our store vessel soon if we are to progress.' Jessop shook his head at what he saw in the distance. 'I thought the Elders of Trinity House Corporation were all supposed to be time-served seamen!'

John nodded in agreement. It seemed a strange location, so far from the reef, but he saw an advantage to it.

'Perhaps now the Elders will consent to our use of the *Neptune Buss*. They won't wish to be reminded that she lies idle in Stonehouse Creek, having spent a great deal of money on her fit-out.'

'Indeed, you be right, John, and I am certain that Mr Smeaton will not miss the point in telling them so! Goodnight to you now.' He made his way down the steps to the cabin below.

It was a calm clear night and, alone, John's thoughts turned to his meeting with Alice Appleford. She had been in his thoughts constantly, particularly when he had time to sit and think during the four long hours on watch. He decided he must visit her again as soon as possible. He got hold of a boathook and raised the cables as much as he was able, to check the mooring for fastness. The moorings had parted on previous nights, when the ground cable was cut through by its constant fraying on the rocky outcrops that lay hidden beneath them. The crew had already spliced and 'wormed' the cables as a running repair until the new chain moorings were ready to bring out. The cable appeared sound.

At last there was a stirring below, then the relief came on deck to take the dawn watch. They exchanged a few words and he turned in for the night.

In the morning, Smeaton landed on the Rock, where he was very satisfied with the progress that Hill's company had made. About a third of the dovetail steps had now been cut to the crayon lines he had laid down himself.

'If we can get our ship and the chain moorings in place, Mr Jessop, I reckon we will complete the shaping of the rock before the weather turns foul,' he said. He was buoyant and clearly in an optimistic mood. 'Look what the men can achieve when they are able to land on every tide.'

Jessop nodded his agreement but he remained cautious. 'The weather determines our progress, Mr Smeaton,' he answered. They cast off to return ashore with Hill's company that evening.

It was now late September, and John Trehearne was on his way to visit Alice. He walked from Millbay the short distance to Plymouth. Since their first meeting in July he had called on Alice regularly. This was during the weeks when Hill's company were ashore, taking their turn in the workyard. Taking off his waistcoat, he slung it over his shoulder, for it was a warm evening that followed a glorious day, and as he strode across the fields he looked seaward past Rame and into the west, where the sun sank low over the shores of Mount Edgecombe. He gave a thought to Richardson's men, out there beyond the reach of his gaze. His path took him across the Hoe and towards the great grey-walled fortress called the Citadel. Alice's residence was just a short distance beyond it, in a fashionable new development that overlooked the Hoe and the Sound. He could see ahead of him the rows of new, stuccoed buildings shining in the evening light.

Alice was expecting him. He had written, in his best hand, requesting to call on her this evening, and she had sent her reply with her maid, that he should call and stay for dinner as soon as it was convenient to him. Over supper he described to her the events of the last couple of weeks.

'The greatest help has been our getting accommodation and stores catered for at sea. Mr Smeaton had the Elders of Trinity House grant us permission to make use of the *Neptune Buss*. Up until a week or so ago we have had to make do with *Hancock's Sloop* and the *Edystone Boat* making regular passage on the tides, bringing us our tools and taking them back to Plymouth for sharpening. But the sloop is continually parting her mooring cables, frayed until cut on the rocks below us.

'Oh dear, that could be disastrous, surely? Still, how do you find the new boat?' Alice motioned to John to help himself to the food on

122

the steaming platters brought to the table and placed before them. 'And are they treating you well at sea?'

'Yes, very well. We have stores enough for our week aboard. The food is simple. 'Tis much less refined than this sumptuous feast, but compared to Navy rations we eat like princes. I'm treated fairly, and the pay is the best I have had in my life – regular too.'

'I am very pleased to hear it, but what of the dangers? I'm told even the Cawsand fishermen are afeared to go there unless it is becalmed. Of course, some are braver than the rest. Dr Edwards of Rame sent a boat to save the keepers from the fire last December.'

'Indeed. Well, I would say the *Neptune* is as safe a vessel as we could wish for. She's well founded and lies quietly at her moorings in the roughest weather – not that we have had any great tempest yet to speak of,' he paused between delicious mouthfuls, 'though her seaworthy qualities, that see her ride well at the moorings, make her the worst possible to sail – indeed I have never known so heavy a sailer! We had the longest passage yet to make the reef. I thought we would be driven back into Cawsand and that 'twould prove nigh impossible to get there. Lord knows how they encouraged her to make Plymouth from London!'

Alice's maid lit the candelabra and the sconces and took away the first course. She returned with the butler, bringing in the main course, seafood fresh-landed in Sutton Pool.

'You may leave us now,' Alice said, dismissing them both. Trehearne noticed how Alice's dark eyes sparkled in the candlelight. For the first time he envied Robert: she was such a beauty! What must he have been thinking in those last few moments, when he knew he would not see her again?

'Now that we are left to ourselves, tell me more of your progress – Mr Trehearne.' She whispered his real name in hushed tones and almost laughed out loud. Despite her period of mourning for her lost husband, there was an unmistakeable secret delight in dining with a handsome fellow who happened to be a fugitive.

'We're proceeding steadily in cutting the formations into the rock, despite the delays we've encountered. The *Neptune* has been secured for our use as a transport station, with great chains. These are held off the bottom using a bridle cable attached to a great buoy. 'Tis a very ingenious method of Mr Smeaton's and Mr Jessop's invention, to keep the chains free from chafing on the rocks beneath us.'

He demonstrated with his watch chain and some items of cutlery on the dining table.

'You see, here is the *Buss* and these are the mooring chains.'

Alice studied Trehearne's features, absorbed in completing the model. 'How handsome he is,' she thought. Their eyes met and she hurriedly looked away.

'Oh, I expect this is not really of interest,' he apologised.

'No, please do continue. I should like to hear everything. All your adventures in that extraordinary place are of interest to me.'

'The weather last week and the week before slowed things up, so we had not more than twenty hours on the Rock, I would say. I'm quite glad to be back. Here in Millbay I am engaged in making timber moulds that will be used to shape the exact finished stones. Mr Smeaton first draws in chalk the shape of every stone in a plan at full size upon the House Rock foundation and we follow his pattern to model the frames for the stones, so. He says we must soon find a room large enough for him to draw the remaining stones in these and all the higher courses. He says there'll be fifty-two courses.'

Showing Alice how each stone is dovetailed to fit a pattern, he asks for paper and scissors, then cuts shapes and arranges them on the dining table.

''Tis only roughly shaped here, but every stone is made specially so that all fits perfect together. These vary in each layer of the foundation.'

Alice listens politely, but her eyes are drawn to his face. He notices, and feels his skin flush at the thought of her intense scrutiny. He changes the subject.

'We had an adventure one night, that Mr Jessop, seeing the danger to an approaching West Indiaman, alerted us and sent us out to give assistance. She were in great danger of driving upon the north-east rock, for there was no wind in her sails and the tide was strong, and if nothing was done they would certainly have struck upon the rock. We went to her in the yawl and towed her off.'

'And saved her?'

'Yes, I suppose so, but it would have been too late had Mr Jessop not seen the danger first and acted upon it.'

Alice is thrilled to hear his vivid account of the rescue. They talk awhile longer; the natural light ebbs away until only the candles and a low firelight from the hearth light the room. At last talk turns to Robert. Alice reads aloud Commissioner Rodgers' letter, stating his findings upon the matter of her husband's punishment and death.

'They have closed ranks on me, Mr Trehearne. I suppose my fighting a case for Robert will only cause them embarrassment. I expect I should be quiet and genteel and then polite society would offer me their sympathy, though the gossips would never cease to remind everyone how Robert died and the shameful guilt upon him.'

'You will not be popular in seeking the truth, Alice, nor will it improve your prospects here in Plymouth. Expect only slander and scandal – 'specially from those with something to hide themselves.'

'I know, can I gain anything for Robert's sake? And I don't want to get you any more involved in this. What if you were caught?'

'They'd see me hang! But for what it's worth, your sacrifice of your good name for your husband's honour does you credit! And you mustn't give it up!'

'Thank you for your kindness, John. Yes, I will write to the Admiralty. If they would investigate the case we might still have justice.'

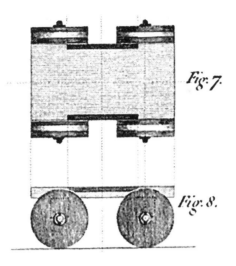

Fig. 7.

Fig. 8.

12

The season's end

It was almost six o'clock on a late September evening when a party of naval officers made their way along the quayside in the King's Dockyard. Picking their way through the assortment of stores, timbers and chandlery that lay stacked up, and avoiding the lines of mooring ropes that stretched across their path, they passed in the shadows of the great leviathans – the battleships of the Western Squadron. Each looked resplendent, painted in bands of black and yellow with their names emblazoned in gold leaf above the banks of latticed windows in the sterncastles. Commissioner Rodgers remarked enthusiastically upon how it stirred him to see them so close – *Duke*, *Antelope*, *Hornet*, *Achilles* and *Dart*.

'Boscawen will deal the French a bloody nose with such ships at his command.' He roused the captains around him. 'There's French prizes for the taking, gentlemen.'

At last, after a long summer at sea, the *Dart* was home once more. Below decks the crew had drawn the cannon up against the ship's sides to make more room and they were joined by visiting wives, women and children in makeshift quarters on the gundecks. Unable to get ashore until they were paid, they made the best of the situation. The hubbub of voices, shanties and laughter carried on the evening air.

Captain Howard had invited the Commissioner and fellow officers from the Fleet men o' war to dine this evening on board. Lieutenant Colquhoun, seeing them approaching, gave an order for the crew to assemble on the main deck to pipe them aboard. The party strode up the gangway and took the salute on deck. They made their way up to the quarterdeck and into the captain's cabin. As the evening wore on, the two great stern lanterns were lit, throwing light onto the slate-grey waters in the harbour pool below. The captain threw open a casement; it remained warm below decks from the heat of the day. He turned and spoke to his guests.

'The hot weather is very welcome. I declare these last few days have been remarkable, fine and clear. Yesterday evening I was walking on the Hoe with Mrs Howard and I could clearly see, in my glass, the light from the lightship upon the Edystone.'

'Quite so, Captain,' the Commissioner agreed. 'The floating light sailed from Plymouth to take up her station only recently. The light has been displayed every evening since.' He paused to take a mouthful of the roast pheasant served them. Looking round, he saw that most of the invited officers had received their plate and were too absorbed in eating for conversation, but the Captain took it up.

'It is a great comfort to all mariners, to see a light thereon once again. I have it reported to me that she is moored some distance away from the House Rock, though, for her safety and self-preservation, so make certain you don't get too close until you have the place firmly fixed in your reckoning, gentlemen!' There was a murmur of consent around the table.

The officers had removed their hats and were sitting around a dark polished table. They were dressed in the full officer's uniform of white waistcoat, breeches and stockings with navy-blue tunics, liberally trimmed with braiding at the lapels and cuffs. Their faces were animated, lit by a lantern that hung from the curved wooden ceiling of the deck. The conversation turned to the *Dart*'s French prize, taken earlier in the year. The Captain was keen to relay how, in engaging the French ship, they had captured it, and brought home the spoils of war. He called upon Lieutenant Colquhoun, who gave a graphic account of the boarding party which he had led onto the *Liberté*, and how they overcame a terrified French crew. The officers cheered at times and applauded him. The dim candlelight from the lantern glinted on the large gold buttons and braid of their dark blue coats. Some of the younger men wore their hair tied back whilst the Commissioner and the older among them wore periwigs concealing whatever lay beneath. They were all engrossed in the story, particularly the details of how the gold was discovered.

'We recovered the gold bullion only moments before she keeled over and slipped beneath the water. But for a chance discovery she would have taken it with her to the bottom.'

'Well done, sir, well done,' Captain Howard interrupted. He felt he was indebted to Colquhoun for finding and delivering up the French bullion. He had not the slightest inkling that a significant part of it had been stolen and secreted away by the Lieutenant's men at Polparra, and he called for another toast to his officers and crew.

'You've made me comfortable in my approaching retirement from the Service, Lieutenant. My "Liberty" has set me free,' he laughed. 'Your health, gentlemen, and – to Providence!'

There had, however, been one incident to mar the ship's log. The entry told of how Robert Appleford had attempted to take for himself some of the French gold held on board and smuggle it ashore. Commissioner Rodgers told them he had received a letter from Appleford's wife and was obliged to investigate her complaint.

'A bad business, that. Unfortunately it happened that her husband was no common sailor.' The Commissioner paused to reflect on his words. 'And what is more, Mrs Appleford is determined, it seems, to seek recompense. She has written to the Lords of the Admiralty. It puts me in an awkward circumstance, d'ye know. She is the daughter of Squire Vasey, a country gentleman in the county and a Justice of the Peace. I served with her father when we were both young midshipmen on board the *Beagle*.'

Colquhoun, seeing the danger to himself, stepped in to steer the outcome of their conversation. To have the subject brought under close scrutiny would not do. His mind raced. If he could discredit her, the Commissioner would surely see her complaint as a malicious accusation.

'It was I, sir, who broke the news of his death and the reason for his punishment to Mrs Appleford. I did so with a heavy heart and with compassion, but I am afraid to say she was most unreasonable and, dare I say, abusive! I believe she suffered from delusions and a loss of her rational faculties, such was her grief upon hearing of his death.'

'Yes, it is never an easy thing, to bear such news to the wife and kin. Cursed the Navy, did she? Thought so, I've borne it many a time.'

'It was impossible for me to convey to her that, under the articles of the law, the penalty for assaulting an officer is automatic.' Lieutenant Colquhoun added that she would, he thought, see reason and accept the circumstances eventually. He was about to change the subject, but the Commissioner was not finished.

'She has brought serious allegations against officers here present. Her letter to the Lords of the Admiralty contained accusations.'

The Lieutenant was outraged, but the others silenced him. The Commissioner continued.

'I have no reason to believe that there is any truth contained in the allegations, and indeed, in her letter Mrs Appleford gave me no evidence to support her claim.' He paused, and looked gravely about him, then spoke softly and deliberately.

'Unless – there is something that I should know?' His eyes moved swiftly around the table from the Captain to the Lieutenant. There was a silence. Captain Howard was visibly taken aback.

'I am dumbfounded, Commissioner, astonished that we should be slandered by this woman. If there were some misdemeanour I assure you I would know of it and would have acted upon it.'

'Very well, but you understand I am obliged to broach the matter,' replied the Commissioner.

'Upon my oath, the man was dealt with fairly. Though I cannot say I regret his loss – had he aimed an inch lower I would have received a mortal wound.' Lieutenant Colquhoun nursed his limp right shoulder, as if to emphasise his words.

The Commissioner's stern look was gone. He felt relieved and was ready to move on to more genial topics.

'Yes of course, that's settled then.' Commissioner Rodgers concluded that she was 'a woman unhinged by her grief'.

The mood and conversation relaxed as the evening wore on. The Commissioner, who had by now taken a respectable amount of wine, insisted on making a further, unofficial announcement. He stood again.

'Gentlemen, I almost forgot, I have a further item of news that I find much more congenial to announce.' His face was reddened by the wine and he took a draught from his glass before continuing.

'I believe now is the moment to tell you that HMS *Dart* will shortly receive her new command. Captain Howard will be taking a new man o' war and I take pleasure in congratulating First Lieutenant Colquhoun, who is to be made up to acting captain for her next voyage.'

The Lieutenant stood and bowed and smiled a supercilious smile.

'I am indebted to you, sir. This gives me great pleasure – and,' he turned to the Captain, 'I can only hope to equal Captain Howard in his most effective leadership.'

'Your orders to sail will follow within the next week. I wish you well and propose a toast to you both in your new commands. Gentlemen – the captains!'

A final round of toasts was drunk to both captains, and then the Commissioner left them, followed by the other guests. They were by now all quite drunk, and one of the invited officers fell down on the deck before regaining his feet. He steadied himself and then staggered down the gangway ashore.

John Trehearne felt a shiver run through him when he heard of the *Dart*'s return to Plymouth. He wondered if he would ever be free of the man o' war and her Lieutenant, and it concerned him greatly. Until now he had felt safe in the Edystone service. He thought he could escape his past, but the news meant his thoughts returned over and over to his pursuer as he made passage in the *Edystone Boat*. As long as he took precautions not to be recognised by any of the ship's company, especially the officers, and Colquhoun in particular …

He suddenly came to at the sound of William Smart's voice.

'Make ready with the line, Mr Bowden.'

Josias Jessop and Smeaton prepared themselves to go ashore. They sailed directly into the Gut, where John quickly secured the lines to the fender piles of the landing place and drew them up tight alongside. Smeaton leapt up the Rock, followed by the older and wiser Jessop, who moved slowly and cautiously.

'Come along, Jessop, see this!'

'I am coming as soon as age and caution will allow, sir.' Jessop laboured up the steps cleft in the rock and joined him, breathing heavily. They had attempted a landing on the previous day, but the sou'westerly wind raised such a groundswell as to make it impossible. Now Smeaton and Jessop found Richardson's company hard at work, using a stone-splitting technique they called the 'key and feather'. With the aid of iron wedges and cold chisels, they were taking great bites out of the incline, crosscutting the strata of the rock and removing several cubic feet at a time. Richardson touched his hat as Smeaton climbed the rock towards him.

'Mr Smeaton, sir.'

'Good day to you, Mr Richardson. Did you sleep well last night aboard the *Buss*?'

Richardson shrugged and made an expression that said more than his spoken words.

'The swell rocked us to sleep, sir; it blew quite hard, but the craft rode well at her moorings. We had nothing more than our own giddiness to contend with. But we are at our happiest here on terra firma, be it ever so small.'

Smeaton cast his eye over each step and dovetail mortise. Some, including the lowest and most difficult to work (being at high-water level), were completed; others were still rough-cut or 'scappelled out' as the men called it.

'Well, the ocean doesn't seem to have affected thy work; this is coming on very well indeed, and the shaping looks more likely now to be completed this season. Tell me, how's tha finding the new method?'

'Very good indeed, sir. Now that we have developed a skill in our practice, we are able to cut with great accuracy.'

'Quite. The rock is naturally more conducive to splitting along the grain.'

'Aye, sir, see here. The men have crosscut down the inclined bed and drilled out the holes for the wedges, they are to be driven in along the bed to break out the waste. They drives the wedges in sideways to break 'er up to the chase, then they cuts in from above.'

'Tha's the added advantage over gunpowder of being able to predict the areas that will come away. Does thou agree, Mr Jessop?'

Mr Jessop agreed. In fact he was amazed at the degree of workmanship and accuracy that the men had achieved in such a short period of time.

'... though I could not see it just a few months ago. When we landed for the first time and you described it to me, I own I thought it would take forever.'

'Might we finish the work of shaping the house's imprint in the rock before the end of the season?' Smeaton asked him. 'How much longer d'ye think we have?'

Jessop part-closed his eyes before he spoke.

'Mmm. 'Tis hard to tell, but not long. The weather can turn at any time, but with luck we might have another month before we are obliged to lift the moorings and bring in the *Neptune*.' His brow furrowed in contemplation. 'I fully expect this calm to be drawing to a close. We need fine weather to raise the moorings and bring the *Buss* home. And we shall have to leave the mooring chains secure for the winter. I propose to fix buoys that will raise them off the rocks below, or a link may break and the whole be lost.'

'And we still must complete the works,' Smeaton interrupted, 'particularly in getting level the sloping top of the rock and preparing it to receive the seventh course – the proper beginning of the solid. I think with thee to help, Mr Jessop, I can get it marked out on our next arrival.'

At that moment, a cheer went up from the men working below. There was a ringing sound as a chain released itself from the split rock. It was a relic from Mr Winstanley's lighthouse. They examined the chain. It was encrusted with oxide, and as red in appearance as the rock it was pulled from. The links were warped and flattened together, until hardly recognisable – crushed between the rock laminations.

Evening came on, the twilight deepened, and as the sun's cast in the western sky turned through red to indigo, they embarked aboard the *Edystone Boat* for Plymouth. It would be almost a fortnight before they would return. Just as Mr Jessop had predicted, bad weather and poor conditions came on and persisted until the end of the month.

When they did return it was the last day of October. On the reduced and flattened top of the rock Smeaton traced the outline of the seventh course. Then the men, using their hand tools, proceeded to cut the rock within this great circle, and sink down its surface to the level of the top of the course below. When they had finished, it appeared like a giant circular imprint or socket. Below it, they would lay the foundation courses, six in total, into the dovetail-shaped steps. The stone foundation would be rooted into the rock's sides.

There was very little further time spent on the rock. Furthermore, they had recently lost the *Great Yawl*, carried away in rough seas on the night of 13th October. It would be foolhardy to stay any longer. Smeaton ordered Richardson to return with his company. They were to bring home the store-vessel. Although sluggish to sail, the *Neptune* had proved very stable at her moorings, riding out the storms of the last month without shipping any water. Her hold, still packed with the fir-wood ballast that Smeaton had seen on the Thames, kept her buoyant in the 'hollow seas' over the reef.

They had done as much as was possible to prepare the rock for next year's building to begin. Mr Rudyerd's original rough-hewn steps were now sculpted into level platforms with precise dovetailed cut-outs hewn in the vertical risers, and three more stepped excavations were added, as well as the sunk, level top. All was made ready to receive the foundation stones, when they returned next year. Only one task remained: they would have to come back to hoist the chain moorings from the seabed and make them safe. Jessop's proposal to attach floating buoys, holding them clear of the reef for the winter storms ahead, seemed a sensible precaution.

As the *Neptune Buss* approached Millbay, Trehearne found himself thinking of Alice and of their arrangement. She was the most beautiful creature, he thought, and he found himself longing to see her again. She had invited him to accompany her on a visit to Breakstone Hall to meet her family and he had procured three days leave, to go with her in the morning. He was exhilarated at the thought of being so close to her and felt a secret joy, but he was also troubled. What were his prospects for happiness when all the while it might so easily be snatched away from him?

The Sound was so calm and serene that the *Neptune*'s wake carried far across to either side, like scissors cutting through fine linen. Autumn was signalled in the blaze of gold and brown that the trees along Mount Edgecombe's shore had become. Not yet stripped of their colour, they cloaked the hills. The winter gales had not yet begun, but the 'Stone' was renowned for its harsh conditions, when often there was perfect calm along the coast. He gazed toward the shoreline, across the smooth inky waters. A naval sloop of war passed before them, and in a short space of time they were in the channel, beating up to the wooden jetty in Millbay. It had been a long, slow and arduous passage, the *Buss* living up to her reputation as a 'heavy sailer'. Trehearne welcomed its end. He cast a line to the hands on shore, and, feeling a shudder as the black-tarred bows struck the fender posts of the quay, drew in the rope.

'I expect you'll want to be makin' the most of yer leave, Mr Bowden.' Jessop was standing at his shoulder. 'Go on, off you go now, we can take care of matters from here. I'll have her warped up tight and the bottom scraped by the time you get back – she'll be lighter in the water – you won't know she's the same vessel.'

'Thanks, Mr Jessop.'

'That's all right, lad, just mind ye get back here safe next week. We need ye with us to see to those moorings before winter sets in,'

'Aye aye, sir.'

Trehearne met Alice early next morning. He set off from his lodging in Stonehouse long before dawn, reaching her house in Plymouth by sunrise. There a carriage awaited them in the mews, and soon they were off, leaving the streets of the town behind and heading north through the country toward the high tors. The Hall was about twenty miles from Plymouth, on the southern edge of the moor. Alice could hardly contain herself. For the first time in months she felt happy and excited at the prospect of returning home, and staying awhile with her family.

The coach arrived early in the afternoon. It was another fine day, and the trees were not yet bare. Rounding a bend in the driveway Alice pointed out the Hall as it came into view.

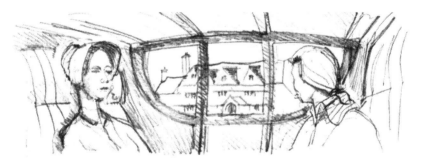

It stood ancient, rambling and comfortable in its setting beneath the high tors of the open moorland, its mullioned windows framed within the oak cruck frames of gabled roofs. A column of smoke rose quietly into the still air from one of the tall stone chimneys. They drew up at the entrance porch where Squire and Mrs Vasey stood to meet them.

'Welcome, my dears, welcome.' Mrs Vasey embraced Alice as she stepped down from the coach, and Trehearne followed. Squire Vasey shook hands with him.

135

'Now, my dear, are you going to tell us who this fine gentleman is?' He took Alice by the hand and kissed her forehead.

'This is John Trehearne, Father. He kindly agreed to accompany me on the journey. We have been acquainted some months now. John first came to see me when he returned to Plymouth in the summer.' She hesitated a moment. 'He was a friend of Robert's and knew him on the ship.' There was a moment's silence but Trehearne took the initiative to speak.

'Robert was my close companion, and a good man. I would give my all for him to be standing here before you in my stead.'

'That is a kind sentiment,' the squire replied, 'but we cannot change what the Lord Almighty has bestowed upon us. Let his soul rest in peace.' Mrs Vasey nodded in agreement and reached out to put her arm around Alice.

'But Father, how can we? I know for certain that he was allowed to take blame – such an injustice is not the Lord's doing, but the actions of evil men!' Alice's dark eyes flashed with a sudden anger, but Squire Vasey was not to be drawn on the subject.

'Come now, here we are to welcome you. Let us not be vexed, your mother has been so looking forward to seeing you. Come, my dear.' He beckoned to her and John to enter the house.

Alice took her mother's arm and they went in through the wide oak door, flung open to admit the warm sunshine. Inside was dark and cool by comparison, but small shafts of sunlight penetrated the traceried casements. They sat in the great hall, bathed in the rich autumnal light. A log fire smouldered, the embers glowing in the fireplace before them.

Tea was served. Alice was listening to her mother speak of the news in the county and the squire was curious to learn about the new stone lighthouse at first hand. In the midst of their conversation Alice's sister Verity came into the room, accompanied by two small dogs. She dropped her basket and ran to greet her sister, who was overjoyed to see her.

'I saw the carriage from the woods, and came as fast as I could. I've been longing to see you,' Verity pouted. Even as she kissed her sister, her eyes travelled to Mr Trehearne, who was caught by her gaze.

'We haven't been introduced – I'm Verity.' She held out her hand. John bowed formally and Alice quickly intervened, making his introduction. She saw the effect her russet-haired sister had on men these days.

'Oh, Verity! Look at the state of your skirts!' her mother exclaimed.

'Oh really, Mother, I'll go and change, but I had to see Alice first.' She turned, and, snatching a cake from the table, bit into it – then, glancing back once more at Trehearne, she left the room in a flurry of skirts. There was a pause while they drew breath.

'And that was my younger daughter,' Squire Vasey sighed. 'Now, Mr Trehearne, you were telling me how your work is progressing on the Edystone.'

That night John slept soundly in a room high in the uppermost storey of the house. Alice had delighted in taking him there, leading him along landings and passages, up staircases that became steeper and narrower the higher they climbed. Later he heard the girls' laughter tinged with excitement. Verity stayed with her sister until she had heard everything that Alice could possibly think of to tell her about him.

The following day John awoke to a knock on the bedroom door. Before he could reply, Verity sailed in with a tray. She laid it on his lap and sat on the end of the bed.

'I hope you slept well, John,' she said. He sipped the tea and looked up at her over the rim of his teacup.

'Yes, very well indeed. I'm not used to such comfort – and to be brought my breakfast in bed is like a dream, If it is a dream, then I don't care to be woken – I could stay here forever. But is it proper for you to be here in the bedroom with me? What will your parents think?'

'Oh, Mama knows I am here, but don't tell Alice.' She suppressed a burst of laughter for fear that Alice should hear.

'We are going out for a walk to the village later, but I think you may be roped in to help pick apples. I heard Alice say that you would both help with the harvest. Mama will want to show you her garden, be warned!'

She leaned towards him and whispered, 'It's a dreary place but she takes all our guests through it. Look out for the "Temple of Antiquity" and her "Sylvan Glade". I like to call them woods. If you like we could go looking for mushrooms there later – the woods are my favourite place.'

She let out another burst of laughter and went to the door, opening it quietly to slip out and giving him a final look before closing it gently behind her. Finishing his breakfast, he dressed and set off to find his way downstairs. He wandered through the house and found Alice with her mother in the breakfast room. The squire had already breakfasted and was out in the home farm.

'Would you like something more for breakfast, John, or perhaps some more tea?'

'No thank you, Mrs Vasey, though I will join you both for your company. Good morning, Alice.'

Alice smiled and told him how Verity was unusually helpful this morning and insisted on taking up his breakfast tray when it was ready. She gave him a look.

'You certainly know how to impress a girl, John; she never did that for anybody else as far as I can remember.'

Mrs Vasey passed him a cup. Alice could not keep a straight face any longer and burst out laughing.

'I thought she would never leave me last night – she wanted to learn everything about you.' Alice appeared radiant this morning. She was happy to be home.

They heard the squire come into the kitchen and call through to them. He'd been down in the lower orchard. The apples were ready and today he wanted their help with the harvest.

'Tonight we shall try the remainder of my best cider, John. That will be your reward – but I tell 'ee that you shall not taste better between here and Okehampton.'

Later that day the women and children made their way down to the orchards. Squire Vasey, conducting the proceedings, was handing out baskets to the labourers' wives and children. The men were mostly out in the fields ploughing for winter wheat and tending the stock. But this was one of the annual tasks that Squire Vasey enjoyed the most, and he would miss it for nothing. From early October he could often be seen, strolling with his dogs down to the orchards at the end of the day. There he would pick an apple and cut it cleanly through to see the pips, and contemplate how long before they could harvest.

The harvest was late this year, but today was perfect for it. An early-morning mist was lifting and the trees took on a green and gold mantle as the sunshine increased overhead. John Trehearne took a long wooden pole with an iron hook attached and under the squire's instructions raised it up into the crown of each tree. Hooking it onto a branch he pulled and shook the tree until it had given up all the fruit on the boughs. Apples rained down to the ground, some bouncing off his head, neck and shoulders in the process. 'Keep your head down,' Alice laughed – and pointed skyward as one caught him unawares, striking him in the eye.

'Ouch!' He dropped his pole and pressed a cupped hand over his brow.

'Oooh dearie, be you alright?' said one of the local women in a deep Devonshire accent. Alice joined in. She lifted his hand and kissed him on the temple.

'Oooh – careful!'

'Don't be a baby,' she answered and pinched him, to the amusement of the others. Then she joined them in collecting up the fruit in the wicker baskets and loading them onto the cart. The children helped for a while, and sometimes ran, playing chase in between the rows of ancient fruit trees. Alice was lost in her thoughts, remembering how she and Robert had played out their courtship amongst these trees. She was saddened, reminding herself how Robert had first seen her at the harvest not so long ago. She had watched him shake the boughs, just as John did now, and she remembered how much she admired him and longed for him to notice her. They had married in the following spring. Tears welled up in her eyes as she remembered how happy they had been together, and how suddenly it had all ended.

By the time all the trees were picked, the sun had sunk low in the sky. The kitchen maid and two or three of the women brought food and refreshment from the house. Verity decided to join the feast. She helped bring flagons of cider to wash down a simple meal of bread and cheese. Long shadows were cast about them in the golden light. Afterwards they made their way slowly back up the hill to the range of farm buildings that stood around a courtyard beside the house. John was held spellbound by the Vasey girls. Verity was a vivacious young beauty, russet-haired and light-eyed, with a precocious air of confidence that he found irresistible. But Alice was as much a beauty in her own right, dark-eyed and determined; her eyes could flash like a sudden storm when provoked.

He knew he had fallen in love with her. When she looked at him he knew theirs was more than just a friendship. If only he could be rid of his fear of his pursuers. Until then he could live only for himself. What use was he if they caught him? He would not have Alice suffer more than she had already.

All too soon it was time for him to return to Plymouth. Leaving Alice to stay on with her family, he set off on foot for the Plymouth road. The squire sent one of his grooms on horseback ahead to wait for him, and they would go on like this, taking turns to ride ahead and walk behind until they reached the town.

Fresh from his travels, Trehearne arrived in the workyard in the morning. Preparations were under way to receive the first consignment of stone from Portland. Any day now they hoped to see the first of the cargo ships bringing the stone, and operations were in hand to complete the construction of the workyard and Smeaton's machinery. Trehearne made his way down to the jetty where a small crowd had gathered alongside the *Buss*. Rain confirmed the onset of November. It fell steadily, enshrouding the estuary landscape in a grey cloak of wetness. Could this be the same country where he had thirsted in the apple orchards at harvest only two days before? He thought this as he walked down toward the group gathered round Mr Smeaton and the shears.

The engineer was testing a new 'purchase' tackle system for lifting the heavy stones of the lighthouse. He stood there, soaking, the rain dripping from the corners of his hat, his hands clasped firmly behind his back.

He nodded to John, who joined the small throng of the company stood about him. All eyes rested upon the huge tackle block that hung suspended on great ropes from the shears. The crossed timbers of the crane rose from the wooden jetty, to which each leg of timber was pinned with cleats and bolts of iron. The ropes grew taut under the strain of opposing forces as the seamen pressed themselves to the *Neptune*'s capstan. Her bow began to lift out of the water and the great pulley rose higher. Suddenly it let out a great crack like gunshot. The men drew back, but Smeaton stood his ground and raised his hand..

'Continue,' he called out.

At this the ship's capstan was given a further turn and an even greater strain was imposed on the ropes and tackle. Smeaton observed every detail, occasionally making notes in pencil in a damp pocket ledger. He calculated that the strain produced on the massive purchase tackle was equivalent to at least four times the weight of the heaviest stones they expected from Portland. His design for the shears and the tackle seemed proven beyond doubt, but he wished to leave nothing to chance. He gave the order to continue with a fourth test.

'D'ye think we need go further with this, Master Smeaton?' Mr Jessop saw no point in driving onward to destruction. There were a hundred and one other jobs to attend to before the ships arrived. 'If we place yet more strain 'pon the shears something must give.'

'Exactly so,' Smeaton replied. 'That, Josias, is the whole purpose for our being here. I want to see it *fail*.' Thinking upon it, he stepped backwards, joining with Jessop and the men at a distance that they considered safe. Once again the capstan turned until the taut ropes quivered like bowstrings. He kept his eye on the great pulley block and spoke in a whisper.

'I think there is no one in the building trade, the entire length and breadth of England, who builds in single blocks of stone of this magnitude.'

'I think there is no greater tackle block either. Five sets of pulleys between six sheaves of timber all bolted through – I certainly have never seen anything to match it in all my years in the dockyard.'

'Well, there we are, it proves my point.'

Mr Jessop started, as another loud crack was emitted. 'Dear Lord preserve me, this sets my teeth to grinding!'

142

'Mechanic powers and their management, Jessop! The common workmen in the building way have not attained an expertness in the use of tackles and purchases, and so in consequence they avoid, wherever they can, the necessity of using them.'

'I dare say, Master, but there are many fine buildings of great magnitude.' Jessop spoke with a pragmatic air.

'Of course, all made in small pieces to be manageable, but it is not well understood that a stone of a ton weight can be as easily hoisted and set, with a proper tackle, as one at a quarter of the weight. And think how much easier becomes the task of filling the same space in the wall, where one stone does the work of four ...'

– another violent crack rent the air. Jessop started once more but Smeaton ignored it and went on –

'... that must themselves be dressed and shaped to fit. Indeed the stones could perhaps be far in excess of one ton, were the quarries able to supply such leviathans.'

'What of the Edystone?' Jessop asked cautiously.

'I think this shows that we are not limited by the laws of physics, but the situation here, as you know best, requires small craft to deliver the cargoes. They would never be capable of landing *very* large stones with safety.'

'Aarhh, there I agree, the swell in the Gut can cause a vessel to rise and fall to a difference of three or four feet, even in calm weather! Were such a stone to be rising out of the hold and the vessel flung upwards by the sea, then it would smash her to pieces.'

'Jessop, I promise thee, the cargoes will not exceed stones of a weight that cannot be swiftly and expeditiously dealt with. We shall have a small number of men working tackles that can be removed from the rock to our store vessel at each tide. For that purpose I think a ton in weight seems a reasonable medium.'

Jessop sighed. 'Glad to hear it,' he said to himself, 'though God knows it's enough.'

Despite the shrieking and cracking of the timber, all held firm – until suddenly, miraculously, the great iron hook opened, and stretched itself as though it were made of some plastic substance with no strength in it. They turned and ran to safety, hearing the shears crash down behind them. There came an ear-splitting crash as the

143

great purchase tackle smashed through the wooden planking of the jetty. In a few moments they regrouped to inspect the damage. Smeaton was satisfied, and the men went back to their work. No lasting damage was done and so the equipment was dismantled and stowed away. Jessop took up again with his work to prepare the *Neptune Buss* and signalled Trehearne to join him.

'She should prove nimbler now that the weed and shells are all scraped off, but there's plenty to do yet afore we go back for the moorings, John Bowden.' John had to remind himself that back here he was known as 'Bowden', the name he had given on his arrival.

'How went your visit?'

'All went very well, Mr Jessop. Perhaps I'll take up on a farm some day, when this is completed and the ships sail past the light without a thought for how it was got there.'

13

Storm at sea

As the year drew to a close John Smeaton wrote to Robert Weston, reporting their progress and reflecting upon the difficulties they had encountered in that first season. The seas had proved most fickle from the beginning. Only a few days before they had courted disaster and he was, he admitted to himself, shaken by it. He pondered on how close they had come to shipwreck off Fowey, only to be driven out further and further into the open sea, almost to Biscay. The *Neptune* was well founded and rode a storm well at her moorings, but she proved difficult to sail in anything except the most favourable conditions. They needed new yawls, too. Smeaton had calculated that if they were to carry out the necessary tonnage of stone within the estimated four-month working season he would need another two vessels. He told this to Weston in his letter, adding that he had decided it best to commission Jessop to build two new purpose-designed boats, to carry the men and stones to the Rock. These were to be larger than the twelve-ton *Edystone Boat* at some eighteen tons each. A further two small yawls were required, that could be hauled up and stowed on the deck of the *Neptune Buss*.

Looking up from his desk and through the window he saw Jessop with John Bowden. They were already preparing timbers for the first of the new yawls. It was as though nothing untoward had happened, he thought, and remembered his own favourite saying: 'let us proceed until there is something to stop us.'

Mr Jessop judiciously advised their being built unusually bold in their bows, and to have a sufficiency of height or depth, to render them very floaty and lively in a rough hollow sea; though by this mode of construction they might not be so speedy sailers ... we determined to build two light yawls, of such size and construction that both might be stowed upon the deck of the Buss at once, and also to build them at home.

The principle of all our vessels, as far as they differed from common ones, was that they were considerably broader in proportion to their length, and remarkably full in their bows; which, though not adapted to make way swiftly through smooth water, yet enabled them to float much more lively upon the surface, when a sharper vessel would almost bury itself in the water; they were therefore not only safer, but even made better way in a rough sea ... Accordingly one of the large boats of 18 tons, and a light yawl were immediately put in hand.

'Pass me the drafts, Mr Bowden.' Jessop was anxious to explain why the new yawls were to look so rounded in the front, unlike the traditional yawls, like those from Deal, which were long and thin.

'I know that the Deal boats are wondrously shaped for speed,' said Jessop, 'with a pointed prow and knife-like keel, they cut through the water ...'

'But they ship it in equal amounts in a rough swell,' Trehearne added as he studied the drafts prepared in Jessop's own hand.

'Exactly, and that's my point – speed but not stability.' Jessop took hold of the drawing and laid it out on the trestle beside them, 'and it's my opinion that these qualities are of no use in the seas around the Stone.' He looked from the draft to the beginnings of the new yawl. Its frame rose upside-down like a thin ribcage from a template blocked out on level ground, the gunwales and keel forming the main support which held fixed the curved ribs.

'She's a very bold shape in the bows, almost round.' Trehearne's voice sounded perplexed; he had never seen small boats of this draught having such a broad shape.

''Tis unusual, I agree – but then they are not intended to be the fastest of their class, though I hope they do prove the safest, and sturdy too.' Jessop raised his finger to emphasise his words. 'They'll each be well ballasted with up to ten ton of stone in the hold, so they must be "floaty", especially in hollow seas when the wind blows fresh at sou'west.'

'You know more of shipwrightry than I, Mr Jessop.' Trehearne, admiring Jessop's craft, suddenly found himself talking incautiously of his own past. 'Though my grandfather was a boat builder of some renown in Cornwall.'

'Was he now? I am old enough that I may even have known him, what was his name?' Jessop waited in anticipation.

'Damn fool!' thought Trehearne, inwardly cursing himself as he fumbled for an excuse to change the subject, but it was too late. If Jessop guessed his true identity, he might be given up to the Navy. At that very moment a young woman appeared before them, walking toward them from the direction of the yard. It was Alice. Thankfully Mr Jessop saw her looking in their direction and forgot his enquiry.

'She's a beauty – seems to be searching for someone – now she's looking this way. Do you know her, John Bowden?'

'Aye, Mr Jessop, she's the eldest of the Vasey girls, daughters of Squire Vasey of Breakstone Hall near Tavistock.' John raised an arm and waved to her.

'Isn't that where you went a while back?'

'It is. You have a memory like an elephant, Mr Jessop.'

'Is that so? I wouldn't know such things but I do know that a man cannot live by bread alone, eh? Surely, such a fine-looking woman ought to be married?'

'She is but recently widowed. I knew her husband, and have made her acquaintance since coming to Plymouth. Her husband served on board the HMS *Dart*.' Trehearne moved closer to the old man and spoke low. 'Though he was a gentleman serving in the ranks it did not prevent his being accused and found guilty of stealing.' Alice was approaching, almost upon them, and John had just enough time to tell how he died from his punishment – a lashing.

Jessop listened hard. 'Go on.'

'I know he was falsely accused, and the truth of it is that he was unjustly punished to keep the guilty out of harm's way.'

Alice stepped over the timbers lying strewn about the new boat.

'Good day, Mr Bowden. I heard from my maid the news. It has caused quite a stir in Plymouth, I believe.'

Trehearne suddenly remembered that he had not introduced her and continued, 'Alice, this is Mr Josias Jessop, general assistant to Mr Smeaton.'

Josias bowed graciously.

'Josias Jessop at your service, ma'am.'

'How do you do, sir.' Alice made a polite curtsey. 'I have heard much about you from Mr Bowden.' She smiled, then looked inquisitively at the beginnings of the new yawl. 'I see you are busy at your work. Perhaps I should come later – it's just that I wanted to know that you are safe.'

Jessop spoke kindly to her. 'Quite so, and I am pleased to say that we all returned safely from our ordeal.' He put a hand on Trehearne's shoulder. 'But I believe none of us would be here now, if it had not been for the skill and bravery of John Bowden here. We owe him our lives'.

John made light of it, and shrugged his shoulders.

'I only did what came first into my mind, Mr Jessop, the Almighty had a greater hand in seeing us safely home.'

The entire company had come close to disaster just a few days before, when the *Neptune Buss* ran ashore in bad weather off Fowey. They had survived largely due to Trehearne's quick thinking and seamanship. The man they knew as John Bowden had steered them to safety, but it had taken days for them to get home. Many in Plymouth had feared the worst, and their return was the talk of the town at the end of November 1756.

Jessop decided that he should leave the two young people to catch up on each other's news.

'Oh, forgive me; I am due in Stonehouse with Mrs Jessop and young William. I'll say good day to you, ma'am.' He smiled and bowed, raising his hat to Alice. They watched his slightly stooped figure disappear into the melee of activity in the workyard. Then Trehearne beckoned Alice to join him in the boatshed.

'We can talk privately here.'

She had received a letter from the Admiralty. It found against the 'allegations' brought against Lieutenant Colquhoun and members of the crew, as being entirely without evidence.

'John, I am afraid! There is no one else I can turn to who knows the truth, and I thought I had lost you!'

'I know, but you need not worry, here I am! Let me tell you what happened.'

'No, not here! Come to my house this evening. You can tell me the whole story there, without fear of interruption.' She reached up and pressed the palm of her hand against his shoulder, then as he placed his own on hers and clasped it tightly, she left him. Alice slipped out through the door, turned and found herself confronted by a strange-looking man. He was standing just beyond the boatshed doors and had been loitering, well within earshot of their conversation.

Had he been eavesdropping? The thought flashed through her mind, as she stood frozen to the spot and caught her breath.

'You're a pretty miss and no mistake. Can I be of assistance? William Hill at your service, ma'am.' He smiled but was not pleasant. Hill mimicked Mr Jessop's courteous bow, and she suddenly felt threatened.

Alice found her tongue. 'No thank you, I have made my business here and now I must be getting home … if you please.' She made to walk past him but he caught her arm and stopped her. She felt his breath in her face; it smelt bad and sodden with gin.

'He's full of surprises, our John. He works for me, you know. But why a fine handsome lady such as you should be interested in him I cannot imagine. He's little more than a tinner, a good seaman, I grant, but not of your society, if I might say so.'

'We are friends. I came to see that he returned safely. I heard the news of the ship's return and I was anxious for news. Rumour was that you were all feared lost.' She pulled her arm away from him and added, 'Now if you dare to obstruct me further I will see to it that your master hears of this.'

'I don't mean no harm, my lady.' He grabbed her wrist and moved closer. 'Now something happened out there that thou knows – I heard thee speak of it!'

'I do not know what you mean,' Alice replied.

'We met with the HMS *Dart* during our troubled voyage. When she came alongside to our signal for assistance, I saw John Bowden hide himself. What is he hiding from? Tell, and I'll let thee go.'

Alice glanced beyond him to a group of men working nearby. 'This is preposterous, Mister Hill. Now let me pass or I shall scream your name out loud and you shall be made to answer to every man here for your behaviour!'

William Hill let go her arm and added dryly, 'Never mind, I shall know everything in good time, I have an instinct for such matters. Was it your husband the Lieutenant had flogged for his crimes? I thought so – but one escaped, did he not? There's some who would pay a high reward for his whereabouts and arrest.' Alice felt her skin flush but she kept her eyes fixed on Hill's leering face.

'Good day to you, Mistress.'

She hitched up her petticoats and made her way across the workyard to the gates without looking back. Hill sauntered away, his eyes following her. Seeing young William Jessop near, he called to him, 'Master Jessop, over here!'

'Yes, Mr Hill?' William was eager to help whenever he could, and came regularly to the yard after his lessons.

'How would you like to earn yourself a ha'penny?'

'Very much, sir!' William was delighted to be assigned a task by the foreman.

'You see that maid leaving by the gate, and heading toward Stonehouse? Hill pointed to the figure of Alice on the road and the boy nodded.

'Aye, sir.'

'I want you to follow her and see where she lives. But you are not to speak to her or let her see you and you must tell no one of it but me. Only then shall you have your reward, d'ye understand?'

'Is she a Frenchie come to spy on us, Mr Hill?'

'Course not, lad. Never you mind who she is or what she's done, you do as I say! Go on, quickly now, or you will lose her!'

'Aye, Mr Hill.' William was already running to make up the ground as he spoke.

Hill began to chuckle to himself, then bellowed with laughter. He could not help himself; his shoulders heaved as an uncontrollable delirium shook his frame till he began to cough. 'Good lad,' he said as he recovered himself, and watched William tearing away towards the Stonehouse road. He rubbed his hands and thought of the precious secret he had overheard her describe.

'Something tells me that Jeremiah Colquhoun will be willing to pay to have such information.' He thought awhile, removing his hat and smoothing the lank hair back from his brow with his hand. 'There's a bargain to be struck, and why not? If John Bowden is this fugitive then I shall have served the Navy well in finding him.'

Later that evening John Trehearne sat with Alice in the small dining room, and after the meal he began to tell her of their ill-fated voyage to the Edystone, and how it had changed everything. It was a dark, wet, late-November evening. He stood over the hearth and placed another log in the firebasket. The fire crackled and fresh flames illuminated his features as he began the story of how they came to be lost.

'In the early hours of Sunday we quit Millbay to attend to the moorings. The *Neptune* slipped away into the Sound on the tide of flood and set a course for the Edystone. I had been aboard the *Buss* since three o'clock and with a fair wind we sailed at four. Smeaton, Jessop, Hill and the company were all on board. And the *Edystone Boat* sailed with us – she took us in tow.' John paused, stood up and walked to the window. He pulled the shutters out from the jamb linings, unfolded them and carefully butted them closed.

'I had a strange feeling of something hanging over us, like a charm that would bring ill luck. I couldn't put my finger on it but from the beginning things happened. One of the seamen climbed the mast of the light yawl following in our wake, as he was used to doing. He must have done it countless times before, but it was enough to overset the yawl and he fell into the sea.' He crossed the room and sat by Alice in an armchair near the hearth.

'We recovered him and arrived at the moorings, around midday. I had by then got to work with the others. There was no time to dwell at leisure, for we spent the entire afternoon lifting and getting in the "bridle cable".'

A knock came at the door, and Alice answered it. It was her maid, Mary, who entered with a jug of hot, spiced wine, placed it on the table, and curtseyed.

'That will be all, Mary. Perhaps you will attend to the candles on your way down. I have a lamp here to light us along the hall later.' Alice bid her 'good night'. Alone once more, she poured a glass and offered it to Trehearne.

'Please do continue with your account, John.'

'We began hauling up the chains to attach the great buoy. Using the bridle chain we carried on until at three o'clock in the morning we got the "swivel" up on deck. Mr Smeaton gave a hand himself to get the forelock of the bolt and shackle clinched, by which the buoy chain was attached.'

'You must have been exhausted by your efforts,' Alice remarked with a look of sympathy.

'We were, and so we left off until daylight, when the *Edystone Boat* came alongside to deliver up the great buoy. Then she sailed for home, with orders to return as soon as the weather permitted. The wind blew fresh at south-east and made hazardous our operations. With the weather worsening (and to catch the favourable winds for our own return), we cut the "clinch" of the bridle cable and, using the buoy chain, lowered the ground chains back into sea. Had we left then, we would have been home and dry by nightfall.'

'Then why in heaven's name did you not?' Alice exclaimed. Trehearne looked into eyes that sparkled in the light of the fire and then raised his glass to his lips. He felt the hot draught suffuse his whole being with warmth. Holding the empty wineglass aloft he looked through it, and nodded thoughtfully.

'You have more sense than the rest of us put together,' he admitted. 'Had we left then …but we stayed to repair the buoy chain. Jessop, God bless him, had found a flaw in a link, where a bolt was driven to hold the chain of the smaller underwater buoy. The *Edystone Boat* had not returned, and the winds grew steadily stronger. "Mr Jessop," said I, "we must make haste and leave soon; it is no longer safe for us to ride by the buoy chain." He had but little time to reply

152

before another piece of ill luck befell us. A cry went up there and then, but it was too late. One of our yawls had broken loose and was sighted too far away for us to recover. I rediscovered then my feeling of foreboding.'

'But what happened – to lose yourselves for more than a week?' Alice interrupted.

'Aye, what indeed! Destiny took events out of our hands.'

'Do go on, tell me all.'

'At last, we launched the great buoy into the sea above the moorings and cast loose, but the wind had veered to north-east, and we could no longer make Plymouth Sound. We steered away before the wind, bound for Fowey. About three hours into our passage Mr Smeaton went down to his cabin to rest, expecting not to be disturbed until we arrived in Fowey harbour. Though the night was dark, we thought to see – by the light of a new moon – the headlands to guide us into the mouth of the River Fowey. The gale was at its height and the rain came in ever-increasing sheets, until we could hardly see ahead.

'Suddenly a great commotion erupted. I heard a voice call from the bows "go about, breakers ahead!" – but it was too late. We were in shallow water, surrounded by the surf and no harbour in sight.' Trehearne closed his eyes for a moment. He could hear in his mind the thunderous roar of the breaking seas on the rocks.

Alice took his hand and clasped it in hers.

'With the seas breaking all about us, our only hope was to put about or be driven onto the rocky shore. I cried out for all aboard to heave hard to bring the mainsail about. I gave Mr Jessop the helm, took up the sheet and pulled with every ounce of strength remaining to me. Mr Smeaton himself rushed up from the cabin and, laying his hands to the rope alongside me, hauled with all his bodily strength. Mr Jessop fell and I took his place, laying the helm as far over as it would go, till, with the stress of the wind in our mainsail, our starboard bow got under. When she dipped her gunwale below the water I thought we would be driven right over. It seemed an age but all this happened within a matter of minutes.

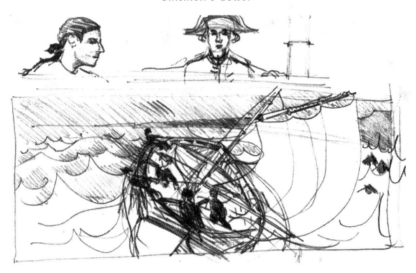

'I altered our course, and could see nothing but darkness ahead. The noise of the breakers remained loud in our ears, for though she answered the helm, we were still not clear of the danger of the shore on our starboard bow. Next the jib shattered and split to pieces, and to save the mainsail I screamed to Hill to lower it to half-mast, which he did straight away. Still she heeled hard over and dipped her gunwale. The men climbed up the port side and clutched at the rigging or they fell down the slippery slope of the deck. Seas broke over us fore and aft against the wind. For two more hours I kept our head pointing south to be sure to clear the rocks stretching from Trewardreth Bay to the Deadman.'

'You were saved – it seems nothing less than miraculous!' Alice clasped her hands tightly together and stood up. 'But why did we not see your return sooner than the 26th?'

Trehearne laughed ironically, and told of how the wind and weather conspired to take them further away out into the Channel.

'The storm continued unabated – we could see no further than fifty fathoms. By daylight, we found ourselves out of sight of land. With the last of our yawls trailing behind us, filled with the spray of the storm, we reluctantly decided to cut her loose. At midday, we sighted the coast and judged it to be the Lizard. The storm had abated and we set a course for St Mount's Bay, but by nightfall found that we had in

154

fact been driven so far to leeward that the Land's End now lay on our weather bow. We again set a course at nor'west by north and stood on this until noon the next day. The wind stayed at nor'east and we had little choice but to lay-to, about eight leagues from Land's End. Taking soundings and finding ourselves to be in some forty fathoms of water, we dropped the anchor.'

Alice lit fresh candles around the room, then returned to the table and poured them each another glass of the mulled wine.

'It seems to me foolhardy that you sailed in the first instance, without adequate provisions and charts for such an outcome.' She gave him a mischievous smile. 'Men are altogether too clever sometimes,' she thought.

'We considered three choices. First (with the wind fixed at nor'east), we could attempt to cross the Bay of Biscay to get in some port of France or Spain. Second, we could stay there until a fair wind blew for home. Or we could make for a port in the Isles of Scilly. We voted the third, to shape a course for Scilly, but without charts or instruments aboard, it was impossible to set the point to steer upon and hope to arrive within sight of the islands.'

He finished his wine and frowned. 'And then the fates struck.'

'What could possibly have made things worse?' she asked.

'We sighted a sail to the east heading toward us. "Make a signal of distress," Mr Smeaton cried out – I recall his words, "It might be a ship of our enemies, but even this would be preferable to our present predicament."'

'And was it?'

'No, but the vessel proved far worse than a Frenchman to me. I knew then why our voyage had been dogged with misfortune and I had felt such foreboding. Approaching, dead ahead, came the *Dart*, as though drawn to me like a magnet.'

'Dear God! But at least you escaped!' Alice could think of little else to offer comfort. She sat down again, and a shiver of excitement, mingled with fear, tingled in her spine.

'When they came alongside I busied myself, attending to the spare foresail in readiness to make sail, with my back turned. I heard Smeaton identify our ship, and request assistance for making a safe course to Scilly. Colquhoun answered him, giving the course bearings.

'I heard him hail us as we passed at close quarters. They were leaving and I was certain I had not been seen, until a shot rang out across our bows. Then I knew I had been discovered. I looked up and saw Midshipman Baines raise the alarm. Colquhoun came to the side and leaned over the gunwale directly above me, all the time staring continually at me. We were but a few feet apart. I held my stance and kept him in my eye whilst the ship slipped past. He walked the entire deck to maintain our relative points until, reaching the farthest point at the stern, gradually, we were carried away from each other. My heart felt as though it were turned to ice, for I knew then, he will some day come to make an end of me.'

'You must not believe it, John. You have friends now and they will do their utmost to protect you.'

Trehearne apologised. 'Yes of course, Alice, and I thank God for it. Whatever happens, I have no wish that my life be different in any particular. Especially the day I met you.' He halted a little awkwardly; but there, he had said only what was in his heart.

Alice felt her cheeks flushing. She felt secretly elated that he had shown his true feeling for her. 'Perhaps you had better finish; it's getting quite late,' she said.

There was little more to tell. By the time they had raised the anchor the *Dart* had long since disappeared over the horizon and a fair wind had sprung up from south-west.

'We raised every piece of cloth we could find and set course for home. Within a few hours came the sight of Rame Head, and with the wind behind us we were soon entering the Sound – tired and hungry, but seeming otherwise little the worse for the adventure. Only I had been changed, and I could tell no one of my fear until tonight.'

It was nearly midnight when Trehearne left. Alice closed the door behind him.

'I must do everything in my power to help him,' she heard herself saying as she turned the key and bolted the front door closed. She took up the candlestick and made her way up to bed, thinking of how much she had wanted him to stay. The rest of the house was in darkness; she extinguished the landing candle and entered her room. The wine sent her to sleep soon after her head lay on the pillow.

But someone had been watching that evening outside, and saw him leave. Hidden in the shadows across the street, a man had waited patiently till all the lights in the house were extinguished. He smiled then spat his satisfaction and stepped lightly across the street and into the darkness of the mews that ran behind the house.

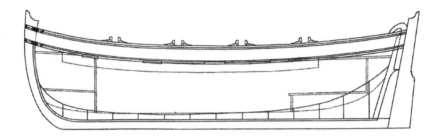

14

Master of the Weston

In the morning the kitchen maid called for the butler and showed him what she had found. There were muddy footprints in her kitchen, and upon investigating further it appeared that they came from the table in front of the scullery window.

'It looks like this is how they got in, ma'am. He tried the window and the sash dropped as soon as his fingers pulled on the mullion bar. 'Tis not damaged at all, it must have been left open. Whoever it was climbed up an' in from the garden, and closed it behind them.' He stood back and gave his mistress a puzzled look. 'The funny thing is that so far I have found nothing at all missing from the house.'

The intruders were the talk of the household and remained so for some time, since nothing was discovered missing, and it was not until Alice sat at her desk some while later that she discovered her bureau drawer had been forced open. She opened it to find that her papers and diary remained, but a letter written to her by John Trehearne was gone. 'Who could have known about it, and why would they risk stealing it?' she thought to herself. Alice told no one of her discovery, and the mystery remained unsolved. Christmas came and the incident was put out of her mind by a hundred more pressing matters.

Christmas came and passed into the new year of 1757, and Smeaton did not return to his new wife in London. Instead he remained in Plymouth, where there was much preparation and preliminary work to complete, before a single stone could be laid on the Edystone Rock. He was determined to return to the rock, in order to trace the outline of the steps they had assiduously cut into it during the previous season. On Wednesday 12th January, finding the sea calm following days of frost and stillness, Smeaton set out with Mr Jessop and the mould-maker, aboard the *Sea-Horse* yawl. Though the weather was fine and the water in the Sound quite smooth, they were met with a swell

> *which increased as we came nearer the Edystone, so that when we came there, we found the sea beating over it with great violence at low water: we ran within twice our boat's length of it, on the West side, to have a view of the work, in which we could not perceive any injury from the late storms, nor change, except that the new surface was of the same colour as the old; being all grown over with dark coloured green seaweed.*

During the late winter evenings Smeaton took to studying the work of Benjamin Franklin upon the subject of electricity, and the effects of lightning upon buildings. On the evening of 25th January, he had watched a storm and seen four flashes in the sky away to the west. Later, hearing that this storm had shattered the spire of Lostwithiel church 'in a very surprising manner', he took the opportunity of travelling there, to see for himself the effects of the lightning strike. What he found intrigued him, and could not be easily explained:

> *It was in this situation when I viewed it, the beginning of March; and I found that the whole of the spire left standing, as well as the lantern was greatly cracked and damaged ... which shewed the effects of an elastic vapour, that wanted to get at liberty by expansion, somewhat similar in its most obvious effects to that of gunpowder ... but there were some attending circumstances ...*

Smeaton observed that, had the effect been due to an explosion, as he at first thought, then the weakest part of the structure would have given way – but the opposite had occurred. What he found was a hole that had 'pierced entirely' through the base of the tower wall at a buttress – which he measured to be some eight feet wide, just inches from a wall only half as massive. It convinced him

> *that there could be no certainty of making any wall so strong as to withstand the action of Lightning, and consequently that no security against the effects of it … ought to be omitted in any building of consequence.*

Smeaton thought of the exposed situation of his lighthouse tower at sea. He decided that he should put into practical use Franklin's theoretical proposal for preserving buildings by means of a 'conductor'.

In the meantime the Portland stone began to arrive from Weymouth. Two ships came in on 8th March, returning with the wooden moulds for the next consignment. Until then they had been for some days without, and to keep the men busy Smeaton had directed them to break off pieces of 'Plymouth marble' along the cliffs, and to cut from these the cubes, twelve inches square on each face, that were to be inlaid between the courses. The yard now became a hive of activity as masons worked to prepare the foundation stones, ready for the coming season's 'outwork' on the Rock. But they were still wanting a number of the moulds for the foundation courses.

By the middle of March the first of the new yawls was completed. The day came to launch the new vessel. A small party of the workmen, seamen, their families and colleagues made up the little crowd attending the launch in Millbay. They gathered round and listened. Smeaton climbed up onto a cask and raised his hands for their attention.

'My good friends, colleagues, men of the Edystone service, ladies and gentlemen,' he looked about him and, seeing a number of wives and relatives present, added, 'and all your kin here today. I have had on occasion the honour of addressing the leading men of science in the country, but I can tell ye that I took no greater pleasure then, or felt so excited as I do now.'

A small cheer and a ripple of applause ran through the crowd, and he went on, 'Mr Jessop, showing great skills of shipwrightry, has devised and built this new yawl in our own yard. I know that she will answer our intentions fully and completely in service in the months ahead.' Jessop raised his hat to a hearty cheer and a further burst of applause. Smeaton again raised his hand for quiet and added, 'I call on him now to christen her on her maiden voyage.'

Mr Jessop came forward to speak.

'Thank you all. Mr Smeaton has asked me to think of a name for her and we are all agreed upon that of our patron and benefactor Mr Robert Weston. And so I name this craft the *Weston*. May God bless and guide all who sail in her.' Jessop dashed a jar of liquor against her bow, and the seamen gathered round ran her down the slip into the cold spring tide. The crowd gave three cheers and a 'hurrah', then Smeaton called for silence once more. William Hill listened intently.

'She is a fine vessel, and she deserves a good master. You will by now have heard of the distinguished actions and presence of mind shown to us by one of our number, on the occasion of our missing the harbour of Fowey. I am certain that were it not for his being with us that night, we would have run ashore and many lives would have been lost. Were I an admiral I should have signally rewarded his services and conduct before; but I have it now in my power to show some gratitude to him on behalf us all. I call upon John Bowden to take charge of the helm as Master of the *Weston*. This is a small payment for his service to his fellow mariners, in their hour of need.'

Hill clenched his teeth. Jealousy ran through him. It coloured everything. 'Now he will be put on the same footing as William Smart, Master of the *Edystone Boat*, and his pay made up to the same as my own.' John Bowden had risen in Smeaton's estimation and was being treated like a hero!

'Still,' he surmised, 'the man is not what they suppose.' Hill stood, chewing a wad of tobacco. His hands were thrust deep into his coat pockets and he spat out stained salvoes of juice whilst he ruminated upon this. It seemed to him that all his life, others were favoured over him. He thought about how from his earliest years he had been unwanted. His mother had died in childbirth and his foster aunt reviled him although he tried his best to please her. As he grew up he had got into bad company and his aunt's family threw him over as

161

soon as they could, saying that he was ungrateful and this was how he repaid them. 'I never had a chance,' he said to himself, and he believed it. It had left him belligerent and dogged, but despite this he had made something of himself. He had got a trade working at the quarries. He was a good craftsman and worked hard when he was sober. His capabilities had got him the position as a foreman here. Had he been of a different disposition and background, he would have seen how fortunate he was. Instead he dwelt upon the letter in his pocket. His fingers went to the document and he turned to the man stood beside him.

'Come, I've heard enough of this – we will profit more from a visit to the Lieutenant. His ship is expected daily in the King's Dock, returned from the Guinea coast.' They slipped away unnoticed.

Soon afterward, the expeditions to the Rock resumed. The consignments of stone from Portland and the first delivery of moorstone from Parr had been delivered. Now Smeaton was anxious to complete making the moulds for each of the stones in the foundation courses. The stones in each course would be tailored to fit the shapes they had tooled into the House Rock itself. For this, the imprint of the steps cut into the rock had first to be surveyed and each corresponding stone drawn in outline, whereupon the carpenter constructed wooden frames (moulds) of each stone. The frames were carried out and assembled *in situ* on the rock to check the fitting. Once fitted together they formed a circular segment that dovetailed into the negative shape of the rock, and Smeaton marked each frame against the next, stretching pack-thread across the assembly.

The wooden moulds all had to be taken from the rock surface, something they had attempted to do since the beginning of the year, but without making landfall until St George's Day.

We made several expeditions of the same nature in the course of the spring, and with no better success, so that it was not till 23rd April that we got a landing. We then went out in our first new boat, which was launched on the 22nd of March, and was called the 'Weston', John Bowden 'master'. There being little wind, we were obliged to row almost all the way. Between twelve and one, when we were about a league from the rock, it became calm; and as we were not soon likely to get out with the great boat, we

162

betook ourselves to the Sea-Horse yawl which attended us, and in an hour landed and got a tide's work of four hours; in which time having marked a durable middle line upon the rock, we got the moulds compleated for courses I, II and VI ...

As it remained calm, we determined to stay in the Weston all night, but, on examination, finding the carpenter had neglected to bring off an additional paper of nails that he was expressly ordered to bring, and reminded of, this trifling incident, however small in itself, was yet likely to put a stop to our further proceedings; for not being able from any expedient to do without nails, the carpenter and three seamen were dispatched in the yawl for Plymouth to bring out this necessary article. The weather continued calm all the night, but in the morning it began to blow fresh at South, which brought on a swell: and not only prevented us from landing, but obliged us to return to Plymouth.

'Trifling incidents' combined with uncertain weather did much to confound him, but nevertheless, progress was made though there was little to show for it yet upon the House Rock. Everything depended on getting the first of the granite stone courses, numbers one to seven, completed. Smeaton had agreed with both Matthew Box and Walter Treleven for two independent consignments to be delivered by Mayday. The smaller quantity, from Walter Treleven, was to be carried to Parr, where they would themselves undertake to ship it home in the sloop, since there were no local captains who would undertake to handle the monoliths. Such heavy stones, averaging over a ton in weight, were beyond the limits of their craft and capabilities. But this did not deter Smeaton. Raising such loads was well within the known capacity of the specialist tackle he had designed and tested so effectively at Millbay.

Granite, although immensely durable, is difficult to work 'easily to an arris' and is prone to spalling. Smeaton was well aware of the tendency for it to 'bruise easily', and took the precaution of sending bigger moulds to the quarry, for the stones to be 'roughed out' by the quarrymen. These arrived at Millbay slightly oversized for finishing at the workyard:

to be cut round all the sides to the true figure of the finishing mould, but they were to reduce them as near the size as they could safely do it by the hammer that they might not leave an unnecessary waste.

When the stones were landed at Millbay, they were handled using a sophisticated system of transportation devised by Smeaton. Carriages running on a narrow-gauge railway track, with turntables, allowed the stones to be transferred from one part of the yard to another, as they underwent a series of operations. Every stone would be carried at least six times, from its arrival as a roughly hewn block to its completion. Finally the stones would be carried from their rows in the yard, down to the wooden pier, for loading into the hold of the yawl ready for departure. In between, their assembly and construction would be tried and tested, by assembling each course upon a specially constructed platform.

> *That we might arrive at perfect certainty in putting the work ultimately together in its place upon the rock, it did not appear to be enough, that the stones should all be hewn as exactly as possible to moulds that fitted each other; but it was further necessary, that the stones in every course should be tried together in their real situation in respect to each other, and so exactly marked that every stone, after the course was taken asunder, could be replaced in the identical position in which it lay upon the Platform, within the fortieth part of an inch.*

To gauge the accuracy of the building's vertically curved profile, the next course was placed upon it and marked in the same manner, which meant that each course of stonework had to be assembled twice on the wooden platform. An efficient means of transport was essential if the work was to be completed to schedule.

Smeaton's concern to monitor the accuracy of the outer face work was due to the construction sequence of the courses. Unlike conventional buildings, where each new level of stone course-work would be set out starting from the quoins at each corner, or in circular buildings by the outer circumference of stone, he had deliberately pursued the idea of setting the centre stone first and working *outward* to complete the course. This had distinct advantages where the power of the sea was a constant threat and could easily dislodge the outer stones if they had no means of support from the inner core. Without the purchase to be gained from interlocking each stone in a single mass, the whole could be dislodged by a single storm. However, this method called for the utmost care in the preparatory work they undertook on the platform, '*that if any defect appeared at the outside, by an accumulation of errors from the centre, it might be rectified upon the platform'.*

It was whilst setting one of the foundation courses on the platform that William Hill learnt of the arrival of HMS *Dart* in the dockyard. That afternoon he sent word to Lieutenant Colquhoun that he had information that would be of interest to him. A reply came by return. The Lieutenant would meet him in an alehouse in the town on the morrow.

William Hill slid his drink off the bar and sat in a dark inglenook away from the general crowd, and awaited the Lieutenant. Hill remembered their last meeting, to agree a price for carrying the contraband and goods landed in the cove a year before. It was not long before his familiar lean figure entered the room. Since the shooting he had not regained the complete use of his right arm but carried it close to his side; it gave him a slightly leaning gait and he now wore his sword left-handed. Lieutenant Colquhoun took his glass and cast his pale eyes around the smoke-filled interior. Spying Hill in the ingle, he made his way toward him and sat down, placing his hat and gloves on the table before him.

'Good day, Lieutenant.'

'Mr Hill? What is it you want of me? Our debt to you is settled.' He looked at him impatiently.

'It is, sir, and as far as I know everything was to your satisfaction 'pon my last engagement?' Hill waited for some acknowledgement.

'Yes,' came the curt reply, 'though there will not be another in that direction from me. I expect my rank of Captain to be confirmed any day now.'

'I get your meaning, sir, there should be nothing seen, to stain your character, that might dislodge your advancement in the Service.' Hill was fishing for an advantage – 'and that is why I thought you might be interested in what I have to offer.'

'Go on.' Colquhoun sipped his glass of port delicately while Hill reached into his breast pocket and produced the stolen letter taken from Alice's bureau. It told of the smugglers and the bullion landed at Polparra.

'She came to the workyard. Pretty young thing, she is. I overheard her speak of this to John Bowden. He has employment with the Edystone service but I believe he goes under an assumed name. I believe him to be the man you lost – the night you were betrayed and shot.'

Hill recounted what he had overheard in the boatshed. The Lieutenant's face was like a mask and he gave away no trace of emotion. Instead he leaned forward and held out his hand. Hill passed him the letter and he took it; he slipped off the tie and unfurled the paper between his hands to study the script.

'As John Bowden he's made himself very popular with the rest of the men and Smeaton. As a matter of fact he's been made up to Master of the new yawl.'

'Come, Mr Hill,' Colquhoun interrupted, 'a yawl? Why that's little more than a rowing boat. Surely he is not grown so great, that the Navy cannot haul him in to answer for his desertion?'

'No, sir, but I think you should not underestimate the favour he is held in by the company. Do you recall our meeting with your ship at sea?'

'I do. It has remained with me during the whole of our passage to the Guinea coast. I saw him aboard your vessel.'

Hill smelled interest in Colquhoun's concern. Perhaps it was *fear* that had motivated him to respond so quickly? He didn't care beyond making a sale of the papers.

'You found us in that situation because we were lost in the storm two nights before. We were very nearly wrecked upon the shore. Trehearne – the man you yourself saw, when you came alongside our vessel – he took the helm and steered our ship to safety. Both Smeaton and Jessop believe he saved the lives of the company that night.'

'Never mind that, he's a deserter. He went over the side and we can hang him for it.' The Lieutenant spoke with a nonchalant air. He took up his glass.

'P'rhaps, but I can't see them handing him over to you – 'specially as he's engaged as John Bowden. There's no record of a John Trehearne. It would be your word against theirs.' Hill paused, then added, 'But I can offer you this written account at a very reasonable figure. The letter proves his identity.'

166

'It's of no use to me without the man himself. Can you deliver him up?'

Hill was silent. The letter was worthless if the Lieutenant refused it. He shook his head.

'In that case the Navy must take him. I will send a cutter to press him.'

The Lieutenant folded the letter and offered it back.

'However, I will agree a price with you – for your assistance in the matter of his detainment. If you will notify me of Trehearne's movements, then perhaps we can intercept him on a passage to the Edystone. You must be on board and on hand, to signal to my officer, which one amongst them is Trehearne.' The Lieutenant produced a velvet purse, heavy with silver, and dropped it onto the table. There's payment in advance if you accept – I will pay you a further sum of five guineas when you deliver him into the hands of the press men.'

Hill needed little encouragement, and the bargain was struck – and, he thought, with the minimum required of him. He would easily be able to signal Trehearne to them and convince the company of his loyalty all the while. What could be simpler than putting on an act of defiance toward the press men that would conceal his own duplicity in the affair? He was well pleased and chuckled in his throat.

Together they set out the details of a plan to take Trehearne. Hill would send word to the *Dart* of their next voyage to the Rock as soon as he was certain of the time of departure. They had still to complete taking the last of the moulds from the rock, for the stones in the foundation courses, and Trehearne would be with him. The *Dart* would launch her cutter, intercepting them off the coast beyond the point of Rame Head. It would appear to be a routine 'pressing', taking four of the men on board. Hill would remonstrate against this outrage, declaring their having Admiralty protection, but he would secretly signal to the naval officer in charge, which of the men amongst them was Trehearne, ensuring that he was taken.

Within days, on 30th April 1757, The *Weston* set sail for the Rock, with the *Edystone Boat* in attendance. They were some three miles from the shore, off Rame Head, when a naval cutter approached and the yawl was stopped and boarded. Mr Jessop looked on from aboard the

Edystone Boat. At first it was a little confusing but as they sailed closer he saw the men being forcibly taken and transferred to the cutter.

'This is preposterous! I cannot believe their purpose – it must be the press men. Mr Smart, can you see how many they have taken? I cannot tell from here.'

'Aye aye, Mr Jessop, sir.' William Smart, Master of the *Edystone Boat*, steadied himself against the mast for a better look. Jessop handed him the telescope. He stretched it open and focused it upon the two vessels. He saw William Hill remonstrating with the naval officer, and then scanned across to the cutter where the men were being got aboard.

'I see four of our company taken aboard the cutter, the two tinners, Joshua Hawkins and James Trevithick, one of our seamen, George Holt, and the last has his back to me – I think he is John Bowden.'

Smart sucked the air through his teeth and grimaced, then looked again. 'Those tars are rough looking fellows. Hill is giving their midshipman an earful. He's struck one of them. That's it, William Hill!'

'Aye, I am well aware of Hill's surly nature, Mr Smart; he's a belligerent fellow,' Jessop observed. 'Still, I am pleased to hear that he won't let his men go without making a fight of it! Come on, lads, we can reach them sooner in the *Sea-Horse* yawl.' Jessop sent two of the men to bring in the yawl, which they had in tow behind them.

'Lay hold of the painter, quick as you can,' Jessop called, but it was already too late. The cutter was under way. Hill had made a convincing act of defiance, though all the while he had secretly signalled to ensure that they took Trehearne. Everything had gone according to plan. The men were snatched before the *Edystone Boat* could reach them and intervene.

They had been hindered by naval press gangs before. To the onlookers aboard the *Edystone Boat*, it simply appeared that their luck had run out on this occasion. As they came alongside the yawl, the cutter was already receding into the distance under full sail. They could just make out the figures of the men on board. Jessop was beside himself with frustration and annoyance. He brought his fist down on the rail of the gunwale as he spoke.

'Well, William Smart, I have never felt as helpless to act as I do now! The men are furnished with Admiralty protections, yet still they are taken. Who can complain of the French, when our own side treat us thus?'

'Navy gangs have been p'ticularly active of late, Mr Jessop. I have heard it said in Plymouth that the press gangs prowl continually, both in the town and on the water. No seaworthy man is safe. They seek landsmen for the war and they don't much care how they go about it. 'Tis perfectly legal.'

'But the men in our service have "express protection", Captain. We deliberately obtained permission that the men are excused entry into naval service from the Admiralty, on account of their "service to all mariners".' Jessop sighed heavily. William Smart took a pragmatic view.

'You cannot blame yourself, Mr Jessop. The Admiralty in London is a long way away from a man o' war in the Sound, with orders to sail and a gundeck to fill. 'Twas bound to 'appen sooner or later.'

'P'rhaps you are right, Mr Smart, though it makes the injustice no easier to bear. I must speak with the master as soon as we make land. This is a bad business.'

The four men sat in silence whilst their captors pulled away from the *Weston*. Trehearne, despondent, his head bowed, eyes downcast, stared into the hold of the cutter. He felt a fear and dread in his stomach. Thoughts came uneasily and uninvited. He wondered, had Colquhoun cast his net? Was he the power behind their being taken? It could happen – he had expected it since their chance encounter at sea. They were now steering a course toward a three-decked man o' war, a seventy-four-gun ship. As they came nearer he saw that he had guessed right, and that he was delivered into the hands of his enemy.

15

Edystone resurgit

When he was not engaged in visits to the workyard, or in drawing out his designs for the stone courses, John Smeaton was fully immersed in conducting a series of experiments concerning 'water-cements'. He looked up from his work table as William Cookworthy entered the room. Smeaton was rolling small, moist and putty-like balls of about two inches in diameter. These he would submerge in pots of fresh and salt water once they had begun to harden. On the shelves behind him were rows and rows of such pots, each containing a similar ball in various degrees of decomposition.

'Good evening, John,' said Mr Cookworthy, 'I am hoping for some improvement in our findings with these new mixes. We must have a cement that is the most perfect possible, if it is to resist the violence of the sea.'

'I quite agree – the sea must give way to the building.'

'Aye, sir, but that will depend upon getting a cement so firm of consistence, and so strong in its adhesion to the stone, that it remains in its place despite the wetness and the waves.'

Smeaton wholeheartedly agreed.

'I cannot rest until we have found one with such magical properties. I shall continue my trials until we succeed. I thought I would try this – an equal mix of blue lyas and puzzolan. Puzzolan I have taken from Belidor and Vitruvius, as being used by the Ancients, though never, I believe, in combination with lime.'

'I am familiar with such quests, John. Here am I, experimenting with the "china stone" and clay I have found in Cornwall. I feel certain that in time I too will find a right formula – in the making of porcelain, that is. As yet I have not perfected the means.'

'If it is to be then you will find the way, Mr Cookworthy. I have much appreciated your help and advice in the "chemistry" of mortars.'

'I thank you, John. I am only glad to have been of some service to you in your work. The lighthouse is such a novel undertaking, that it seems to demand "invention" in every part of it, to make it firm and lasting.'

There was a knock at the door and Mr Jessop was shown in. As he entered the room his mind was filled with what had happened that day and he wore a heavy expression on his face.

'How was your passage home?'

Jessop was able to hold back no longer, and he burst out with the news of the loss of the men.

'Not good, sir. All went well upon the Rock; we finished the moulds – but we ran into trouble off Rame Head.'

'A moment, Josias, while I clear these away, and we can sit.' Smeaton indicated the table and chairs. William Cookworthy and Jessop sat down together in the warm glow of the coals from the hearth. Once he had put the newly labelled pots upon the shelf and wiped his hands, Smeaton joined them. He placed a jug of ale and some bread and cold mutton before them.

'Go on.'

'A navy cutter stopped the *Weston*, about five hundred fathoms ahead of us and not more than a league from Rame. They boarded her. We were too far off to lend assistance but we saw them press four of the company. There was nothing we could do.'

'And did they know our purpose?'

171

'Yes, sir, they did. Mr Hill told them in no uncertain terms. They took not the slightest notice that the men were really and bona fide employed in the Edystone service.'

Cookworthy took the jug and poured ale into the tankards. Jessop supped the ale slowly. Smeaton got up and moved around the room. He attended to the fire and said nothing, but he wore a worried expression. Then he rejoined Jessop at the table and ate in silence whilst the old surveyor told them what had happened and the names of the men who had been taken. Mr Cookworthy was indignant.

'John Bowden! But he is your best seaman! What of your immunity?'

'I know, sir,' said Jessop, 'Mr Hill insisted on it, but he says they had no means of proof and he was forcibly put down. The men are doing all they can to discover which ship has taken them.

'Good!' Smeaton exhorted, 'but we must act quickly if they are to be found. I will attend the Commissioner in the morning and demand that this "misunderstanding" is put right. What is the point of our having the protection of the Admiralty, if every young midshipman takes it upon himself to determine our identity? We must look to some means of redressing this.'

Jessop was distraught. He chewed at a piece of mutton and ruminated in silence, but Cookworthy suddenly had an idea and made a suggestion.

'If it could be made plain who you are, by painting some sign upon your mainsail ...'

'Yes of course, then they would not have any excuse to molest us! And what else than a large figure of the lighthouse! This would appear distinctly as our emblem at a good distance. There would be no possible excuse for the Navy to approach our vessels again. That was well said, Mr Cookworthy.'

'Aarhh, that's the answer at sea! But what of the times when the men are ashore?' said Jessop.

'Mmm, happen you have a point! They're liable to press them in Plymouth without our knowing. We must give them some means of identifying their service.'

The fire in the grate burnt low; they pondered this a long while. Smeaton took a taper to it and lit another candle for the table. In the flickering candlelight his eye caught the gleam of silver coins that lay between the dull grey pewter of the dishes.

'There it is before us! A piece of silver stamped with our mark; something that cannot be counterfeited. We shall give to each man a silver medallion, stamped like a coin, that he might keep it in his pocket; and 'twill serve as proof, should he be accosted.' He resolved to put this in place right away.

'I shall write to Mr Weston. He will see to it in London.'

'That's it, sir. Mr Weston will do everything in his power to help.' Jessop reached forward and took an iron poker from the fire. He plunged it, hissing, into his tankard. 'I cannot partake of too much cold ale at my age, makes my belly grumble. I likes it warm as broth. What a day! I shall have to be making my way. Mrs Jessop will be waiting 'pon my getting home.'

Jessop's head tilted back as he hurried now to quaff the warmed ale in his tankard. Then he swung forward and banged the empty tankard emphatically down on the table. He took his hat, placed it firmly over his periwig, and leaned both forearms on the table to raise himself up.

Then another knock came, this time at the door leading into the workroom from the street. They looked at each other.

'Who can that be? Are you expecting anyone tonight, Mr Smeaton?' asked Cookworthy.

Smeaton shook his head and shrugged his shoulders. 'See who it is, Josias.'

Jessop walked a little stiffly to the door and the knocking came again, louder this time. 'Alright, coming, I'm coming quick as I can!' He slid across the iron bolt and pulled the door open.

'Oh, good evening, Miss, sorry for my barking so. It's Mistress Alice, b'ain't it?'

'Yes, good evening, Mr Jessop. May I come in?'

'Of course, my dear.'

Alice stepped inside and Jessop closed the door and motioned her to join Mr Cookworthy by the fireside. Smeaton hurriedly cleared the remains of their meal from the table into the scullery and was now attending to the embers of the fire. He emerged from the shadows into the candlelight. Mr Jessop introduced Alice to him and Cookworthy.

'Good evening, sirs.' Alice curtseyed and her eyes shone in the soft candlelight of the sconces. Smeaton stepped forward and took her hand. She waited for some remark but nothing came. Looking at him she thought his looks quite handsome. He had a strong determined look about him. At last he managed a few words.

'Good evening, ma'am. What brings you to call upon us at this time of evening. Mr Jessop seems to know – tell me, what can it be?'

'Forgive me for venturing forth so late in the hour,' she faltered, but Smeaton's calm expression encouraged her and his eyes seemed to will her to speak.

'I have heard much about you and your scheme, sir. Mr Bowden has described your progress in great detail. I apologise if I have disturbed you, coming here this late in the evening, but I had no one else to turn to.'

'There now, tell us what is the matter,' Mr Cookworthy said kindly.

'John is missing. He was expected at my house this evening and when he did not come I sent my maid to his lodging but they told her that he was not returned and that one of the men from Millbay had called with news that he was detained by the press men.'

'I'm afraid it's true, mistress,' said Jessop. 'He was taken with three others from the *Weston* this afternoon when they were homeward bound. We tried to reach them to lend assistance but could not get there soon enough. They are pressed into service, even though our men have exemptions.' Jessop sighed again.

'Mr Jessop, Mr Cookworthy and I have talked of little else this evening. But try not to concern yourself. I shall go to the Commissioner and demand his release at the first opportunity tomorrow. The men have Admiralty protections; he will be obliged to cooperate in the matter.' Smeaton's face wore an expression of calm benevolence, mixed with genuine interest as he studied Alice.

'If she carries a candle for John then he has done well indeed,' he thought to himself.

Alice had loosened her cape and revealed her pale neck and shoulders. He thought of Anne in the same moment – it seemed an age since he had left her in London. He longed to be with her again now that she was with child.

Tears were welling in Alice's eyes and she looked visibly shaken. 'What is it, my dear?' William Cookworthy asked her. Alice fought to gain control of her emotions, taking deep breaths.

'Forgive me, gentlemen, but if I tell you my innermost thoughts I shall be breaking a confidence that I am sworn to keep.'

'Then how can we help you? If you seek my counsel then I must know everything that causes you to come here at this late hour.' Smeaton's reply was typically forthright.

'Will you give me your word that nothing will go beyond these walls?' Alice pleaded.

'Everything you say will be in strict confidence. I give you my word,' Smeaton said firmly. 'And I too,' Jessop added, 'though I must leave you now, or Mrs Jessop will be sending out the watch to look for me. Good night to you, ma'am, Master.'

'Good night, Josias, rest you well. See to it tomorrow that the sails of all our craft are painted with our emblem, the house in outline, black and large. Mr Jessop touched his hat. Pulling on his greatcoat, he lifted the thumb latch and let himself out into the night.

'I must attend to my household. I will leave you in private, but if you have need of anything, we are in the parlour across the hall.'

175

Cookworthy bowed politely and left the room.

Smeaton now settled himself into a chair by the fireside to hear Alice's story; he spoke softly and deliberately.

'Speak plainly, Mrs Appleford. As I have said, in order to be of assistance to you I must have all the facts, so I can make proper judgement of how we are to proceed with this matter.' He looked intently at Alice.

She began, telling him everything as she remembered it, and he silently considered the details as she spoke.

'John Bowden is a fugitive on the run from the Navy. His real name is John Trehearne and he served with my husband aboard HMS *Dart.*' She recounted the details of the events that led to her husband's tragic death and Trehearne's escape to shore. She paused and drew a deep breath to steady her voice.

'When Mr Trehearne, the man you know as John Bowden, came to my house for the first time, he told me all this in great detail. I believe it to be the truth. He also told me how afterwards the launch from his ship succeeded in landing the stolen gold in the very cove where he himself had made landfall and lay exhausted. He wrote of it in a letter and put his signature to it, with permission that I might use it in my efforts to prove my husband's innocence and the injustice he had suffered.'

All this time Smeaton listened intently without interruption. Then Alice ended abruptly, giving him the opportunity to speak.

'Have you this document with you now?

'No sir, and that's another thing. Only a few weeks back, my residence was broken into in the night. We found a scullery window left open the next day and there were footprints left on the table and floor. The house was searched from top to bottom but nothing was found to be missing. That is, until I went to my bureau in the study, where I discovered the lock on the drawer had been forced open. When I opened it I found that this letter to me from John had been stolen.'

'And did you tell anyone of this?'

'No. Not a single soul. Not even my sister when she came to visit me from the country soon afterward. Why anyone would take it has puzzled me ever since. But I could tell no one – until now.' Alice's lip trembled to fight the onset of tears. Closing her eyes, she pursed her lips tightly and her voice wavered.

'Now he is taken, I fear the worst will happen.'

'Come my dear, in my dealings with the Navy I found that, though desertion is a martial offence, it very rarely happens the accused is sent to the gallows. Mutinous actions are regularly overlooked.' Smeaton distractedly ran his fingers through his fine wavy hair, releasing the tied pigtail at his collar, and placed his hands on top of his head, the clasped fingers interlocking over his scalp.

'Yes I know, sir, but this is different. The very same night that my house was broken into and the letter stolen, Mr Trehearne had called on me as my guest. We supped together and he told me the story of the *Neptune*'s escape from shipwreck at Fowey.'

'Indeed we cannot forget it, nor the debt we owe to Fortune and to him. Oh happy day, when he came to see me in my yard and I took him into the Service.' His arms suddenly dropped down and he slung his large frame forward in the chair, clasping his hands and pointing with both index fingers in combination at some invisible thing before them.

'Mind you, I thought then that there was more to him than met the eye. How right I was! 'Course if I had known the truth of it, I would not have had him, and now we should all be drowned for my knowledge. What a good thing it is that we cannot see the future!'

Alice nodded her consent.

'Yes, but John saw it. He saw plainly what lay ahead for him and even spoke of it as though it had already happened!' She looked at him as though seeing afar. 'You recall your encounter with the *Dart* out in the Channel?'

'Indeed, at the time it was a most welcome sight, to see one of our own men o' war. Especially in these times, the war with France was foremost in my mind. Try as we might we could not beat up-channel, but were carried further and further out to sea .We were almost in sight of Finisterre, without means of protecting ourselves and unable to sail except in a direction that would take us further into the hands of our enemies.'

'Yes, it was a welcome sight to all your company – except, that is, for John – as your ships came alongside. It was close enough for him to be spotted by their Lieutenant, the hateful man who has caused all my grief. I believe he will stop at nothing ...' Alice fell silent, though her eyes blazed anger bright as the embers in the hearth.

'I spoke with him across the bows.' Smeaton paused and he looked up whilst he remembered what had taken place. 'They came up close and gave us direction to set a safe course for Scilly. I had no idea of the risk to John Bowden.'

'Now that you know of his past, will you help? I fear there is no one else who can. Colquhoun will see to it that John is silenced forever – he will do anything to protect his reputation.'

'I will, lass, if only it means that you will stop thinking such dark thoughts. It does not become a woman as young and beautiful as yourself.' Smeaton smiled as she looked away in every direction and her cheeks and neck coloured involuntarily. She suddenly laughed, despite her annoyance at the embarrassment.

'I would have you know, Mr Smeaton, that looks are but skin-deep. I have a mind to see justice done, as determined as yours is to see a light upon the Edystone.'

'Well said! 'Tis assured that I am as determined to protect all who serve under me as though they were my own family. I have no truck with injustice and foul play. Our men have Admiralty protections. We shall do all we can to secure John's release. And I dare say that his case might yet be investigated, if we can raise it with the Admiralty Board.'

It was past midnight. Alice stood up and thanked him for his kindness. She pulled her cloak about her and raised the hood to cover her head. Smeaton gave her a look of concern. He could hear the wind rattling the sashes and the driven rain drumming on the panes.

'It's quite alright, sir. My manservant has a carriage awaiting me across the street.'

'Indeed, but I insist on seeing thee to it.' He took up a battered tricorn hat and coat and, throwing it on, led her out to her carriage.

A week passed, then two, and despite his meeting with Commissioner Rodgers there was still no news of Trehearne. John Smeaton was working on his hands and knees in the mould room, carefully setting out the lines that described the intricate geometry for the seventh course at full size. This, the first complete course, would form a circular base to the 'solid', from which the great column would rise. Smeaton worked with the utmost care and attention to achieve the accuracy required.

'Begging your pardon, sir?' He had been so engrossed in drawing the lines on the floor that he had not heard her come in. It was the cooper's wife.

'Yes, what is it?'

'There's a Mr Weston arrived here from London to see you, sir.'

The engineer rose to his feet, brushing himself down. 'Capital. Please be so good as to show him in, Mrs Coates. Never was there a better time for him to come. See how it is that we translate our models and drafts into the real thing!'

Mrs Coates was polite toward her husband's employer, but she had no real enthusiasm for the enterprise, beyond the thought that it would provide her husband with an excellent steady employment for the present. She had not anticipated, when Mr Jessop came to ask for the use of the rooms, quite what would happen next. He had offered to rent the three ground-floor rooms and they had gladly accepted.

'It's for the Master's use in carrying out the works,' Mr Coates had told her. Well, naturally she thought he meant that Mr Smeaton would use the downstairs living room and the kitchen, along with her husband's workshop as an office to the nearby yard. The house, being situated as it was off the Stonehouse road, between the village and the new workyard at Millbay, seemed the perfect place for him to set up. But no sooner had he moved in than a gang of men with irons and hammers followed, and to her horror began to lay about them until the whole place shook. It was very distressing, and she was not to be consoled until Mr Smeaton himself assured her that this was not a wanton act of destruction and all would be put back as new when he had completed his work of drawing the stone course patterns. The workmen continued to remove all the walls and partitions between the rooms till it appeared scarcely recognisable as the cosy little apartment she knew. When she and Mr Coates walked around upstairs she could feel the floors 'very springy and lively'. She had told Mr Coates she feared the children could not run about in case they might 'disappear in an instant, falling through'. Her husband said there was no cause for worry, and that the extra money made a little inconvenience worth bearing.

'He's famous for his skill at building, Mrs Coates, have no fear.'

But then she showed him the gap that had opened between the wall and the bedroom floor, and sure enough the next day the men came with ropes and pulleys to rig up a support from the top floor above.

'Now it is more like a brig than a house,' she thought, as she led Mr Weston past ropes stretched taut with strain and lashed down to great heavy baulks of ship's timber. She entered the mould room with Mr Weston following close behind. Smeaton was drawing a chalk line along a ruler made from a length of planed timber. Hearing them come in, he looked up, got to his feet and stood in the midst of the now vast room, brushing chalk dust from his breeches and waistcoat.

'Mr Weston, very glad to see you, sir. You come at a very agreeable moment.'

'I'll leave you to it then shall I, sirs?'

'Yes Mrs Coates, that will be all.'

'By the by, Mr Smeaton, it seems the house is stopped settling now. You will be putting back the walls for us afterward?'

'Yes, of course. This will all be returned to the condition in which we found it, upon your kind offer of letting. And I can assure you that the whole is safe and sound.'

'I can't say I understand the workings of it but the floors do now feel firm again. My husband reckons there's no harm done.'

'Quite right. It might appear to stand without any means of support, but this is not the case. I have devised a means by which the whole of the upstairs is made secure. We have hung the upper floors from the roof trusses using the small purchase tackles and the cables are brought down to these Kent ledge anchors below.' He pointed to the heavy baulks that were themselves strapped down to the floor. 'The floors are drawn upward by the strain. I daresay you might invite all your neighbours for dancing and there would be no ill effect upon the frame.'

Mr Weston turned his attention from the ropes stretched taught from floor to ceiling and studied the chalk design laid down upon the floor. Within the circumference, lines zigzagged in tiers of geometric patterns from the outside to the centre. He recognised the dovetail shapes as those of the stones with which the tower would be constructed. The sheer size and magnitude of the pieces was impressive. Moulds for the foundation stones were strewn about the room and some were placed neatly over the chalk patterns on the floor. Weston carefully stepped forward over the course patterns and they shook hands, greeting each other warmly.

Smeaton told him how he had taken the ground-floor rooms in the house and removed the partitions between, in order to create the mould room with a floor of sufficient size to lay out the courses. Pointing to the wooden frames he launched into an enthusiastic explanation.

'You see here, Robert, the very roots of the column – the foundation moulds taken from the Rock.'

'It is impressive, but how do you manage? I had imagined you would use another place for your work, something a little grander perhaps?' Robert Weston looked about him as he spoke. Although the room was large and wide, the low beamed ceiling gave it an unnatural proportion, more akin to the lower decks of a man o' war than a building. It made the giant blocks of the timber moulds appear even larger than they actually were, in the dim light admitted through the casements.

'You could use better light for your eyes, too.'

'This is not my first choice. Last month I applied to the Mayor for the use of the Guildhall, but he absolutely refused. When I asked his reason, he told me "the chalk lines would spoil the floor", be damned! As you can see, I need a large floor and so afterwards I requested the Assembly Rooms for use of theirs and, I am bound to say, I succeeded no better. So rather than be subjected to any more denials I removed a partition between these two rooms, which were the garrets of our cooper. Though as you say this is not much to look at, it will serve my purpose. Had Mrs Coates known our intentions I expect we would have been turned away again, so happen I must make the best of my luck.'

'They ought to be ashamed of themselves. The elders of the town know how important it is that the unlit reef is made safe.' Robert Weston shook his head in disbelief. 'If they think of the increased trade and commerce that they themselves stand to benefit from, surely more ships will come into the Sound and to Plymouth harbour if there is nothing to fear and a light to guide them safely past the rocks.'

Weston reached out to touch one of the timber moulds, a wooden framework that described the outline of the stone block to be cut. The mould was shaped like a dogleg and had an indented side and front face. He studied it closely.

'Perhaps they're not fond of putting up with a man from the north country,' Smeaton said, and smiled wryly before adding, 'who insists that the column can be raised in stone. I am forever hearing them say that *nothing but wood will last upon the Edystone.*'

'Really? Perhaps it is only the sceptics who speak out loudest.'

'I wish it were so, but no, I would say 'tis the "general" opinion, and anyone who wishes to hold forth tends to fall in with it.'

Mr Weston looked again at the mould.

'Show me how this foundation works.'

'If you will help me carry these.' Smeaton turned away, walking over to the far side of the room. He began to slide another mould forward. Robert Weston took hold of the opposite side. Soon they had half a dozen of the shapes aligned and Smeaton was arranging them carefully so that they fitted exactly with the chalk lines on the floor.

'The blue line is the vertical face of the rock, where we have cut it and shaped it into the negative imprint of our stones.' Smeaton bent down and placed his hand level with the top of the moulds on the imaginary surface of the rock shelf. 'This is the bed for the next course to follow.'

'Very ingenious, sir.' Robert Weston nodded as he grasped the simple ingenuity of the engineer's methods. He saw in his mind the precise shapes of the stones, first keying in to the rock face and then to each other. Again he examined the white lines that zigzagged outwards across the floor, away from the row of moulds that were now locked together in a row. They traced the geometric pattern of the stones to follow and complete the course.

'These moulds are taken from the rock face, as we have cut it, and the remainder we have made here from my lines traced out as you can see. The masons are cutting and tooling each stone to fit the exact dimensions of its corresponding mould. Mr Tyrrell has come from Portland to oversee the masons' work in the yard.'

'Is he the man you told me of in your letter, who fashioned the Portland stone for the new bridge at Westminster?' Robert Weston asked.

'Yes, an excellent craftsman and master mason, he has the necessary capabilities. At first the ships would not come out of Portland without a naval escort, but they "ran it" here and we have all the Portland stone we need for this season.'

'Good. You told me of the French privateers in your letter. I am relieved that they kept from harm's way. But I understood the material for construction was to be Cornish moorstone?' said Weston.

'Yes, in part. We are using both. The Portland will make up the solid mass of the interior with the facing in moorstone, from the quarries at Lanlivery and Constantine.' Smeaton pointed to the outer circumference of the pattern.

'And the Portland is suitable?'

'Indeed, Portland is very suitable, easy to cut and work precisely though not as durable as the moorstone that shall protect it. Hence all our facing work is in the moorstone. I was obliged to send John Bowden who sailed in *Hancock's Sloop* to fetch it from the quayside at Par, for none other would carry it, believing that the stones could not be managed. He did say the captains there were astonished at the sight of our crew lifting them into the hold of the sloop.' Smeaton's laughter echoed in the empty room. 'Apparently it drew a large crowd of the idle and the curious.'

Robert Weston was keen to understand everything. 'I want to be able to describe your methods to the body of the Proprietors on my return.' He gestured to the moulds and the lines on the floor.

Smeaton obliged him. 'The remaining moulds for this course will fit into the pattern I have marked out. This is course number five; there are seven foundation courses, until the first full circular base course, that which I am laying down here alongside.' Smeaton gestured to the huge circular pattern beyond.

'I see each stone will be locked to its neighbour, something like a carpenter's joint,' said Weston. 'I recall the model you showed me last year in London, and indeed I saw such an ingenious design in the stones of the new Westminster Bridge.'

'Aye indeed, the very place and example that came to my thoughts – where the dovetailed tie-stones hold fast the kerbs from being loosened if they are struck by a heavy cartwheel. The stones for the Rock are very much like that, only the purpose of their dovetailed shape is to hold fast against the great power of the sea. Especially when they are newly laid and vulnerable, before the circle is closed.'

They heard the sound of voices and hurried steps approaching; Smeaton spun round and called out toward the men who burst into the room.

'How many times must I tell ye, I am not to be disturbed at my work! What is it, Jenkins?'

'Sir, we have news of John Bowden's whereabouts. Some of the men got aboard the Gunship *Duke* at her mooring in the Hamoaze. They spoke with the crew, who said he was interned below decks and not seen since. Wanted for deserting ship, they said.'

'Did they say when?' Smeaton's expression had turned from annoyance to anxious concern.

'Who is John Bowden?' asked Robert Weston.

'He is our best seaman. I made him Master of the *Weston*, the new yawl we named after yourself.'

'And what's this about desertion? If he has run away then they are at liberty to do with him as they please, are they not?'

'Word has it that he will be sentenced to hang, sir,' said Jenkins boldly. 'The men are all for a riot; we are ready to go to the Port Admiral's house if need be.'

'Thank ye, Jenkins, we must act upon this news quickly if we are to get him back. Tell Mr Jessop to make ready the *Edystone Boat*. We shall make sail right away to the Hamoaze.'

'Is it wise to involve yourself?' asked Weston, 'when there is so much to be done here?' He was concerned that they should not fall foul of the Navy.

Smeaton was adamant. 'Four of our men were taken, and only three have been returned! Tha knows the lad may well be a fugitive, but ...'

'Then why are you willing to protect him?' Robert Weston broke in.

'In our service he enjoys Admiralty protection from the impress officer the same as the others,' said Smeaton loudly, ''tis a point of principle.'

Then he lowered his voice to barely more than a whisper. 'A friend of good standing in society came to me and told me how both he and another were falsely accused and made to suffer an injustice that rightly should be the subject of an investigation. I promised I would do what's in my power to help.'

'I have brought the medallions you requested for proof of the men's protection,' Weston added, in an effort to make amends. Smeaton was delighted.

'Mr Weston, have you brought written proof from the Admiralty of their status?'

'Yes I have, along with three dozen medals cast from the die. They are in silver, as you asked for in your letter, and about the bigness of a crown.' Weston signalled for his coachman to bring a box into the room. The man returned a few minutes later with a small but obviously heavy wooden chest. Placing it on a work table he took a key from his pocket, unlocked the chest, and threw open the lid.

Mr Weston took up one of the medals and placed it in Smeaton's palm. He read aloud the motto running around the circumference – *In salutem omnium* – and the words *Edistone resurgit*, with the year *1757* marked below.

'For the safety of all ... Edystone rises again ...,' said Weston. 'I was obliged to make an application to the Secretary of State to permit the minting of them.'

'What a fine piece of work!' exclaimed Smeaton.

'Yes, I agree, they are rather fine.' replied Weston, with great satisfaction.

Smeaton held the medal close up. In the centre was a relief showing the new lighthouse upon its rock at sea. The hand that engraved the die had gone to great lengths to make it as truthful and intricate as was possible. Here were inscribed the blocks of stone, and billows of smoke issued forth from the orb that crowned the lantern.

'I fear it is perhaps a little too valuable for its purpose.' Smeaton inadvertently spoke his thoughts whilst he admired the shiny silver piece. 'Too much so to be handed out hither and thither,' he added.

'I thought that perhaps you would restrict their distribution to, say, the Commissioner and the Admiral at Plymouth and any persons whom you think might assist you in completing the scheme.' Robert Weston paused to thread a leather lace through the hole in the top of the medal and, tying it, put it over his head to wear. 'As for the rest, they might be worn thus by the workmen in the out-service and then surrendered to their opposites in the succeeding company as the work goes on.'

'I see, they share the use of the medals, but do not have the property. 'Tis well considered, Mr Weston, and we will take up your suggestion.' Weston slipped the medal off over his head and handed it to him. He held it aloft. 'But first we must make use of this one to get our man. Come, we have tarried long enough, there is not a moment to lose.' The men headed out onto the road and made for the yard.

'Edystone resurgit!' Smeaton cried to Robert Weston as they emerged into the near-blinding daylight. As they strode along the dusty road, he reflected on the motto.

'Do not think me feeble, Mr Weston, but there's an old proverb we use frequently in Yorkshire; not to reckon our chickens before they are hatched. Some may think we speak too soon – we have yet to lay a single stone!'

'No, the Proprietors have all agreed the wording is most apt, and the rest of the world shall know it. You have our complete faith and our trust.'

'I thank thee for it. We will show you what can be done this season, I am sure of it.' Smeaton strode ahead and Robert Weston followed close upon his heels as they headed off down toward Millbay. His face was set in a determined look that Weston thought could only inspire confidence in those around him; indeed he felt inspired and uplifted himself to be part of the adventure. Who would ever have thought that here he would be, following his 'engineer' like a schoolboy hero about to take on the might of the Royal Navy? It was absurd, but such was this man's charisma and sense of purpose that he felt it entirely right to do so. Smeaton's strong north-country voice roused him again.

'Let me tell thee, Mr Weston, we would all be shipwrecked now were it not for Bowden's courage and resolve at Fowey. We must not be intimidated; John Bowden belongs to the Edystone service. This medal shall be his, to prove it.'

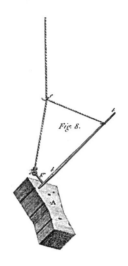

Fig. 8.

16

The outwork

'This is beyond endurance!' John Smeaton exclaimed. They were making sail out into the channel called Cremyll Passage, between the King's Docks and Mount Edgecombe. Beating upstream, they headed toward the great natural harbour in the lower reaches of the Tamar estuary where the King's ships lay at anchor; it was known as the Hamoaze.

'As if this is not hindrance enough – it's time to take matters into our own hands, Mr Weston,' said Josias Jessop. Smeaton had already represented to the commander at Plymouth the matter of the press gangs, and that there was no reason for their detaining anyone further.

'Commissioner Rodgers has given orders that the men are all to be released. Yet still we have difficulty in getting them back,' Jessop continued.

'Mr Jessop, I know it already from Mr Smeaton that this man is a navy deserter.'

'Oh, I see, sir,' replied Jessop. He was a little embarrassed and his manner became subdued.

'I have brought you the medals and I hope that from now on they will afford your men all the protection they require,' said Weston. He placed a hand on the old man's arm as he confided in him. 'Know too that I have heard the full story pertaining to your man – I believe we know him by the name John Bowden.' He smiled and gave a knowing signal. 'Mr Smeaton is determined to see him returned to the Edystone service and he has my complete faith and trust, as do you, Josias. I could not wish for any better anywhere. Let us get our man and then we can get back to our business, eh?'

They watched as the chequered sides of the *Duke* came into view. Smeaton felt in his pocket and ran his fingers over the raised surface of the Edystone medallion. He turned it over and over between his thumb and forefinger and thought of what he would say to the ship's captain. Robert Weston had volunteered his attendance to offer any assistance he could. Their mainsail filled in the breeze, showing the newly painted silhouette of the Edystone Lighthouse, the emblem of their Service.

The voyage was a short one and they were soon approaching the man o' war, but there was time enough for Smeaton to describe in more detail his building, the experiments to make a 'water-cement', and the method he was formulating for creating as hard and impervious a surface as he thought possible for the construction.

'The solid will consist of fifteen courses of stone that will lift the base of the tower up to the entrance level. When we complete it, it will be as one mass of stone, made immovable by the hardened mortar cement I am to use for the bed joints and the grouting.'

'I should like, perhaps, to return when you have reached a completed stage in the work,' Weston interrupted.

'Capital idea. I suggest tha comes back when we have laid the stepped foundation courses. Then we shall have brought the masonry level with the rock for the first course to form a complete circle. Course number seven is of the greatest diameter.' Smeaton held his hands wide apart to give a greater emphasis to his words.

'I should like very much to see it,' said Robert Weston.

'Good, that's settled then. The whole pattern of dovetailed stones emanates from a square stone in the centre – the stones then keying together around it, laid from the centre to the circumference.'

'Will you allow me the honour of placing a stone on behalf of the Proprietors?'

'Most certain! Why did I not think of it sooner? You shall place the centre plug stone – a cube of marble let into the surface very like a wood mortise and loose tenon.'

Smeaton went on to describe how another eight marble cubes surrounded the centre plug like 'pips' in an apple, each of one cubic foot in size. 'Each drops into a pocket in the surface of the completed bed and keys it to the underside of the course of stones to follow.'

Robert Weston listened attentively until they came alongside the man o'war's beam. A line dropped and ladders followed and they proceeded to climb up her side to the main deck where the captain awaited them. They were led away to his cabin below the quarterdeck and he begged them to sit and make themselves comfortable.

'Bring us tea,' he ordered his steward.

'Well, Mr Smeaton, how goes your enterprise? Will we see something raised this year on the Edystone?'

'It goes very well, sir. We expect to lay the first foundation stone as soon as we have good weather, I hope it will be this week.'

'Excellent news! A light upon the Edystone is most welcome to British men o' war returning from all the four quarters of the globe.'

'Indeed, Captain. Let me introduce our party: Mr Jessop, who I am sure you know of as the surveyor for the Edystone; Mr Weston, our patron and representative for the Proprietors of the Edystone Lighthouse; Mr Richardson, foreman; and our secretary Mr Harrison.'

'How d'you do, gentlemen – I for one know well the dangers of seafaring. I served aboard the *Victory* when she foundered on the Casquets in '44.'

Jessop raised his voice to exclaim, 'I remember her well!' Josias Jessop had been a master shipwright in the Royal Dockyard and he knew every post ship in the Western Squadron.

'Let me see, that would have been Captain …'

'Faulknor,' the captain prompted.

'Captain Faulknor! Aye, indeed,' said Jessop.

'He was a good captain, but on returning from Gibraltar we lost our reckoning – and the rest was fate.' The captain mused for a few seconds. 'Still, here we are! To what do we owe your visit? We hardly venture beyond the Sound. And then only to exercise our men at the great guns!'

'Though not in the direction of the Edystone, I hope!' said Robert Weston.

There was polite laughter at this amusement. The steward returned with tea and served them whilst Smeaton came directly to the point. The captain sat back and listened to what he had to say.

'We have good reason to believe that you are holding one of my company here.'

'Are you certain?' the captain replied coolly.

'I am, sir – and that he is held against his will and despite his having got a valid protection from the Admiralty.'

'Then what do you propose to do about it?'

'We want him back.' Smeaton took the medal from his pocket and placed it on the table. 'This is his token of protection, minted under the permission of the Secretary of State.'

'There are well nigh twenty dozen souls in my ship's company. Forgive me, sir, if I cannot place the man as easily as you would like.'

'We know him as John Bowden, but perhaps you know him as John Trehearne,' Smeaton replied.

'I will ask the purser to consult his register. We can send a message to you later. I am sure you would not want to be kept from your business by this matter,' said the captain.

'On the contrary, we cannot undertake our business until we know the whereabouts and safety of this man. He is an essential member of our crew – master of our yawl.' Smeaton leaned over the table and spoke in a barely audible voice, words that were lost to the others but had the effect of a full broadside on the captain. His face reddened and the cool reserve of a few moments ago was lost.

'We have instructions to hold this man pending his trial,' came the curt reply.

John Smeaton was in no mood to be rebuffed, but he remained calm.

'Lieutenant Colquhoun of the *Dart* did not release him when he should have, but sent him here. You will save yourself a great deal of trouble, Captain, if you release him now. If you do not, then I shall have to request Mr Weston here to petition the Admiralty for it.'

There was a moment's silence until it was broken by the sound of Smeaton's voice again, calmer now. He spoke in a more conciliatory manner.

'Let us not quarrel. I am sure this man is of no consequence to you and I will personally assume responsibility for insisting upon his release.' He smiled a placating smile but then resumed his stern timbre. 'But I can assure you that I will be calling upon the Lords of the Admiralty to hear evidence, should you decide to keep him! I have the ear of Admirals Anson and Boscawen, and I will see to it they are fully acquainted with our testimony.'

It was enough. The captain, who clearly saw himself challenged by a man who had both influence and position, suddenly changed tack. He deferred, politely granting Treherne's release, making an excuse of not knowing the man's assumed name and throwing in a suitable apology all at once. A few moments later Trehearne was brought up on deck, apparently none the worse for his detainment.

June was fast approaching. There was now a tremendous sense of urgency to get out to the rock to continue the 'outwork' as soon as possible. Everything depended on the weather. For weeks the stores, tackle and tools had been stowed aboard the *Neptune*; but the year was marching steadily on and it was now the beginning of summer.

Then, early on the morning of 3rd June, Jessop came to the mould room, where he found Smeaton at work.

'Mr Smeaton, sir, wind and weather are favourable to get under way. I have it from Cawsand.'

'Praise be! At last I can get off my knees!' Smeaton staggered to his feet and stretched himself. 'How soon?'

'Will you be coming with us, sir?' Jessop enquired.

'Of course, thou knows how impatient I am to see our work begin. This blasted weather has been such a nuisance.'

'Aye, contrary – but it can be high summer in Plymouth and you will find it blowing hard upon the reef. But we have it from the fishing fleet that conditions are perfectly calm there this morning.'

'Capital! I cannot tell thee how glad I am to be out of this dingy room.'

They sailed later that afternoon. The conditions at sea were so balmy that they were becalmed about a 'league' from the rock and dropped anchor until the morning. They hoisted sail again at dawn the following day, reaching the buoy and the moorings by six o'clock. Then began the arduous task of raising the moorings. For this they used the great tackle blocks that Smeaton had designed and tested to great effect at Millbay. Slowly the chains rose out of the calm waters and were brought up on deck, over the rail.

Then suddenly one of the seamen, standing near the davit, cried out, 'Hold hard! The chains are breaking!'

'Stand to,' Jessop gave the order to halt. The men secured the ropes, then backed off along the deck to what they considered a safe distance and waited. Smeaton raised his spyglass and observed how the link now upon the drum was bending with the strain placed upon it. This he immediately saw was due to the length of the link and the small diameter of the iron roll.

When these links came to a strain upon the Davit roll, which was of cast iron (and not above nine or ten inches in diameter) they began to bend upon the convexity of the roll; and as I was apprehensive of the ill consequence that might attend their breaking, the following remedy occurred to me ...

'Mr Bowden,' he called out, 'fetch me an oak trenail, cut into short lengths about three inches long, and split these again in two!'

'Aye aye, sir.' Trehearne duly produced the pieces of oak cut neatly to the sizes asked for. Smeaton took these in his hand and made his way bravely forward.

'Begging your pardon, sir' said Jessop, 'but I'd rather you let one of the seamen perform the duty?' And he continued in a hushed tone ''Tis extremely dangerous for you to be stood there, if any of the links should snap ...' He halted, an expression of acute concern twisting his features.

'I am very well aware of it, Mr Jessop. That is why I wish you to proceed as carefully as you can, and I will take it upon myself to carry out the post of honour here.'

The buckled link might snap at any moment, sending the chain lashing across the deck. It would cut through anything in its path. The thought was uppermost in Smeaton's mind as he made his way up to the davit. He took one of the wooden wedges and placed it carefully between the chain link and the roll.

'Now, Mr Jessop, have the men take the strain.'

The men took up their stations and on Jessop's command resumed the slow deliberate heave. When the next link rose, Smeaton placed another wedge between it and the davit roll, thus preventing the link from bending under the strain. It seemed to be working. As each link passed over the roll, the wedges dropped out, and he gathered them up from the deck to use again. He continued, assiduously placing wedges between the chain links and the iron roll, while the crew hauled in the remaining eleven fathoms of chain link by link, until at last the great swivel of the bridle chain was raised. Some hours had passed, and Smeaton was exhausted, but at last the buoy chain was raised up. By midday they had added another five fathoms of new chain to the bridle and the *Neptune Buss* rode securely at her moorings.

'That was bravely done, sir,' Jessop's voice drifted down from above as Smeaton eased himself down the steps into the cabin below. 'I'll see to it that you have fresh coffee brought down.'

'Oh yes, tha's a good fellow, that would be a treat! I confess I am ready for it,' he called out without looking up. He was stiff with cold and constant bending. Lighting a lantern, his eyes adjusted to the dim light of the cabin. The relentless minding of the chain had taken his full powers of attention, with no opportunity for his mind to wander. He felt suddenly drained. Removing only his coat and without bothering more, he fell into the cot bed. He slept heavily. Later the sound of the cook approaching roused him, and there came the strong delicious scent of coffee. The coffee revived him and, helping himself to a third cup, he rose and took up his journal. Writing in a neat freehand he recorded the events of the last few days, still fresh in his memory. It helped to pass the time aboard the *Neptune* to enter the daily events of their progress.

Years later, at Austhorpe, his journals enabled him to write the *Narrative.*

On Saturday the 11th of June the first course of stone was put on board the Edystone Boat with all the necessary stores, tools, and utensils.. We landed at eight on Sunday morning, the 12th of June and before noon had got the first stone into its place, being that upon which the date of the year 1757 is inscribed in deep characters; and the tide coming upon us, we secured it with chains to the old stanchions, and then quitted the rock till the evening tide, when it was fitted, bedded in mortar, trenailed down, and compleatly fixed; and all the outward joints coated over with Plaster of Paris, to prevent the immediate wash of the sea upon the mortar. This stone, according to its dimensions, weighed two-and-a-half tons. The weather serving at intervals, it was at the evening of Monday June the 13th that the first course, consisting of four stones was finished; and which, as they all presented some part of their faces to the sea, were all of Moorstone.

The following day began very calm, but by the time the *Weston* came into the Gut to land her cargo of five stones, the wind had sprung up fresh again at north-east. John Trehearne at the helm needed all his skill, along with a secure line fastened to the transport buoy, to deliver up her cargo and get away out of the Gut. Relieved of her ballast, the yawl pitched and rolled in the confusion of white waters about the Rock. She made headway toward the mooring, but here she lurched and rolled on staccato seas foaming with breakers whipped up in the gale, and driving her hard toward the *Buss* alongside. The *Weston* rode violently up and down, pitching her bowsprit into the spume. It was too dangerous to remain.

'Signal our leaving. We must bend a sail for home or be dashed to pieces here!' Trehearne bellowed against the wind.

A reply came running up the *Neptune*'s mast.

'Let out a pennant and slip.' The sail frapped and flew out till it caught the fresh breeze and they shot away clear of the reef. Behind them they could see the men on the Rock struggling to lash down the unfixed stones with chains and ropes. Then a great swell suddenly rose up over everything and hid them from view. When the spray cleared they saw, to their relief, the figures now crawling down to their boats and hurriedly quitting the place for the refuge of the *Neptune*.

In the next few days Richardson's men set the first two courses, but they suffered setbacks. The gales took away five pieces of stone that they had not had sufficient time to fix and these would have to be remade before the work could continue. There was nothing for it but to come home in the *Sea-Horse* yawl as soon as the weather allowed. At low tide Smeaton and Jessop went out in the light yawl, powered by four oarsmen. They passed close by the House Rock and he scoured the rock's surface with his glass. As the breaking seas fell away Smeaton spoke aloud the numbers of the stones that he could see were missing. Jessop recorded them by noting down as best he could in the wet.

'Number 9 is gone and also the ladder it was chained to, number 5 and 6 are gone, number 3 has broke its cramp and is gone, the lead weight is also gone.'

'Is that everything?' Jessop enquired as he wrapped his book with a piece of oiled tarpaulin.

'Aye it is, we must make immediately for Plymouth. We have the moulds for these and enough spare blocks for replacements. I shall want a couple of men on each, working night and day until they are ready.'

There was nothing for it but to accept the delay. Whilst the masons worked unceasingly, chipping at the great blocks of stone within the moulds, John Smeaton was dressing himself for a visit to the Assembly Rooms. He was the invited guest of Lord Edgecombe. He had thought to decline, but now he might as well enjoy the interruption in their schedule.

'A pity that Anne could not be here to accompany me – how she adores a dance,' he said to himself as he drew himself up before the mirror. He wore his finest silk shirt and a dark blue coat of best Yorkshire worsted cloth. He made a final adjustment to the grey periwig. It was a while since he had worn it, preferring to wear his hair tied back in a ponytail whilst engaged in the day-to-day business at Millbay. The timepiece in the room sounded the half hour. He glanced over to look at it on the mantelpiece, then looked out of the window and, seeing Lord Edgecombe's coach drawing up in the street outside, took up his hat and made his way down. Mr Cookworthy was calling him from the hall. He was anxious not to keep the Edgecombes waiting.

'What time are we meeting Mr Trehearne?' Verity demanded. She was growing more and more impatient as the day wore on. Her eye caught herself in the dressing room mirror. She smiled at her reflection and admired her new gown of russet-coloured silk, trimmed with lace. It set off the colour of her hair. 'Do you not think that this perfectly matches my hair?'

'Yes, it does. You will have the eyes of all the young gentlemen and officers upon you, like moths to the flame. It might be a little uncomfortable?' Alice supposed. Then she thought better of it. 'What harm could there be in making an impression,' she thought. Besides, her younger sister craved the attention that her looks bestowed on her and here was the perfect place to be seen.

'I hope John likes it,' said Verity unthinkingly, as she twirled her figure before the mirror. 'He is such a handsome fellow, and it has been more than a half year since he came to the Hall, and I have missed him so.'

'Well he has had rather a lot to contend with. First, being lost at sea, then meeting with the naval press gang, and then not released until his rescue by Mr Smeaton. Imagine how he must have languished aboard that awful guardship in the Hamoaze knowing that he lay under threat of a court martial.'

'I wonder if he thought of me.' Verity was unspeakable at times, thought Alice. Verity carried on preening herself, thinking of Trehearne and speaking her thoughts.

'Is he safe in Plymouth now?' she asked.

'He has a silver medal, that affords him greater protection than any civil authority here in the town,' replied Alice, 'but you're not to mention it to him or anyone there tonight.'

'Why? Will they catch him and hang him?'

'No, of course not! Thanks to Mr Smeaton. And I expect that he is far the smallest of the Navy's concerns. There is a war being fought, or didn't you know?'

'Of course I know! Honestly, Alice, I may not have your years and connections, but neither am I wholly concerned with myself and the fashion.'

'Yes, I know, I'm sorry.'

'We may live in the country but Father has the newspaper every week and we are up with politics and news of the war as much as anyone.'

'I know, please forgive me, but I mean what I say – that there is one who will stop at nothing to see John harmed.'

'What can he possibly have done to deserve such malice, I'm sure?' said Verity as she took up her cloak and followed her sister downstairs and out into the street.

It was a wonderful, warm summer's evening. So warm that there were great crowds walking upon the Hoe. A full moon was rising and hung low in the evening sky. It cast reflections upon the serene waters below them, as they passed beneath the grey stone bastions of the Citadel. Alice and Verity had decided to walk to the town; it was such a beautiful midsummer's eve. Their coach was to attend them later, under instructions to come to the Assembly Rooms not before ten o'clock.

'Look,' Alice gestured to a coach as it passed them, approaching the entrance portico of the Assembly Rooms, 'there is Lord Edgecombe's party.' As the coach drew up, the footmen jumping down and opening the doors, she recognised one of the group emerging from the cabin. 'And that is Mr Smeaton with them. My word, he looks refined; I hardly recognise him.'

'Do you really know him?'

'Well, yes I do. I visited his lodgings and made his acquaintance there. I was so desperate that John was lost or taken.'

They made their way carefully through the street, now filled with carriages arriving at the Assembly Rooms. The horses stood patiently whilst their drivers and coachmen gathered around to talk in their own company. Verity picked her way through the melee; she was looking at her feet and stepping carefully, holding her skirts aloft to avoid the piles of fresh horse dung.

'Ahoy there, good evening, Mistress Appleford, Miss Vasey.' Trehearne stepped forward and bowed before them. He looked a gentleman in every detail, from the landsman's silk stockings and breeches to his lace necktie. Gone were the seaman's trousers and jacket. Instead he wore a long coat over a waistcoat, and his hair was tied neatly back beneath a black tricorn hat.

'I say, Mr Trehearne, you look splendid!'

'Thank you, Verity, put it down to my pay and prospects in the Edystone service. I thought that if I was to accompany you tonight then I must appear in every way a gentleman.' He offered his arm and Verity took it, Alice walking alongside her. They joined the procession of people now making their way up the grand stone steps and entered.

The dancing had begun. 'Come, Mr Trehearne, will you dance with me?' Verity pleaded.

'I may appear a country gentleman, but I know only jigs and hornpipes, my dear,' he spoke with genuine concern.

'Never mind, I can show you; just follow the others and do as I do. You're in good company – all these naval lieutenants and young midshipmen know little else.' He looked to Alice and she smiled her approval.

'Do, John – I cannot tell you how long Verity has been waiting to step out in Plymouth society.'

Alice observed as they joined the line of couples for the next dance. From high up in the gallery the band struck up an air that she recognised, but could not recall the name. She watched with amusement as John did his best to follow in the steps by watching Verity and those around him. It made him a little slower than the rest and gave him the appearance of comic clumsiness. But he was not the only one.

She stood for a while taking in the splendid spectacle. The vast room was filled with the best society from all over the county. Great chandeliers hung down above the dancers and cast a glittering light. Beneath them moving shadows intertwined, as the dancers promenaded the length and breadth of the floor. Around the perimeter of the room stood an audience of young women and men, the men mostly naval officers in their dress uniforms. The older set formed small cliques, like tight knots, and were engrossed in conversation. They observed the dancers and their audience casually. Mr Cookworthy stood out in his simple, black and white apparel, recognisably a sober Quaker, but his face was animated. He was a great conversationalist and he lost no time in introducing Smeaton to a wide circle of friends. A small army of footmen waited upon them constantly.

'Tell me, Alice, who is that man dancing with your sister?' A friend she recognised immediately interrupted Alice from her thoughts.

'Oh Sophie! How glad I am to see you. I was lost in the spectacle of it all! It's been so long since I have attended the Summer Dances. Not since my husband ...'

'Yes, it's been too long. You look charming; how that colour suits you!' Sophie admired her cream damask gown. 'And how your sister is grown. I swear she was not more than a child when I saw her last. Now she is a beauty – and tell me, who is her dark handsome beau?'

'He is our friend Mr Trehearne, of Polruan, near Fowey, in the county of Cornwall.' Alice hid her annoyance from Sophie, who obviously saw them as the perfect couple.

'Has he estates there?'

'No, he has no especial inheritance that I know of. He is yet another poor Cornishman who ventured to sea to better himself. They are uncommon good sailors, I believe, or so my husband said when he lived.'

'Yes.' Sophie was a little lost for words. Alice knew she would be thinking of the scandal she had caused a year before when she publicly refuted the details of her husband's death in the Service, accusing the Navy of 'concealment' in a terrible miscarriage of justice. The news of it had got round and for months she received few if any of her former acquaintances. Sophie to her credit had remained loyal, though she was one of the few to do so. Time had mended the damage, but Alice could not forget what had happened, and could not forgive the man who had caused it.

'Still, he's a devilish handsome Jack, and they make such an elegant couple,' Sophie said, her head rested to one side with eyes half closed, and seemingly in a dreamlike state. Alice atoned for her off-hand remarks.

'And he has excellent prospects in the Edystone service. He has been made a master, and the company worship him; his bravery and seamanship has already saved their lives.'

'I recall hearing of it. They were thought by everyone to be lost at sea. It was a great talking point in Plymouth upon their return.'

'Yes it was,' Alice agreed. She had heard of it.

'You know that very few in Plymouth believe it will succeed? Everyone says that a building made in stone cannot last upon the Edystone. Indeed it is said that even Lord Edgecombe has his doubts. And they are saying how much it all costs, that it will bankrupt the owners, and that the sea will knock it over like a child's toy when the greatest storms come.'

Lord Edgecombe's party were held in thrall by Smeaton's up-to-the-minute account of the progress on the new lighthouse. William Cookworthy was delighted with the impact his guest was making upon them. Sir Joshua Reynolds had joined them. He too was a native of Plymouth, born in nearby Plympton, and would give up London when on occasions his busy work and social engagements allowed. He was curious to meet the engineer, having heard about him in London from their mutual friend, Mr Wilson the landscape painter.

'We have a mutual acquaintance in Mr Wilson, the painter. He has told me how Lord Macclesfield sent to him to find you and that he was the only person in London who knew where you were.'

'Indeed, were it not for our friendship I might still be in Northumberland and the scheme for the Edystone in some other person's hands.'

'Tell me, is it true that he wrote twice to convince you of accepting this commission?'

'I dare say it is. Had I known more of the nature of it, perhaps I should have declined entirely.' There was laughter at Smeaton's remark. The party found him amusing and good company, and warmed to his ready wit and humorous remarks. Smeaton thought it equally gratifying to be in such exalted company. He had grown fond of the men in the Edystone Company; they were his 'Plymouth family', but theirs was a gritty and eccentric humour, almost child-like. He appreciated their loyalty and devotion, like (as he imagined) a good ship's company for their captain. But he missed the learning, sharp wit and brilliant insight of the members of the Society. Tonight was a welcome variation in his diet.

'Can you can paint a picture in our minds of your experiences on the Edystone, Mr Smeaton? Do you think it a foul hellish place, as the sailors know it, or perhaps one of awesome beauty?'

'There you have me, Sir Joshua. I confess I have not given it much thought, for all my efforts are concerned with the technical difficulties it presents. We are engaged in the most difficult and dangerous phase of the work at this very moment.'

'Really? How so?' Sir Joshua sipped at his glass and listened with interest.

'Our gaining access to the rock is limited by the tides, and *terra firma* is at a premium. We are constantly washed over by breaking seas, often struggling to preserve ourselves, our materials and stores. There's mortar buckets, tackle blocks, shears and such like, as well as our souls – all at risk of being washed from the rock with one rogue swell.'

'It sounds terrifying.' Lady Edgecombe placed a hand on Smeaton's coat lapel and gently patted, 'we will pray for you in our chapel at Rame.'

'But how do you manage should the weather take a sudden turn? I imagine a squall at sea can be disastrous in such circumstances,' Lord Edgecombe asked. 'Why, I remember a passage to Madeira when sudden storms wreaked havoc 'pon the *Halsewell*.'

'Then we must be nimble, stow everything in our small boats and make all speed for the *Neptune Buss*, our store vessel and station. Once on board we are as safe as we can be, though the journey can be near impossible at times.'

'Do tell us of it, sir. We on land have little idea of what it must be like to be cast away upon the agitated waters around the Stone.'

'Very well, if it does not tire thee to hear more.' He described how on one occasion they were caught by increasing winds and tide and struggled to reach the *Buss*. 'The wind and seas had so increased from the north-east quarter, that we found it quite impossible to make headway. Compelled by necessity, we risked a passage through the rocks to southward, aiming at the interval betwixt the Sugar Loaf and the House Rock, and both boats providentially got through unhurt, it then blowing a hard gale of wind. Mr Jessop and I rowed with two of the hands in the light yawl, and Mr Richardson and a crew of eight pulled in the other, the *Sea-Horse* yawl. We took them in tow but got into so much wind and sea and current of tide that we were carried away and had no choice but to part.'

'Cast away upon the seas – it must have been awesome and terrible to be in those small boats! Whatever did you think?' Reynolds saw a heroic scene in his mind's eye.

'We determined to make the *Buss*, while the *Sea-Horse* yawl had no choice but to make for the floating light to leeward.'

'Which I am told is some way from the House Rock, is it not?' Lord Edgecombe added. Smeaton nodded in confirmation.

'Yes, though the *Neptune* was near, the tide's flow was agin it. We would labour at our oars for an hour and a half more, until at last recovering her – to our great joy! Next morning it blew so hard that the *Weston* signalled her distress and left us to make her best port. It was not until the afternoon that conditions and tide allowed the *Sea-Horse* to return safely. We discovered her crew did manage to get onto the floating light and were eternally thankful for it.'

'It sounds awesome. Dare I say it would be a wonderful, dramatic subject to paint? Though I prefer the comfort of my studio to the open sea.'

'Indeed, you must visit us again at Mount Edgecombe, Sir Joshua, and perhaps you will come, Mr Smeaton? We have planted a great many trees and the gardens are looking their best. We have some new garden structures and ruins that I think would interest you both.'

'An excellent proposal, my dear.' Lord Edgecombe turned to Smeaton. 'You might bring your great spyglass, sir, and place it in the chapel on Rame Head. There you will have the best view of the Edystone from any part of the coast.'

Reynolds and Smeaton both agreed it would be a most agreeable visit.

'Good! We'll make a day of it.' Lord Edgecombe's word was final. They fell silent and watched the next dance begin.

Smeaton caught sight of Alice. She was dancing with John Trehearne. How happy they looked. Alice had thought that she could never be this happy again, but when she looked at her partner she knew that she was. No words were needed to explain the warmth she felt within.

Verity was dancing the same dance with a handsome young officer. She had received the attentions of all of them and she had danced with as many as she could. Now it was nearly ten, she decided that this young lieutenant from the *Amazon* was her favourite. Alice caught site of them for a moment as they passed down the line. Her parents would hear of it but she didn't mind. Verity was old enough to have a care.

Alice was at her happiest – when suddenly she caught sight of him. At that moment the dance brought her and John together, and she leaned forward and spoke in his ear. Trehearne looked up in the direction of the gallery and felt a crawling sensation as the hair rose on his neck. He saw a face in the crowd that that he knew could be no other.

Lieutenant Colquhoun stood watching them. A young woman seemed to be talking to him. She clutched at his arm, but he took no notice. His pallid stare fell first on Alice then on her partner. When Alice glanced in that direction she was met by a look from his pale eyes that sent a chill deep into her. When the dance finished, they lost sight of him in the crowd. Though he hid his feelings well, Trehearne could not forget the cold panic he had felt on seeing that face. His enemy lurking in the shadows – there would be no end to his nightmare. It haunted him always. But he determined to put such thoughts out of his mind, at least while Alice stood by him

The evening was drawing to a close and there was now a general confusion as the hall began to empty. Everywhere people were taking leave of friends and acquaintances. Alice bid Sophie goodnight, they held hands briefly, and then she turned to look for Verity.

'Don't be anxious. I expect she's slipped off to say her goodbyes to that officer she was dancing with.' Trehearne politely offered her his arm and they joined the slow procession towards the great doors that now were thrown open. Framed in the open portal, Alice saw that the night sky had turned a deep indigo and showed the bright stars within it. The evening air was cool under the portico. Upon the call to 'make way' everyone stepped aside. Alice and John followed suit, providing an aisle that led straight down the stone staircase to allow the party of Lord and Lady Edgecombe to pass. A lantern cast its sallow light on the giant columns that supported the great stone frieze and pediment above them. The Edgecombe carriage had drawn up below. Everyone waited patiently as the small group made its way outside and down to the carriage awaiting them.

'Look, Alice,' John whispered in her ear, 'there's John Smeaton, and who's that with him?'

'Sophie told me he is Sir Joshua Reynolds, the famous portrait painter, down from London.'

Smeaton saw them and he raised his hat to them in passing. Alice curtseyed and they exchanged a few words.

'Good night, sir.'

'Good night, Alice. I saw you dancing this evening, and if thou were not spoken for, or I a married man, I should have made sure to set my cap at thee. Look after her, Mr Bowden.'

'I promise I shall, Mr Smeaton.'

'You sail more skilfully than you dance, sir, and I thank Heaven for it.'

He smiled benevolently towards them, and headed down the steps to rejoin the party and climb into the coach.

Lieutenant Colquhoun hardly heard a word his partner said. She carried on, seemingly unaware of his distraction, and he made the barest response to her questioning, the simplest 'yes' or 'no' and 'of course my dear'. She would have begged an explanation for his far-away look and his loss of tongue. But she was quite content to be seen out on the arm of the First Lieutenant, especially as he was now made acting commander of his ship. Jeremiah attended to her every want, and he bought her dresses and jewels – paid for, he said with prize-money, but she was not so sure. His gaming debts amounted to a great deal, and he was not always so lucky as when they took the *Liberté*. She hoped that soon he would receive confirmation of his post, and they would be married, and she thought how, as the wife of a captain in the Western Squadron, her life would become easier. It was everything she wanted.

'I mustn't upset him now; he's obviously got things on his mind,' she consoled herself and took another glass of sherry. She downed the drink. Flushed by the alcohol she became bold. Her thoughts began to run. She saw Alice. The one he cursed so openly, the one who accused him of lies, the widow who threatened to make more trouble for Jeremiah than her own husband was ever worth, even if he was a gentleman.

'Isn't that the widow, you know, the one who called for an inquiry to be set up from the Admiralty?'

'What, oh yes, she could not accept the truth of it. That her husband was a thief.'

'Then who is that man she dances with?'

'No one, my dear – he is but a rogue in fine livery.'

'She seems very happy with him.'

'He got away from me.'

'Really?'

'Yes, he is a deserter from my ship, my dear ... A bad man.'

'Then why is he at liberty?'

'Why indeed! At first we all thought he was drowned. When I caught him I had him imprisoned aboard the *Duke* awaiting his court-martial, but that fool of a captain let him go. Now he mixes in the best society like a lord, and no one will touch him.'

'That's terrible, ain't it? But do not fret so, Jeremiah – you look so cruel, it frightens me!'

'Believe me, Harriet, he must be dealt with,' he replied. 'I can't have him at liberty, hanging about my neck,' he told himself.

'Perhaps we should speak with her, warn her of his deeds.'

'No, don't do that, my dear – I can manage it myself. You must promise me never to speak with either of them. Never, you understand?'

'Jeremiah, you're hurting me!'

He loosened his grip on her arm as he led her away. She was frightened until he apologised for his behaviour.

'It is a kind of madness, but I can confide in no one else.' He stopped himself.

'Jeremiah, are you quite well?' She had never heard him speak in such a way.

'Yes, quite well. I am sorry to have troubled you with it. It's nothing, honestly. Come, let us away now before the crowd. Let me take you home.'

He offered her his 'good' left arm and they slipped away down the steps, beyond the line of coaches awaiting their passengers and through the cobbled lanes into the town. All the while his mind was racing. 'He knows too much to run loose; how can I rid myself of him?' Then he hit upon an idea. 'Trehearne could meet with an accident at sea – that little boat of his sunk, perhaps by one of those heavy stones crashing down upon it. William Hill will know how.'

Alice and John were growing more concerned by the minute, but at last Verity joined them. They had been looking for her for nearly half an hour and most of the coaches were gone. Alice was grown anxious that she might have agreed to go off with her officer to some ship in the port. What might happen she dreaded to think – and what would she say to Mother? An elopement? She was so worried that she asked John to look for her in the nearby streets and taverns. Alone, she remembered Colquhoun, and worried that he too was out there somewhere and that John Trehearne might be taken again. She sighed a sigh of relief when he came back empty-handed, and then suddenly there was Verity, standing before them.

'Where have you been, you minx?' Alice's concern hardened into anger; she was very cross with her younger sister. But Verity had had too wonderful an evening for this to spoil it now. She had also enjoyed more sherry than was good for her.

'Oh, Alice, he says he will take me on a tour of his ship, the *Amazon*, on the morrow! May I go? Please!'

'He's obviously no gentleman to leave you wandering the streets, that's certain!'

'He had to get back for his watch. We have only just parted. I was not abandoned! May I go? Please!'

'That depends on your shaping up here and now, and you can apologise to Mr Trehearne; he has been searching the town up and down, to find you. Everyone else has gone home!'

Verity looked at him with her head to one side. 'I am very sorry, John, I loved you before but now I love another. Ooh dear, I feel a little dizzy.' He took her arm to steady her and walked her on.

'Come on, Verity, we have the coach waiting.' John and Alice managed to get her in and could not help laughing together when she fell sound asleep. Alice soon put any thought of the gaunt lieutenant completely out of her mind, but Trehearne could not altogether forget the face he saw stare out at him from the shadows.

17

Mutiny and combination

It was a warm summer night. In the west, streaks of light remained, and Smeaton could see in the deepening dark the mast-lantern of the floating light. Jessop was leaning on the rail in his shirtsleeves, staring into the turbid waters below. The stillness calmed the waters but the slow heave of the swell gave the impression of an oily solution, black as bitumen and thick with matter in suspension. They looked down into the barely moving water as it slopped against the *Neptune*'s sides, then up at the stars.

'A perfect night, Josias.'

'It is indeed, Master, sea's almost a millpond. And not a breath of wind.'

'Yes, I find it very hot and airless below.'

'Aye, this is how it is in the tropics; there the sailors choose to sleep on deck.'

'I was writing my journal. Will you give me your witnessing of the wreck of the *Charming Sally*. It proves only too well how ineffectual the floating light is, so far from the reef.' He nodded in the direction of the dim lightship a couple of miles away.

'Always thought that they was too far off to be of much use, Mr Smeaton.'

'Tell me what happened.'

'Betwixt eleven and twelve o'clock that night, the watch espied a sail on the rocks; so I dispatched the yawl to their aid. They returned with the crew of the *Charming Sally* of Bideford, a vessel of some 130 tons burthen. By daylight we could see her, sat upright upon the rocks all that day, but smashed herself to pieces in the following night. The Cawsand fishermen came to pick up salvage later in the day, but was too late and found nothing.'

'What a piece of luck it was that you were on hand to bring her crew off.'

'Aye. They told us how they had mistaken the dark reef for fishing boats! In the morning we sent them ashore in the yawl. They were intending to make their way home by land.'

'By the by, have ye enough mortar for the week?'

'We have. We've overcome the shortage by lashing the casks to the shrouds of the yawls.

We had all but run out. Now with the casks hanging in the shrouds, we send out a rope from the *Buss* and the lashing being cut, the casks fall into the sea from where they can be towed on board.'

'Capital. Thou knows, Josias, I believe that we have accomplished the hardest part.'

'Aye indeed, sir, but there is something concerns me.'

'Go on.'

Jessop wore a worried expression, furrowing his brow.

'It's Hill, sir, he favours some in the company whilst mistreating others. He is hard on John Bowden in particular, ever since his release.'

'I fear the same. He has too much influence and not for the better. I will see to it; there is no room for mutiny and combination here. If he has a grievance than he should bring it to me, not seek to poison our authority with his surly contempt.' He paused and placed a hand on Mr Jessop's arm, telling him not to worry himself unduly and to get some sleep. 'Rest you well, Josias. Soon we will finish the foundation, and start on the solid.'

The 'fundamental solid', as Smeaton called it, was to be all one mass of stone up to the entrance passage floor at course fifteen.

'The higher we climb, so at least the drier we shall be, Master Smeaton.'

'Right enough. Good night to thee, Josias.'

A few days later John Smeaton found himself back in Millbay, where he lost no time in seeking out Hill and speaking his mind. As a result William Hill's fury with Smeaton had led him to the nearest tavern. He drank until he was unable to stand, for Smeaton had publicly reprimanded him, and afterward Hill had spent the whole day brooding in sullen quiet. Now he roared his displeasure.

'Damn his eyes, I believe he bears nothing but contempt for me. And that's all the thanks I get.' He belched loudly into his ale and there was a protracted silence as he quaffed it, then banged the pot down onto the wooden sideboard. A hardened group of supporters had gathered round him, drawn from the ranks of the tinners and stonemasons.

'And old Jessop has too. Richardson is a good fellow, William Smart a fine master, and John Bowden – our saviour – can do no wrong; but I am not worthy.'

'You been done down proper, I says,' one of the men consoled.

'Aye, I have nothing but insults I do not deserve. He'll push too hard if he's not careful. The tinners will follow me, not him.'

'William! You can't go sayin' things like that! Better vent your spleen elsewhere.'

'I tell you, he shall know where loyalties lie, that's certain.'

'Here, drink away your madness and forget the cruel world.'

'Come along now, have a care for the hour, there's good fellows.' The innkeeper was ready to shut up for the night and he was having

211

trouble in shifting them. They had drunk until their ability to be civil and reasonable was as dislodged as their balance. With Hill at their midst they became belligerent and rowdy, and it took all his skill and powers of persuasion to see them out into the street. Eventually they reeled out into the night air, and the bolts of the tavern door slid home so hard behind them that they sounded like musket shots in the evening quiet.

The following morning there was no sign of Hill, and those who had managed to rouse themselves for work were a sorry sight. When Jessop asked them to explain his absence they looked blankly at each other, shrugged their shoulders and said nothing.

'Gone to earth to lick his wounds, I shouldn't be surprised,' he said in a low voice, more to himself than to anyone in particular. 'Very well, be about your business and look useful.' Then he made his way to the wooden shed that served as their office. He shoved open the door and, hearing the sound of Smeaton's voice, hung up his hat and greatcoat.

'Mr Weston will be returning shortly to visit us and set his hand to work upon the Rock.' Smeaton spoke his thoughts out loud, interrupting Mr Harrison the clerk who was in the middle of his arithmetic; he murmured his annoyance at losing count. Smeaton had written, taking the opportunity to invite their employer to return in the coming month and perform the ceremony of laying the keystone into the first entire course.

'Good morning, Josias, what say you that we give Robert Weston the marble cube, to lay in its plug at the centre of the course.'

'That sounds very agreeable,' said Jessop.

The morning passed easily as they attended to business and reviewed the day-to-day matters that stood neglected when they were engaged in the 'outwork' at sea. There was an atmosphere of quiet concentration, as each focused upon the work in hand. Suddenly Smeaton broke off and, laying down his pen, stood up and stretched himself upright.

'Will you take coffee, Josias? Mr Harrison, rest from your figures and have a fresh pot brought in here to share between us.'

'Gladly, sir, I will go and fetch one. Let me clear these ledgers away and bring out the cups.' He busied himself about the desks, drawing board and table, clearing away papers and ink, and then went outside. Returning a few minutes later, he shouldered the door open and pushed it shut behind him using the heel of his shoe. He held a pot of piping hot coffee with a cloth, placing it down on the makeshift kitchen surface, between his account ledgers and a drawing board. A distinct aroma wisped upward from the coffee-pot spout and reached their nostrils. 'You may take the post of honour, Mr Harrison. Coffee is a marvellous creation to be savoured, don't you say?'

'Yes indeed, very pleasurable.'

'My wife is taking to it,' Jessop added.

'Mrs Jessop knows a good thing, I'd say.'

They fell silent as each sipped at the delicious coffee.

'William Hill is not with us today. No one will say what has happened to him, but by the look of his associates I would guess that he took himself off to the ale-house last night and now cannot work because of it.'

'I feared it, Josias. He has a rock on his shoulder as large, and hard to shift as any of our stone pieces.'

'He has taken his grievances to heart,' Jessop answered.

'And in doing, he proves himself unworthy of the position we have entrusted to him. He is both disobedient and, worse, untrustworthy.'

'And he gathers the weaker men to him; playing on their grievances, he is a sower of discord amongst them. Only yesterday he complained that they should receive greater inducements ...'

'I have heard it all before. Why, 'tis harder to control workmen than the elements! It is in part the reason why I undertook to produce this.' Smeaton held out his hand toward the large printed foolscap sheet that was affixed to the wall. The 'Plan for carrying on the Works and management of the Workmen' listed, in twenty-two articles, the rules for their engagement. He got up to study it and read aloud.

'*First. The Edystone service should by all reasonable inducements be rendered preferable to any other common employment.* There! It says so in black ink on white paper. Though I fear that having no other kind of persuasion by no means teaches them submission and obedience.'

'I fear it to be human nature, sir.' Harrison had been listening

213

intently and now agreed wholeheartedly. 'In my observation, it can on the contrary make matters worse –being treated fairly, they get an inflated opinion of themselves, and suppose every success to be owing to their own merit.'

'And had they not been employed then the thing could not have been done,' said Smeaton.

'Exactly so,' Jessop agreed.

'Hill has a tendency to mutiny and combination, would you not say?'

Jessop and Harrison nodded balefully. They finished the coffee and were about to return to their business when who should enter the office but William Hill himself. Harrison quickly busied himself and observed from behind the safety of his open ledger, as events unfolded rapidly. Hill was clearly intoxicated by liquor, and just as Harrison had described, he now acted. His sullen face scowling, he swayed menacingly before them, demanding recognition of his grievances.

'I'm sick of your whinging, disobedient ways,' Smeaton barked. He leapt up and stood directly before him. He was a big man and physically capable of trading blows with the rough-cut Hill. 'Tha doesn't frighten me, sir. I find you irregular and disorderly and if tha cannot take an order, then sir, tha must go!'

'To hell with you,' Hill growled, 'if I go then what of the others?'

'You will go, sir, as an example to them. You are bound by the conditions set out here,' he pointed to the plan of work before him. 'As are your employers!'

It was the first time that Jessop, or indeed any of the company, had heard Smeaton raise his voice. It made the silence that followed almost unbearable. Jessop kept his eye fixed firmly on Hill but he reached down slowly for his musket. Ever since goods were stolen one night, the night watchman was armed with it, and Jessop kept it handy. Carefully he cocked the hammer and raised the gun behind the desk and then stood to present it straight in Hill's face; Harrison grew smaller behind his desk. Hill was rough and belligerent but he was no fool. He scowled at Jessop.

'Would you shoot me like a dog, old man?'

'If I am forced to,' came the steady reply. 'We can always find another foreman.'

'Now listen here, man, what is wrong with you? Mr Harrison, remind us of what a foreman is entitled to,' demanded Smeaton.

A small voice, dry with fear, rasped, 'One shilling per hour extra pay – and Mr Hill did receive in one week, with landings on the outwork, near five guineas (including his constant wages).'

'Good wages – as good as any you will find elsewhere, Mr Hill.'

'If you throw me off, then I will take all the rest with me,' Hill smirked.

'I see. Then, sir, tha leaves me no choice but to lay the axe to the root of the tree.'

William Hill stood staring at the barrel of the musket as Smeaton, ignoring him, picked up his hat and headed outside. Jessop, wondering what would happen next, ordered Hill to turn about and proceed 'easy like' into the yard.

'Here, take this,' he said to Harrison, handing him the gun once Hill was outside. He took up his cane and broke into a trot to catch up. Harrison followed at what he considered to be a safe distance.

Smeaton gathered the men. They stood about him in a half circle as, climbing up onto the stone platform, he raised his hands for quiet and spoke to them.

He pointed a finger at Hill.

'Mr Hill has made it plain to me that he no longer wishes to have an attachment to the Service. For his ingratitude and disobedience of orders, I am obliged to take it upon myself as supervisor of the works and the men in this Service, to dismiss him.'

He climbed up higher onto the courses of stones that lay fitted on the platform, and searched their upturned faces for any sign of dissent.

'Let him be an example to any would-be offenders amongst you,' he cried.

'I have done nothing to deserve this.' Hill came amongst them to rally support, seeking out his drinking companions of the night before.

'You have done nowt to prevent it, sir,' Smeaton jibed. 'We had hoped to persuade you otherwise, but you've given us no choice. You had better collect your tools and be off! Mr Harrison, see to it that Mr Hill receives his wages in full.'

'If I am discharged, the rest will follow.' Hill looked around into the faces of the men gathered about him. 'Come on, lads, they can do nothing if we take away our labour.' At this, the men in Hill's company looked uncertain. Their eyes, shifting furtively to and from each other, were avoiding Hill's manic stare.

Smeaton spoke again. 'Those of you that have any dependence upon or attachment to William Hill can fetch your tools and leave with him now.'

Hill, like a cornered animal, began to shake the men in his company, to bring them to their senses, but each stood, as though in a dream, unable to see him.

'What of you, Joshua Hawkins, cousin? These others are all afraid – to hell with them – but you are my kinsman. Do not be a turncoat.'

The men crowded around Hill and pushed him up toward the entrance. He struck out with his fists at any who came too near but he was defeated. At last he broke away and, cursing them, he ran from the yard. Hawkins picked up his tools and followed, leaving in silence.

'Back to work, everyone, we have a lighthouse to build.' Mr Jessop raised his cane toward the two courses of stone on the platform.

'We've to mark out and shift that lot, and place them on the Rock before Mr Weston arrives!'

'Tha's right, Mr Jessop. Let us put this behind us and proceed.'

But William Hill was not finished with them. He was furious with the men for betraying him, with Smeaton for accusing him and publicly humiliating him, and with himself for throwing over the best-paid steady employment he had ever had. He had been proud and vain, but mostly he had been drunk. He stumbled along through the sultry summer heat.

'What shall I do now?' he thought to himself. Apathy turned to anger and bile. He despised and cursed them all, Smeaton, Jessop, Bowden ... Then an idea came into his head. He was not the only one who had a score to settle with that man. He smiled to himself, as he thought of how he might yet profit from his mistreatment. Turning onto the road, he made his way toward the newly built officers' quarters in Stonehouse. Later that day, Hill also visited his cousin and told him of his plan.

'We both will profit from it, Joshua!' The Lieutenant had made him a very attractive proposition. He had promised him payment in gold for 'making necessary arrangements' to see to it that Trehearne would suffer his death upon the Rock.

'It's madness, William ... he is a skilful sailor and well thought of. There's no one would do such a thing.'

'I can think of just the man. He stands here now before me.'

Hawkins was sickened; he could do no such thing.

'Joshua, I am entered into a contract to do it.'

Hill saw that his cousin bitterly regretted his actions earlier that day.

'And where am I to find new employment?' he heard him say.

'Alright, I know I made a mess of things through my drunkenness. But listen to me, Joshua; there is still time for you to go back if you do so straight away. Smeaton needs all the experienced hands he can get right now. They know we are cousins; tell them you were confused in your mind and did as a loyal kinsman would. Ask their forgiveness and beg them to reconsider.'

'It's worth a try. I might get a reprieve.'

'You shall, I am certain of it.' ('That's a good fellow – I need you there as my eyes and ears for when the moment comes,' thought Hill.)

'I want no more trouble, William, I have had enough of your hell-raising and mutiny.'

'There'll be no more, never you worry!' Hill cried out. He spoke earnestly, his hands held aloft to declare his good intent.

'You swear to it?'

'I do, but you shall have a substantial gain when the time comes. It will be nothing, a mere accident – with no one at fault, I promise thee.'

'Who's there with you, Joshua?' Mrs Hawkins called to him. They heard the baby crying.

'What am I to do?'

'Go back, Joshua, be my eyes and ears and serve me as my right hand – or be damned!'

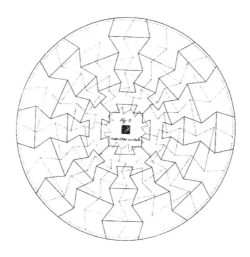

18

Closing the circle

5th August, 1757. This day our additional boat, that had for some time been fitting out, called the 'Assistant', brought out and landed her first cargo of stone. Samuel Medling I appointed to be Master. On visiting I found Course no. V containing twenty six pieces to be closed in.

Two of the outer stones had fallen an inch beyond the line of the circumference but were otherwise sound, and once the mortar was hardened these were tooled to fit in their situation. He moved on to the next entry, and dipping his quill he wrote of today's progress:

the eight of August at noon, the weather being exceeding fine and with a low neap tide. I took the opportunity to draw a meridian line upon the platform of Course VI. This was the first time that the sea had not washed over all since we began to build.

Smeaton laid down his quill pen and meditated upon their progress in the last few days. He had gone out with both companies, directing them until they were familiar with handling the stones and in the sequence and methods of fixing he had devised. It had been the greatest test, working at just above the high-water mark, constantly showered by spray in continual wetness, the waters regularly coming over all. They had little more than a circle of thirty-two feet in diameter within which to operate, and had on more than one occasion been surprised by the groundswell. It was crucial, judging when to cling to the rock and when to abandon it, knowing that if they stayed too long they might easily be swept off.

He paused and thought of how easily the stones, each over a ton in weight, had been carried away from course number two a few weeks earlier. Though it seemed a catastrophe at the time and had undoubtedly set them back, it had been a valuable demonstration, vindicating his measures for fixing and securing them. Everywhere the work was completed, the stones had held fast. They had successfully repaired the mortar pointing in the damaged joints where the sea, washing over everything, had washed it out. Smeaton's own worst fear was that the impact and violence of the sea could lift the fresh-laid stones in the uppermost courses. This had happened, but only where the untimely need to abandon the Rock had left stones unfixed (they being loosely placed in their positions, interlocking with their neighbours, and not mechanically tied down using the oak trenails).

The troubles caused by Hill had come to a sudden head, like the midsummer storm that had swept away their work, and he was relieved that he had sent him packing.. Ahead lay the task to repair and make good the last of the damage to the foundation. Hill's company was now under Jessop. They had shifted Richardson's men from the rock, and took the opportunity afforded them by the calm summer weather of grouting and pointing up any areas where the rough tide had got to the stonework and washed out the fresh mortar. On his next visit he was happy to observe how in every case the pointing withstood the wash of the seas, once it had been given time to harden.

'The puzzolan, for hard service, cannot be beaten, Josias.'

'No, sir, we've tried some other tests in that "Dutch tarras" pointing as you asked, but it's nothing like as hard. No, your lime and puzzylan mix is the best thing in water-cements I have ever seen. After a single tide, by God, 'tis as hard as iron.'

'Good! The sea must give way to the building, remember?'

'Aye. Already there's so much seaweed about the base, it looks as though this might have stood here since the Creation.'

The men about them were busy beating up fresh mortar in purpose-made buckets of wood hooped in iron. They came one after the other at the call of the masons, who having got their stone fitted, were ready to place the mortar bed joint. Another single-handedly heaved the stone up from its recess, using the double tackle and lightweight triangle. This was easily transportable and yet capable of managing almost all of the stones, except the very largest. The stone block now hung in the triangle. The pulley block creaked above them as the taut ropes rocked and the great block swayed in the gusting wind, pinched by the lewis. Beneath it, the mason deftly and expertly spread the mortar to a constant thickness and then signalled for the stone to be lowered again, fitting firmly into its place. When he was finished the carpenter took over. He dropped long, thin oak wedges head-first into the chases or grooves that were pre-cut in the sides of each stone. These aligned with corresponding identical chases in the neighbouring stones to make a pocket. Then, taking another wedge, he dropped it down point-first and carefully drove it tighter against the other to lie 'heads and points' together. As the second wedge slid home, tamped down with an iron bar, the timber exerted a tensile force upon the stones that kept them in place. Once wetted by the sea the oak would swell and become increasingly tight, exerting an even greater pressure by which all the stones resisted each other and became much more difficult to dislodge.

'Have a care not to ram the wedge too hard.' Smeaton made it very clear not to over-tighten them, since they could exert an even greater force that might cause the stone to split. The carpenter wiped the sweat from his brow, and with the wedges driven fully home he took up his saw. He cut off their ragged tops neatly, to lie flush with the top of the stone.

'That's neatly done. Now, just a couple of thin wedges in the butt face will keep it secure from a rough sea till the course is closed,' Smeaton instructed him. They worked late into the night. That same evening's tide the basement was completed, and the centre stone of the seventh course, the first complete circular course, was landed. It was very nearly dark when they left the rock.

Tired from his exertions, Smeaton slept well that night and awoke at dawn to the sounds of stirrings beyond his cabin door and voices above him. He heard the sound of running feet on the deckhead, as the company answered to Mr Jessop's commands and made preparations to go off to the Rock. He lay in bed and thought for a few moments of what the day would bring. There was a knock at the door.

'Enter.'

It was Samuel Medling, his head appearing round the door. 'Coffee, Mr Smeaton?' He entered the cabin with a pot of hot coffee, poured a cup and passed it over, holding it out for Smeaton to take hold.

'Thank you, Samuel. What's the day looking like?'

'Dry and fine since dawn, sir, very much like yesterday.'

'Then we should make good progress. Tell Mr Jessop he may join me in having some breakfast, if you will; and tell Cook to bring me at least three rashers of bacon, with eggs. There's a hard day's graft ahead.'

'Aye, sir.'

'How are you managing? What have you to eat?'

'We have brought our own with us. We have meat pasties and a flagon of ale for later, and some brandy if need be aboard the *Assistant*.'

'Good, and how d'you find her?'

'Very reliable and seaworthy, Mr Smeaton, sturdy and yet easily managed. I turned her on her beam yesterday to tack through the reef.'

'Aye, we saw you putting her about – very handy she was, and with a fine bow wave.'

'Mr Jessop should have the credit, sir. She's a well-made yawl.'

'Will you take me across to the Rock this morning?'

'Aye aye, sir. We will be ready to leave when you are.' He raised his closed fist and touched the brim of his hat with thumb and forefinger, then closed the door behind him. Smeaton was up and helping himself to a second cup as he gazed out to sea through the small casement panes in the stern. It was indeed another fine summer's morning. In the clear morning light he could see through his glass the small chapel on Rame Head, and beyond it the coastline of Plymouth. There were numerous ships in the Sound. Sloops, brigs, men o' war and cutters, their sails let out or furled into the masts and yards.

'Most waiting for a fair wind in this calm,' he thought to himself.

After breakfast they were ferried across to the House Rock in the *Assistant*, whereupon the early-morning ritual of setting up the triangle was got under way. The *Weston* hove into view with a cargo of five stones belonging to course seven.

'She will be here shortly with the first of the pieces.'

'Indeed, that's a splendid sight. I hope Mr Trehearne has the joggles.'

'The marble cubes? I think I see them lying in the hold,' Jessop reported as he scanned the vessel with his spyglass.

'Capital, Josias! The plug and joggle stones provide the means of purchase for keying between the courses, above the rock itself. The local Plymouth marble serves well for these.'

'Very – the masons tell me they find it suitable for working, being hard, with great accuracy of fit.' Smeaton no longer stood beside him; instead he was strolling around the perimeter of the circular platform, enjoying the novelty of having a level surface to walk upon. He looked out to sea and then turned and came close to watch. The marble plug stone, exactly one foot square and eighteen inches tall, was being lowered carefully down and guided into its square socket, cut in the centre of the platform in the course below. It took quite some time for the stone to slide down into the full depth of the socket and settle on the mortar bed. Hands gently rocked the lewis to encourage the stone when it stuck fast to the sides of the hole. It had fitted in the trial putting-together on the wooden platform at Millbay, and so had the surrounding stones of the course above, which were slid down over it, so there was no real cause for concern. Suddenly it let in to the full depth of the mortise. The workmen poured a wet slurry grout into the joints on all four sides and again thin oak wedges were driven into the joints until the plug was fixed firmly and rigidly in place. After a while they continued to pour more grout, which disappeared down inside the joints until all the remaining spaces were filled. Satisfied that all was completed, Smeaton told Jessop to stand the men down.

'Well done, lads, you can rest while the shears is got up for the next.'

There was a murmur of approval, and an atmosphere of contentment spread amongst them as they relaxed as best they could. Smeaton enjoyed the company of these rugged hard men and they enjoyed his yarns and observations at moments like this. Whilst they sat around, John Trehearne produced a fishing line and they took turns to cast out for mackerel for supper that night, if they could but land one.

The centre stone weighed nearly two tons and could only be lifted by using the great purchase tackle. The stone had been landed the evening before and raised to the platform with the shears. Now there was to be a considerable delay as the heavy lifting equipment was raised into its place. Jessop recalled how it had been made to the engineer's entirely new design and tested so impressively by him in the yard last year.

Smeaton sat calmly, watching the preparations. He was not a great theatre man but he thought of it now. It reminded him of his visit to Drury Lane with Anne soon after they were married. He recalled how 'one must wait patiently for the scene changes, from behind a heavy curtain, so that the audience can only imagine the goings-on from the bumps and bangs, until all becomes quiet and the curtain goes up to reveal something entirely new.'

In the meantime the slow and methodical preparations here afforded them a welcome opportunity for rest and a small meal. They took some food and drink brought up from the boat for all. Smeaton sat with Jessop on the centre stone.

'Will you have some more porter, Mr Smeaton?' Jessop showed him the flask.

'What? – oh, no thank ye. I was lost in my thoughts. How like a stage this all appears, except there is no one to see us.' He stood up and strode around the platform, surveying the extraordinary sight, the smoothed and levelled natural rock with its manmade counterpart toothed into the carved rock. A little more than one half was now made in dovetailed stonework, leading away from the rock shelf in an almost symmetrical pattern. Smeaton jumped up onto the marble plug arising at the exact centre.

'What a magnificent pavement! White Portland stone, edged in such distinctive grey granite that carries flecks of white crystal quartz and veins of red iron. As fine as any street in Westminster, don't you say?'

'I believe so, Mr Smeaton, but I have only your opinion to rely upon. I should like to see the capital myself one day. Mr Tyrrell, our foreman from Portland, was himself in London and often talks of the great edifices there!'

'Quite, Josias – he spent many years working on the new Westminster bridge – but I believe he has excelled himself here.'

Half the circle was made up of Portland stone surrounded by a granite margin. The remainder of the surface consisted of layered red rock, the flattened top of the House Rock. It was a beautiful sight, soon to be hidden away. Eight recessed pockets lay in a circular pattern about the plug, cut into both surfaces and ready to receive the joggle stones. Smeaton stepped down again and it was while negotiating the timber leg of the shears that he inadvertently put his heel into one of them. He fell backward and went over the perimeter, falling headlong to the seas below. Jessop and the men watched helplessly as he disappeared before their eyes. They sat for an instant, dumfounded, completely taken aback.

'Quickly now, a rope, look lively!' Jessop coughed on the remains of his bread and porter. Dropping food and drink, he was up in an instant and calling out over the edge.

'Hullo there, can you hear me, Master?' There was no reply.

Had he fallen in the water, he wondered. It was all so sudden he could hardly take it in. 'Quick lads, get a rope over the side – he may be in the water!'

With an expertise born of years spent at sea, John Trehearne hurriedly tied a knot into a length of rope taken from the tackle and slipped the noose over the marble plug.

'Here, Samuel, you and the others take hold of the slack!' Sam Medling caught hold of the coils of rope. He passed it between the four hands and, looping it around the stone, told them to take the strain. Trehearne tied the opposite end about himself.

'Are you ready, John?' Trehearne signalled he was, and leant back over the edge of the platform. Slowly they payed out the rope, Medling keeping his foot on it at the plug. Trehearne walked out over the edge, descending down the splayed foundation to the rocks below. He saw where Smeaton lay in a crevice.

'Master Smeaton, sir, are you hurt?' He turned him over. Smeaton groaned but managed to say something.

'I seem to be all in one piece except for this.' He lifted his hand by the wrist. The thumb was bent double.

'Can you stand?'

'I can with your help, John.'

His fall had been fortunate, since this was the highest part of the rock with the shortest drop from above. He had lodged in a shelf between rock and stone, with the seas washing just below.

'Can you put your useful arm about my shoulder?' Trehearne enquired.

'Yes, thank God, there seems to be no great damage to any other part of me.'

Trehearne called up to the onlookers waiting anxiously above and peering down cautiously from the rim of the platform.

'I need a plank for to make a seat in the rope.'

Jessop cupped his hands around his mouth to direct his reply. 'Stand by, we'll lower a timber down' – and almost immediately a short length of wide board came over the side, lowered on another line. Taking hold of it, Trehearne expertly made a pair of loops in his rope and placed the piece of timber into it, for the injured man to sit on. Smeaton leaned on him as he bent to lift his legs into the chair. After a few minutes he signalled all was ready. Jessop got to his feet and gave the order to pull.

'Steady now, easy does it.'

The rope became taut as they hauled, and Smeaton's chair was raised up. He walked his legs in front of him up the curving stone face, and, holding onto the rope with his good arm, slung his damaged hand in his waistcoat, close to his chest. Trehearne climbed hand over hand alongside, using the other line. Nearing the top, he placed his foot on the stone arris, and with a final heave pulled himself up onto the platform. Sam Medling was directing two of the men to help the injured Smeaton and clear away the ropes.

'Sit you down on the centre stone, Mr Smeaton. Tell me, are you hurt bad?'

'It hurts like the very Devil, Sam, but I will live.'

'Here, take this and drink. It will steady your nerve. We carry a reserve stowed away on board the *Assistant* – just for emergencies, you understand.' He lifted the brandy flagon to Smeaton's lips. He gasped as the hot liquor burned his throat, but then felt the comforting warmth infuse his being.

'Quite. I hope 'twill dull this infernal pain. I thank the Lord that I am with you now although it appears I have put my thumb out.'

'We can give you passage home.'

'Thank ye, Sam, but I can bear this pain in the meantime. The nearest surgeon is several leagues from here, and there's no guarantee of finding him at home.' He winced as he raised his hand and inspected his bent thumb. It stuck out at an odd angle.

'Besides, the idea of Dr Spry performing some horrendous operation upon me is one I cannot tolerate. You know he pours hot lead into animals since his experience with the old light-keeper. Mr Jessop told me 'tis common knowledge. He thinks he has made an important discovery that will gain him admission to the Royal Society.'

'It looks broken. Can you move it at all?' Trehearne had joined the ring of concerned faces. Smeaton shook his head to say he could not.

'No John, I am certain it is not, but it is dislodged from its proper place. Give me another draught of your elixir and I may find enough false courage to push it back.' After a liberal helping from the jar, he took hold of his damaged thumb and snapped it back into its socket. He let out a yell but soon found that the pain was eased, and afterward he rested for a while by lying down in the hold of the yawl. The brandy had taken effect and he was snoring loudly when Jessop and the company came down from the platform.

'Let us get you back to the *Neptune*.'

There was no reply. Jessop saw how peacefully he slept. 'Still, it could have been much worse,' he thought.

'I believe we should thank the Lord in our prayers for saving thee,' he breathed whilst they boarded as carefully as they could to avoid disturbing him. Sam looked at Smeaton's swollen hand.

'That won't stop him – why, it would take more than a bent thumb to tear himself away from this place.'

'Cast away, Mr Medling, I myself have seen enough of here for one day.'

Austhorpe Lodge, October 1792

Old Smeaton's face was animated as he told the story of his accident to his guests.

'I was always so methodical, and quite unprepared for my clumsiness when it came.' Laughter followed his remarks.

William Jessop had arrived and had joined them for dinner. Smeaton directed his attention to the man sitting before him, and remembered the boy whom he had made his ward and apprentice when Josias died in 1761. Smeaton had made the arduous journey to Plymouth for the burial. His visit to the lighthouse found everything in order and remarkably well kept.

William had been taken on as a pupil and had spent the next fourteen years assisting John Smeaton in all his works. It had been an incredible journey. After the Calder Navigation there had followed a constant stream of proposals and projects – new bridges, harbours, and inland navigations. Then there was the steam engine, built for winding and pumping water in mines and mills, and to supply drinking water. Smeaton had made many ingenious improvements to Newcomen's 'atmospheric' beam engine and was undoubtedly the greatest exponent of water-powered mill design. William remembered how Smeaton would say that his 'constant price for water mills for thirty years past has been twenty-five guineas each sett and windmills thirty guineas.'

'Can't tell thee how much it pleases me to have thee with us this evening, William.'

'I would not have missed the opportunity for a moment. Especially in such company.' He bowed to acknowledge Mr Trehearne.

'When I was thirteen years old I wanted nothing more than to be the Master of the *Assistant*, but you set me to making ironwork,' he said.

There was a ripple of laughter. Everyone appreciated this since William Jessop had already spoken of his new venture, an ironworks in Derbyshire that he had just come from to visit Austhorpe. Trehearne remembered only too well the thin young lad who knew all the ships and who joined them whenever he was allowed on their passages to the Edystone.

'You hated school because it kept you out of the yard and land-bound. We took you as often as we could, and though you did not know it, your hiding amongst the stones was the very thing that saved me!'

'I don't follow you, Mr Trehearne.'

'You will, sir. Your father told me afterward, how your playing amongst the stones had given him the idea of a hiding-place. Is that not the truth, Mr Smeaton?'

'Absolutely. You see, William, when I wrote the *Narrative of the Building of the Edystone Lighthouse*, I had in mind to tell the reader how it was achieved in every detail ...'

'Indeed, I remember now. I had got my first passage with you to the Rock, but without my father knowing. I did not think he would come that day, but he did. I saw him first in the *Edystone Boat* and so thought that I would crouch down between the great blocks and make it impossible for him to see me there – I hoped he might miss my being there on the Rock that day. He made a point of looking at the shears there almost beside me, but did not say a word or make any sign of anger. I had no idea that he must have seen me!' said William.

'Oh yes, he did! And likewise in my book you will find no hint of it. For it concerns another story – held a secret within the very stones of the lighthouse, the story of the man who was pursued there to his death. 'Twas shortly before the house was completed and lit ...'

'But I thought no one died there. Indeed, Father often made a point of how proud he was that in carrying out the works in such a perilous situation, not a single soul was lost.'

'And he spoke the truth,' Smeaton added with an air of mystery. He looked first at William, and smiled benevolently, then turned to the others. There was a knowing look between them and a pregnant silence.

William was baffled, but he chose not to pursue the subject, instead recalling a favourite story of his father's regarding Smeaton's own brush with disaster.

'It was lucky you fell when you did, Mr Smeaton, and not later! I remember the tale my father told of you climbing aloft with Roger Cornthwaite, standing upon nothing but four planks to fix the screws into the neck of the gilded ball.'

'Ah yes, there was nowt for it. It thou wants a job doing well, thou must do it thyself. I was not going to leave such an important task to the care of other hands. Besides, it were such a beautiful thing. I could see myself reflected in it – the amber varnish sealing over the layers of gold leaf.'

'Roger was your counterbalance – prevented you both falling from the very top.'

'True, he was a brave soul. I believe it must have been far worse for him than for me. He had nothing to occupy him other than the horizon and the seas one hundred and twenty feet below. Though we did take great care to synchronise our movements about the ball.'

The guests listened appreciatively. William was himself a respected engineer but his admiration and affection for the elderly man was undiminished. In particular he never tired of hearing the stories and reminiscences of the Edystone and Plymouth. It had been a great adventure, one that changed the course of his future and perhaps still cast an influence over him. He would not have missed this evening's reunion, and luckily his work had brought him to within a short distance of Austhorpe.

Mary Smeaton entered the candlelit room and sat opposite her father, beside William Jessop. 'We have your favourite this evening, Father, roast beef and dumplings.'

'You see how well attended I am, William, I could not ask for better in my latter years. My dearest daughter has assumed the responsibilities of running the house. I was always too busy in my work or travelling abroad to take charge, and now I am too old and weak – and my dear Anne is gone – my own time is at hand.'

'No, Father.'

'Yes, lass, I doubt not that I have but little time remaining to me. I ought not to complain, I have my house and books, though I am confined to the ground floor and I cannot manage the steps to the observatory.'

'Are you suffering from the effects of your seizure?' William asked him.

'No. I am grateful to have recovered with my faculties remaining to me.'

Mary interrupted to lighten the mood.

'Yes, it is almost a year since Father announced his retirement, to continue his new work, the description of his "several works". The *Narrative* has been so well received by the general public. Father has a bound volume that he has given to Mr Trehearne. Would you care to see it afterward, William?'

'It would be my great pleasure. I feel as though a part of me will always remain in Plymouth. Tell me, is there mention of my father in your account, sir?'

'Of course. It would not be complete without a good deal of Josias. I owe a great debt to the Surveyor of the Edystone Lighthouse.'

'After the house was completed, and you left, he often spoke of you, and he kept a keen interest in the welfare of the house and its keepers up until his death. He would have been so proud that you came to attend his burial.'

'There was no question; I was determined to pay my respects. When I offered myself as your guardian, your mother told me that Josias would have wanted nothing more. We both knew you had a talent for mechanical matters, and I promised your father that I would see it was put to good use. I had my eye on you even then.'

'I hope some day to have the opportunity to repay you.'

'You have already, William. Your generation will do great things. Steam, that's the future thing. I could only tinker with Mr Newcomen's engine. But now we have a revolution in James Watt; he has made such a machine for motive power!' Smeaton paused and looked around the table into the old and young faces.

'In my day there were no engineers. There were only thinkers and pragmatists. Few, if any, applied true method to their understanding of structures, but now it is more commonly understood. This is my comfort, that I wrote to pass on what little knowledge I have gained in my own experiments.'

'You give a great deal of importance to the future, Mr Smeaton, but will it go well? Will the trouble in France spread amongst the poor here at home? I have never seen such poverty in the countryside as during these last few years.' Alice had spoken for the first time during the meal.

'Quite right, it is an uncertain time, but I see great benefit from the changes and advancements in our field. We built our lighthouse under sail and muscle power. We were beholden to the limits of natural laws and the elements. Now a new age is coming, though I shall not be here to see it.'

'Well, we shall not see it either, shall we, Mr Trehearne. I dare say that we can leave it to William and Mary here, but tonight we give thanks to you, our dear John Smeaton.' Alice Trehearne laid her hand on his arm and then took up her glass.

'Listen, everyone! I wish to propose a toast to the light that shines this night upon the Edystone, in the tower where once a fugitive was saved from his enemies. Here's to the secret of the stones!'

19
Tall ships

'What's all the fuss about?

'There's been foul play, Mr Smeaton,' Mr Jessop said between gasps of breath. He had just returned from the shore. 'Seems there has been an attempt to wreck the punt. Medling discovered it first thing this morning.'

'What has happened?' John Smeaton's brow furrowed with anxiety, expecting the worst.

'The low tides at present prevent us from loading our vessels directly from the jetty and so we are using the punt to carry out stones into deep water, where they can be hoisted into the yawls.'

'Yes, yes, I am perfectly aware of it, but what has happened?'

'When Mr Medling arrived at the mooring on this morning's tide he noticed that the salvagee had been all but severed, just below the waterline.'

'D'you mean to say that someone deliberately cut it?'

Trehearne joined them.

'Aye, Master, that was a new rope spliced to the punt only a fortnight back. We fitted the salvagee so that we could haul her out

233

safely to moor overnight. It could never have worn in that time.' Just as he was speaking Sam Medling joined them.

'What's all this about wrecking, Sam? Speak plainly, lad, for I still know not whether we have lost anything!'

'The rope was cut, sir. I discovered it as Mr Bowden was hauling her up to bring the punt back into Millbay. All but one of the rope strands had been cut through with a knife just below the water line. Had it not been for the calm last night she would have broke free and been carried away on the ebb tide and lost at sea, or wrecked.'

'But nowt actually happened?'

'No, sir. Providence chose to smile upon us this morning, despite our unwanted guest.'

'What a mindless act of gross stupidity! Or is it the work of an unseen enemy? It makes my blood run cold to think on it.'

'One of the men thinks he saw someone rowing out toward the mooring. A man he thinks looked very like William Hill.'

'I dare say! That wouldn't surprise me in the least. I suppose he considers himself aggrieved, having lost his place here.'

Joshua Hawkins stood amid the crowd of men that had gathered about them. He felt uncomfortable at the mention of his cousin's name, for he knew William Hill continued to watch the yard. He could see him in his mind's eye, rowing out into the channel, intent upon an act of revenge for his dismissal.

The group dispersed. Mr Jessop saw to it that they each had their work and busied themselves with it.

'There's no more to see here. Let's be about our business. Don't tell me you've no work this morning. I can find plenty for idle hands and busy tongues!'

Hawkins followed, walking the short distance from the jetty to the yard along the track of the new rail-road that ran between the ships and the compound. He passed the stones that were set out in rows, resting on pallets like dusty books awaiting their turn to be taken down from their shelves. He thought to himself how, luckily, no one suspected him of having anything further to do with Hill since his return. He had hoped to put all that had happened behind him, though now he could think only of Hill's resentment, and he remembered his cousin's words, 'They will pay.'

Hawkins was unnerved. He had not forgotten how Hill had imposed on him to be his 'eyes and ears', and he resolved to visit his cousin that night, to put an end to his foreboding.

Around him everywhere the sounds of industry invaded his thoughts. The works were proving something of a spectacle to the curious, who came to see for themselves the hive of activity that this place had become. They saw stones lifted and then carried on the specially constructed 'rail-way'. Local gentry, naval officers ashore, and their wives would visit Millbay in parties and stand alongside the idle and the beggars observing them through the fence. The roll carriage used to manoeuvre the stones amused them. This was a flat-bedded timber trolley supported on iron frames having two solid timber rollers that ran over wooden planks laid in the aisles between the rows of stones. There was applause and cries of encouragement as each transported stone was expertly slid across onto a sturdy railway carriage, constructed in iron and timber. It resembled the trolley and both were of a size and scale that was determined by the pieces of stone they were designed to carry. The crowd followed as the workmen heaved against the carriage and it gathered momentum along the iron road.

'I wonder that folk have the time and inclination to come here.' The increasing numbers that were coming to view the works genuinely surprised Smeaton. Jessop agreed.

'We've had such a crowd I have had to ensure that they remain on the other side of the fence, if only for their own safety. Last week I found them interfering with our work upon the platform. One was even switching the railroad turntable to see how the carriage is turned onto the track to the jetty!'

'This is astonishing. Many of them come from the higher ranks; they ought to know better.' John Smeaton looked out at the crowd beyond the palisade.

'I am altogether in agreement with you, sir, but as Mrs Jessop says, it's a nice spot and the Quality are always on the lookout for a new entertainment, something to satisfy their curiosity. We lesser folk must work for a living.'

'Quite, though let us take comfort that our labours serve the common weal.'

'I have notified Lord Edgecombe's agent 'bout it, sir. He is of the opinion that 'tis better to let them come than to strive to keep them out.'

'Very well, let them see that we truly are building our house in stone, Josias.'

All day long the carriage trundled up and down the track carrying stones to and from the compound. Course number eight was brought up and assembled on the platform. Then the next was placed on top. Everything fitted.

'Check the lewises are sound and that the trenail holes line up, and make sure each stone is marked along with its neighbour.' Smeaton walked around the platform studying the completed courses assembled and occasionally thrusting a cane into the drilled holes to see if they corresponded with those in the course beneath. When he was satisfied the masons took up their bolsters and chisels and began making their way methodically from stone to stone, cutting a V-shaped line across each joint. Now that the work was approved, they could mark the stones to ensure an exact realignment during the reconstruction upon the Rock. When this was done they began the lengthy reverse process of dismantling the courses and returning the stones along the track to their original places.

'What a laborious exercise.'

'It's my experience, Mr Weston, that if anything is to fit upon the Edystone, then it needs must have been checked for fit with all due care in Millbay first.'

'I quite understand, Smeaton. I find it admirable to see such diligence in the carrying out of your duties.' Robert Weston had come straight to the yard on his latest visit to view their progress.

'Time, sir, is always at a premium on the Rock. A day spent in preparation here is worth perhaps an hour at most, in a tide's work out there.' He gestured, raising a bandaged hand toward the open sea. 'This wooden platform is the template for our construction. 'Tis not unlike a tailor's pattern, around which he can cut his cloth, being confident that the suit shall fit afterward.'

'And here with less risk of falling more than a few feet! How is you injury?'

Smeaton's face coloured as he spoke, but he made light of the episode.

'Oh, much better, thank you. My thumb was dislodged from its socket when I fell, but fortunately I was able to put it back in, without hindrance. It was really very careless of me. I was too busy admiring the completed foundation, then about to receive the first full circular course, when it happened.'

'You must have a care, Mr Smeaton. You of all people!'

'Aye, happen I will, but we have got on well since then, with no further mishap. We have gone forward with course seven, and safely. They tell me there was such an enormous swell in the Gut – 'twas greater than any we have experienced and due to a strong easterly – that when they came in to land the stones, the boats rose and fell full four feet perpendicular!'

'By Jove, was any damage done to them?'

'No, the men handled the purchases swiftly and with skill. Their determination meant that all the stones were landed safely. Though in more than one lift the boat was raised up under the stone with such force, that it was unhooked from the tackle and deposited in the hold once more.'

'Oh, I feel my sea-legs going from under me; I do hope we have smooth passage for my visit,' Weston implored, his eyes looking to the heavens.

'Now that all is ready here, we ought to be able to sail on the morrow if it suits you.'

'That will do. At what time?'

'The tide turns before seven. With a favourable breeze I would expect to make the Rock by ten,' Smeaton thought aloud.

'Very well, it's been a long journey and I am ready now for my supper and a good night's rest.'

'Where are you lodging?'

'At the Angel.'

'I will have Mr Jessop send a carriage for you in the morning, calling say at a half past six? We will be waiting for you and ready to leave when you come by.'

'Very well, thank you. Goodnight, Smeaton.'

The sun sank lower in the western sky and Robert Weston turned away, walking the short distance across the fields to where his coach awaited him, at the gates to the Stonehouse road.

237

That evening Joshua Hawkins went over on the last sailing of the Cremyll ferry and landed in Cornwall. He headed for a small village near Mount Edgecombe, walking along the tree-lined shore until he came around a small headland, and there was the hamlet. Lights showed in some of the windows, reflecting in the calm black waters of the estuary. It was not yet dark but out in the Hamoaze he could see lanterns lit on the sterncastles of the ships at anchor, and beyond them the smallest flecks of light, which he guessed issued from dwellings along the opposite shore, as far as the Hoe. He fancied he could just see the great dark mass of the Citadel, high upon the Hoe, commanding the approaches to Plymouth Harbour. Hawkins drew his collar up and pulled his hat low. He passed longboats and small sailing boats drawn up on the shingle and headed into the cluster of houses and boatsheds, along a slipway that became the village street.

A loud rapping came at the door.

'All right, all right, I am coming.' William Hill opened the door to find Joshua standing on the doorstep and anxious to come in before he might be seen. Hill had returned here since his departure from the Service. It was cheaper to live on this side of the water, where he could borrow from his Cornish brethren, until his next employment. Joshua also felt safer from prying eyes on this side of the water. Even so, he was taking a risk, especially since the attempt on the punt. As soon as the door opened wide enough to pass, he was inside.

'It was you, was it not?' Joshua spoke gruffly.

'Good day William, good day Joshua, might not go amiss,' came the reply.

'Come now, the night watchman thinks he saw you out on the punt.'

'Don't know what you're talking 'bout.'

'Someone went out and cut the moorings. The punt was fully laden with stone for the lighthouse. They think it was you.'

'Do they indeed?' Hill smirked. His face took on a queer expression, a wry grin spreading slowly across it. 'I am owed a greater debt than that. Why would I waste my time? But I take satisfaction from hearing of it.'

'Then you swear you had no knowledge of it?'

'I do. It was more likely the work of some drunken saps, bent on tom-foolery.'

At this Joshua Hawkins heaved a sigh of relief. Hill was not impressed.

'There, you see, there's nothing to worry yourself about. Only "poor Will" must take the blame for every single blow the lighthouse builders suffer. I think I might as well take the opportunity of dealing one for myself, if I am already to hang in their eyes.'

'How can you? You 'ave lost all means in your power. Smeaton says he'll have you before the magistrate if you set foot in Millbay.'

'Maybe – but I've no need to, as long as you are there!' Hill's words chilled him.

'You cannot count on me!' Hawkins spoke firmly. 'I have worked hard to make amends, for they have given me a second chance. I've a family to keep. Mary would cut me if I lost such fair employment.'

'Fair! Not to me it wasn't. They owe me, and I shall have my revenge.' Hill whispered the words darkly. Hawkins felt a coldness creeping over him as he listened to his cousin's words.

'I shall soon have my purse from a grateful lieutenant. He burns to see an outcome.'

'What d'ye mean?' Hawkins spoke gravely.

'There's to be an accident, exactly when the *Weston* is to deliver up her cargo on the reef.'

' I want no part of it.' Hawkins felt the hairs rising on the back of his neck.

'You must. Or by God I will kill thee!' Hill spat the words.

Joshua was frightened at his ferocity. 'For God's sake, I cannot do it!'

'All I ask is that you loosen the pin of the shears. It will be an accident. Do this and Nature and mechanics will do the rest.'

'For God's sake, William, this is murder you speak of.'

'I cannot go back on my oath. John Bowden-Trehearne knows too much and I have promised to make an end of him once and for all.'

'Who is behind this?'

'I cannot tell, but they spreads among the high ranks in the Navy – stealing prizes – but never you mind.'

'Why, if you know of it, do you not tell someone? The Port

Admiral – or even Smeaton might help! He has connections at the Admiralty,' Joshua added, 'it would make amends ...' but William Hill only stared bleakly.

'No, it's too late! I'm in too deep. They would stop at nothing to silence me, if they thought I was a turncoat. You must help me, cousin, or I swear I'll take you with me.'

Night had fallen while Joshua had been at his cousin's house. Despite the warmth of the August night, he felt a cold dread upon him.

Wednesday the 17th August 1757. My much esteemed master and friend Mr Weston has come from London to be witness of our proceedings. I went off with him early this morning, attended by Mr Jessop and his company, and landed on the Rock at ten.

Mr Richardson and his men were about to start setting the next circle of stones, the fifth belonging to course number seven, working outward from the square 'plug' stone at the centre. He turned and hailed them as the *Edystone Boat* approached the landing place. Within minutes he was greeting them as they came ashore.

'Good morning to you, Richardson,' said Smeaton. 'A fine day so far. Here is Mr Weston come to see how we are getting on.'

'Morning, sir. We hope to complete the fifth tier before we go.' Seven large dovetailed stones lay placed on top of the platform; the last was being hoisted up from below, held in the shears. The stones appeared identical in size and shape and would be lowered into the pockets formed by the outline of the previous tier now set in place, radiating like spokes in a wheel. Weston appreciated the pure geometry with which the stones spread out from the centre. He noticed how, beyond the innermost ring, they were a simple dovetail shape that was repeated, growing proportionately larger from the centre to the circumference. The star-shaped pattern grew from its beginnings as each circular tier was added.

The men returned to their work and Smeaton took the opportunity of explaining to Robert Weston in detail their method of fixing the stones. He pointed to the oak folding wedges driven into vertical chases in the joints, explaining how these acted to force the stones apart and exert a mechanical force to hold fast each dovetail. Even in fine weather it was difficult to hear him speak over the continual pounding and booming of the waves against the rock.

'What's that you say?' Weston cupped his hands around his mouth.

'These lock the stones together,' Smeaton cried out. He pointed to the squares of fresh timber that filled grooves and to the stone chases that could be seen on the vertical faces of one of the stones about to go in. 'But the force of the sea is so great, that even when the entire course is laid seawater might thrust its way in, and cause the whole tier to be lifted from its mortar bed. That is why we must defend it until the mortar is hardened.'

Seeing for himself the rising surf drift across in a mist, Weston was coming to terms with the immense forces that had to be withstood.

'Tell me, Mr Smeaton, is it safe? I mean, will it last?'

In Robert Weston's face Smeaton saw all the fears that plagued him in the early hours. The small but constant nagging voice of doubt, that 'a building of stone would be overset'. He looked away for a moment along the clear coastline and gathered his thoughts. Another thunderous boom filled the air, followed by a fine spray that rose up and blotted out the distant land.

'I am unable to say,' he said. His words were lost in the beating of the sea and the raining white water that followed.

'It's no use, I cannot hear you,' Weston mouthed.

Smeaton took his arm and led him around the westward-sloping cliff into the lee. It was quieter here.

'If what you see here proves too little, then it is beyond my power to know what is enough.'

'I mean no criticism of you, Smeaton. What I see you have done amazes me in its depth of consideration, and in its execution. But standing here and observing the power of the sea, I ask for your truthful opinion – will it last?'

'I cannot say that I have accurately solved the problem, but I have endeavoured to do it, so far as my *feelings* rather than calculations will bear me out.' Smeaton paused to gain his composure. 'The column is proportionate in every part to the stress it shall have to bear and of equal strength throughout, and in the total cohesion of its stones and combined weight, less subject to the heavy stroke of the sea.'

Robert felt his fears allayed, and wished now that he had not raised the subject. It was a sign of their friendship and respect for each other that he could ask the unthinkable. John Smeaton, having answered truthfully, was moved to silence.

'But why the need for timber to hold these parts together?' said Weston.

'Observe.' Smeaton pointed to yet another swell that threw up a wall of water against the solid. 'Until the mortar is hardened, and become as strong as the surrounding stone (as it does very quickly), there is a chance that the impact of the waves will lift the uppermost stones from their mortar bed. If that happens they will become at best defective in their union with the other parts, or at worst unhinged and thrown down.'

'And if defective, allow the sea to force itself into the joint,' Weston said.

'Good. I see you follow, Robert. To answer this a pair of holes are drilled in each stone.' Smeaton pointed to the holes made with a jumper hand drill.

'These reach down into holes corresponding in the stone of the course below. Ah look, see, we can watch Richardson setting a stone now. See the carpenter about to drive in the trenails ...'

They watched as he took a long oak dowel and drove it down into one of the holes.

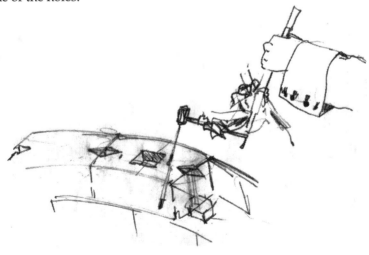

'He cuts in a small wedge, let into the end. When the trenail hits the end of the hole, it will spread the wooden nail and prevent its working loose. The sea will do the rest – swell it to fill the hole and make a tight-fitting plug.'

Smeaton laid his bandaged hand on top of a sawn trenail, dressed flush with the surface.

'The vertical joints are grouted, and once hardened, will combine with the stones and the marble cubes between the courses to form one entirely solid mass of stone.'

'And what of the cubes?' Robert watched fascinated as the masons came in and laid a liberal amount of mortar over one of the marble cubes. Above it hung the next huge dovetail piece about to be lowered and fitted over it.

'One plug at the middle, eight joggles of a foot cube each of the hardest marble, along with the additional security of the trenails; an infinite number of indentures 'pon the surface and the lewis holes, all filled with an *extuberance* of mortar, which going hard each becomes a steady pin ...'

'And all are needed?'

'The forces of Nature being subject to no calculation, I endeavour not to omit anything that can be done without difficulty. Besides, the *solid* would not be complete if it were held together only by these wooden needles! But they do give security from the start.'

Robert Weston now understood both his theory and his meticulous methods, to overcome the difficulties of building on the Edystone. Around them the companies got on with their work. There was a sense of order in their progress as if, to these rugged men, there was no question of failure. They had a simple faith in their ability to complete the task and now more than ever Smeaton warmed to their loyalty and steadfastness.

'The sea shall give way to the building, sir!'

'Well said, Josias! Aye it must, though few believe it.'

In the swell of the Gut the newly arrived *Assistant* struggled to hold her station whilst more stones were taken off.

'Mr Weston, if this weather holds we will soon be ready for you to lay the plug for the next course.'

'I am indeed honoured, Mr Jessop.'

Mr Jessop touched his hat and called out new instructions.

'Clear away all for this tide's work every man! Look out below!'

The tide was risen and a swell now suddenly reared up, causing a huge wave to force itself through the gully. It lifted the boats up against the fender piles like small toys, running up onto the sheer surfaces of the House Rock and overtopping the Sugar Loaf. Weston and Jessop helped to carry down the buckets and tools and stow them away in the boats.

'Quickly now, let's be away before the next wave floods into the gully.' Mr Jessop was just aboard and gave the order to 'slip' when they felt themselves lifted up and cast out from the Gut by the next great wave. Weston felt queasy and put his head low, but soon they were making for Plymouth with a steadying breeze behind them.

The weather broke, and for days they were obliged to quit the rock and ride out the storm aboard the *Buss*. Smeaton and Weston had to wait days for an improvement. When at last a break came they returned to Millbay in the yawl under a strong south-westerly. Theirs was a flying passage but thankfully it was quick; Mr Weston could scarcely take any more time at sea. He soon recovered, though, and entered the office at Millbay on the morning of 29th August in high spirits, where he found Smeaton at his desk writing in his journal.

'Good morning, Mr Smeaton. Did you hear? 'Twas well that we returned when we did. Yesterday's gale brought the *Antelope* close to shipwreck!'

'I know, I saw her dragging her anchors and driving away across the Sound. Thank the Lord the *Assistant* brought Jessop's company back when she did. I am told she had to go out, for they were down to their last crust of bread!' said Smeaton with a grin.

'I wonder how Richardson fares aboard the *Neptune*.' Robert Weston spoke his thoughts.

'So do I. Let us see if we can find them with my telescope from the Hoe.' Smeaton threw on his overcoat and dark grey tricorn hat. As he rose up the chair scraped noisily back over the bare floorboards.

'Look in the cabinet behind you, Robert. You will find my telescope and stand in there. Can you bring the stand? I will carry the 'scope.' Weston handed him his valuable telescope and shouldered the wooden tripod.

'You're in charge, Harrison. See to it that no one enters unattended here, and tell Mr Jessop we are gone to the monument on the Hoe.'

The door slammed shut and Harrison returned to his figures. 'He'll spend hours up there just looking at the Edystone,' he pondered to himself, until he became engrossed in his accounts for materials and purchases once more.

The wind blew hard, tugging at the coats of the two figures standing beside the tall white obelisk overlooking the Sound. The ground fell away before them, down to the cliffs and rock pools of the promontory, where the sea drove wave upon wave, and showers drifted up in a salt spray that wetted the seaward faces of the great stone needle. Robert Weston drew his coat collar up and held onto his hat with one hand, whilst carrying the barrel of the telescope with the other. Smeaton fixed it onto the level top of the tripod, then, training it on the bearing for Edystone, he found the *Neptune* and then the Rock.

'Ah, the *Buss* rides safe!'

'What of the Rock? Can you see it?' Weston asked him.

'Mmm ...' Oblivious to the gale, he scanned the horizon and looked again into the eyepiece, whilst adjusting the focal point. 'I can make out very little through the breaking water. Ah yes, I see it!'

He drew himself up, a serious look on his face. Putting his hand to his lips he was pensive, then gestured to Weston to see for himself. Still holding his hat firmly, Robert bent forward to look through the eyepiece. It was a marvellous instrument, made by Smeaton himself. Suddenly he was within clear sight of the House Rock and the Sugar Loaf. The heavy seas heaved and rolled all about the place, and then all was lost in an explosion of surf, rising many times higher than the level platform of the 'solid' stump. When he saw the *Buss*, he spoke out with alarm.

'Dear Lord preserve us!' Weston watched spellbound, alarmed by the sight. 'The storm tosses them about with ease; 'tis a wonder the moorings are holding. The seas pass right over her!'

He broke off and stared open-mouthed at Smeaton.

'This is the worst weather, I admit, Weston, but I believe the chains will keep her secure; she's no sailor but very sturdy made and well-ballasted.' Smeaton took a last lingering look into the eyepiece and saw something that worried him. He turned to Weston with as troubled look.

'There is no time to lose, Mr Weston – I must get back! I shall go on board the *Edystone Boat* and sail as soon as the storm eases.'

'Are you mad? The seas are huge!' Weston forgot himself in the moment. It was incomprehensible that his engineer should take yet another risk with, it seemed, his life in his hands. 'You should not take such risks! What disturbs you so suddenly?' said Weston.

'The shears are lost!' Smeaton began to dismount the telescope. 'Mr Jessop shall have to make us another! But I must go to see for myself. They will have had to leave stones unfixed, and the storm might take them too!'

Placing the heavy telescope under his arm, he headed off down the hill toward Millbay. Weston picked up the tripod and followed, bent double into the wind and hugging his coat about him.

There was nothing for it but to wait until conditions improved. It was summer but nothing could be done. August turned into September, and at last came a fine spell as good as any they had seen all summer. Smeaton had guessed rightly, and in his reconnoitre about the besieged House Rock he had found two stones swept away, along with the shears and the triangle, and the windlass smashed. In the meantime, though Richardson and company could not land again before the 3rd, Mr Jessop had re-fitted on shore, and the new shears, along with a new windlass, were stowed aboard the *Edystone Boat* for their return.

'We thought the deck itself would be stove in,' Richardson told them on his return, as he described their ordeal aboard the *Neptune* at the height of the storm. 'We were helpless, shipping water in the heaviest seas I ever have seen. I reckon we gave some seven fathoms of cable out, to ride safer, but feared to let out any more lest the *Buss* should drag upon the rocks.'

Smeaton gave him a sound pat on the back. Despite the damage he too was delighted that they were all returned safe. Weston thought he detected a sigh of relief too. It could have been disastrous, he saw through the general good humour, and the tired looks in their faces told him how near they had all come to disaster.

At last there came a change for the better.

'What a difference a day makes,' thought Weston as he leant upon the gunwale of the *Edystone Boat*. They sailed in the early hours before dawn. Day was breaking, fine and calm, as they entered the reef. A communication had come to them from Mr Jessop, that he had found the stones lying in the water, having gone out to retrieve them a few days before. Though the largest stone had dropped back in, it too was eventually raised by getting a chain fixed around the waist of the dovetail, and so there was no need to make new ones. By now Jessop had closed, pointed and grouted course number seven and they were set to embark upon the next.

As soon as the *Edystone Boat* tied up alongside, Smeaton was making his way up the wooden rungs notched into the fender pile. Weston followed. Above them two men were turning the handles of the windlass to wind in the lifting rope. It stretched out taut, passing under the snatch-block pulley anchored into the rock, then rose up to two great purchase blocks slung from the head of the new shears. As the men wound in the rope onto the windlass roll, the great wooden pulley blocks were drawn closer together and the centre stone emerged out of the boat's hold, rising upward. Above them, another man was steadily drawing in the runner-tackle that drew the head of the shears backward until it stood vertical, and the stone was placed down on the surface of the solid. Robert watched them adeptly manoeuvre it; the whole operation went smoothly in the still conditions. Smeaton looked pleased with the workmanship

'Perfect, Josias. All has been brought to level; I see not a single irregularity,' he said as he cast his eye over the completed surface of course seven. 'All neatly dressed and done.'

'Thank you, sir. Would ye believe, it has been so calm here that the platform has not been wetted these past three days!'

'Happen that's the longest since we began. Let's hope it lasts till this season's end. What d'ye say?'

'Aye. It's most pleasant in this balmy weather, except it has become very hot mid-afternoon.'

'Ah, still – better than a soaking, eh?'

'Most definitely. It promises another fine day today, judging by that sky.' Josias looked away to the brightening east.

It was not long before they were ready for Robert Weston to lay the centre plug of course number eight. The square marble stone hung from the lewis pincers. One of the tinners brought forth a freshly beaten bucket of mortar and Mr Weston trowelled a liberal amount of it into the square recess onto the top of the previous marble plug, to his own and everyone's satisfaction. Then he raised his hand and signalled for the stone to be lowered. He held it steady, assisted by the masons who gently rocked the sides to release the tight-fitting block, encouraging it to drop under its own weight. The plug dropped and came to a stop and Jessop placed a rule alongside to measure the height.

'Well done, sir. That went in better than the previous, I'd say.'

'Thank you, Mr Jessop.'

'P'rhaps you'd like to say a few words, sir.'

All work ceased and everyone gathered round to hear the dedication. Smeaton and Jessop sat down on a block of Portland. Robert Weston stepped up onto the plug stone and then he spotted something behind them in the distance.

'Look, what a sight – we are to be entertained by a great spectacle!'

Out in the Channel, he could see a fleet of ships. Within minutes more and more appeared over the horizon. A great convoy of more than a hundred sail was heading toward them.

Sam Medling was busy counting ships and Jessop handed his eyeglass to Smeaton for a closer view.

'West Indiamen and merchantmen, I think,' he surmised.

'Most likely, Master,' replied Jessop.

The fleet was in full sail, and as it came nearer the ships divided into two streams, surrounding them on all sides. The ships' passage took them inside and outside the Edystone reef, as they passed to south-west toward the open seas. They watched in silence, mesmerised by the splendour unfolding all around. Robert Weston was moved to speak.

'Gentlemen. This magnificent fleet serves to remind us of our purpose. Mr Medling says he has counted upward of one hundred merchantmen passing. There must be thousands of souls aboard. Now I ask – instead of looking upon them here, sailing down-channel with a fair wind on a fine day, imagine them returning in a storm, unable perhaps for days to make any observations, doubtful of their station, uncertain of their ship's course and tossed to and fro at the pleasure of the wind and seas ... weary souls longing for sight of home, sailed from the Americas, or the Indies, or perhaps China? They look for the light upon the Edystone, as a star to guide them safely by.'

'Indeed, Mr Weston – very well put,' said Smeaton, gesturing him to go on.

'Let this scene add strength to your sinews, let it inspire you with fresh ardour to complete what you have begun, and may God bless and keep you all from harm.'

Jessop followed with a rousing 'Three cheers for Mr Weston – hip, hip HURRAH; hip, hip HURRAH; hip, hip HURRAH!'

They raised their hats in a final salute, and it seemed the spell was broken. Soon only the topsails and gallants remained in sight as the fleet faded from view. By ten o'clock that morning, the centre and all four surrounding stones were set and Mr Weston took his leave of them, returning to Plymouth in the *Edystone Boat*.

20

The accident

Almost a year had passed since the dedication of the work, the day they had seen the great fleet beating down-channel in a favourable wind. John Trehearne cast his mind back to the events that had followed. The outwork had ceased early in October with the completion of course nine. Mr Smeaton, recalling the near-disaster of the previous season, when they had continued until November and had come close to shipwreck, determined that it would be best to leave off, having completed an entire course. He left Plymouth for London soon after, to return in the April of this year, whereupon he had almost straight away to return to London, to attend a committee of the House of Commons concerning the River Calder Navigation Bill. This, Smeaton had told them, was to be his next work.

Though steady progress was made in the yard, the storms of winter and continuing bad weather in the spring had caused the loss of the moorings. Under orders from the Master, Trehearne-Bowden and the other seamen had taken every opportunity to sweep the waters in search of them, until at last the chains were recovered, all except the great buoy. Still the weather would not allow the outwork to proceed.

> *Yet such however is the uncertainty of human affairs, and particularly those that depend upon the state of the winds and waves, that, from this time till the 2nd of July, instead of prosecuting the work, our thoughts and attention were wholly employed to remedy disasters.*

Now at last August was proving kinder, the good weather allowing them to inch closer to completion of the great mass of stone that Smeaton called the 'fundamental solid'. Trehearne stood at the helm of the *Weston*, his hand guiding the tiller whilst they approached 'the Stone'. He saw before him the massive spreading base of the tower rising up some twelve feet above the great slanting slab of stone that was the House Rock.

A light breeze carried them steadily along. Above, the wind filled out the great curve of the mainsail, showing the large black silhouette of the Edystone Lighthouse. Ahead, the jib sail flew out, and the *Weston* ploughed her broad rounded bow through the water. In the hold lay the four great centre stones of course number sixteen. Each had an identical hook-scarfed outline that would lock together and form a complete circle. They were the beginnings of the well-hole. When completed it would contain the staircase leading from the entry passage to the rooms above.

His mind focused on the approaching Rock. Though they had made this passage many times now, there was always a danger of catching upon one of the hidden rocks that lay, like sharpened teeth, just below the surface of the water. Steering a safe course through the reef demanded all his attention and skill, but today in this fine weather all seemed calm and serene.

'We approach on a full tide of flood, Mr Jenkins, it should give plenty of water beneath us and the tallest rocks below.'

'Aye sir, though I'll keep an eye ahead and take soundings to be safe.' In a few minutes they would enter the Gut and make landfall.

Joshua Hawkins tried not to think of what he must do that morning, as he worked upon the topmost completed stone course, tooling the smallest irregularities in the surface of the Portland blocks. He dreaded the expected arrival of the *Weston* with her cargo, because he knew what was to happen. Things had gone from bad to worse at home. William Hill frequently came to the house, often drunk and dishevelled. He had not worked since his dismissal, over a year ago, and he blamed his situation on Smeaton and the Service. In the depths of drink, despair and self-pity he had turned up unannounced, just two nights before. He had one burning intent.

'Remember your promise to me, Joshua – you are my eyes and ears 'pon the Stone.'

Joshua had felt sick when he was reminded of his cousin's plans.

'The time has come for you to earn your reward, and you shall not refuse me. If you do as I ask you will have a purse of fifty pounds, half the agreed payment to me. But if you refuse me … I cannot say what that would bring upon you and your kin.' His eyes glared from a sullen face.

'What is it you want of me?' demanded Hawkins.

'An accident, remember?'

'But how?'

'Loosen the pin that holds back the guy rope of the shears.'

'I will hang for it!'

'No, you heard me wrong. An *accident*, I said. The shears is weakened but not broken, so that it will fall under the strain of raising a load upon the *Weston*. Only make sure that *he* is aboard.'

'Who?'

'Trehearne, Joshua, Trehearne! John Bowden to you. What is he, except a deserter and fugitive? A common criminal no one will take much notice of. Such accidents are a natural course of events. The outwork is a perilous occupation; people are daily expecting losses.'

Hawkins was frightened into submission. Since his cousin's visit he had become silent and brooding as he set his mind to the deed. His attention came hurtling back to the present when he sighted a sail away towards the north-east. As it came nearer he could clearly see the tiny black emblem upon it. It was the *Weston*, bringing with it John Bowden. A sinking feeling of despair and panic entered Joshua's stomach. He hoped that this would instead prove to be Samuel

Medling aboard the *Assistant*. Then he could 'discover' the flaw – the broken pin – and save them from harm.

Again Hawkins re-lived his last meeting with Hill, and it drove him to act. Seizing on a quiet moment with no one about, he approached the crane. Holding in his hands a mallet and bolster he dropped down and drove out the metal pin. The block that anchored the 'in-hauler' guy of the shears to the rock was loosened and ready to break free. He felt the blood thundering through his veins, dizzy from the fear and excitement, mingled with anticipation. The sensation abated. No one had seen him, and he resigned himself to what was to happen next.

The *Weston* arrived with her cargo. Hawkins observed every move of the figures of Trehearne and the two seamen as they prepared to offload in the Gut below. All went smoothly in the calm waters. One of the crew jumped ashore with a rope, and tied the yawl up tight to the fender piles. Joshua felt his heart pounding inside him. Watching closely, he saw Trehearne signalling to the men on the rock to lower the great iron hook and tackle. The shears dipped forward until they were almost horizontal and level with his eye. Down below in the yawl's open hold, her master took the lifting hook and slipped it under the short length of chain attached between the lewises. Checking first that they were firmly secured in the lewis-holes cut into the stone, he gave another signal to haul it up. Slowly the stone rose up beneath the purchase tackles, and at the same time the head of the shears lifted in an arc over the *Weston*. Soon the first of the four great Portland blocks was landed on the stone platform, alongside Hawkins.

'Perhaps it will hold after all,' he told himself as two more identical blocks came up and were safely deposited beside the first. Only one remained, lying in the hold of the small wooden vessel. With the stones landed, the other hands were busy all about him, as preparations got under way to set these new blocks. The slow rhythmic sound of fresh buckets of mortar being beaten mingled with the chinking and rasping of chains and the voices of Richardson and his men, as they busied themselves.

'Mr Hawkins, lend a hand here.' Richardson beckoned and Joshua turned from his silent watch to join them. At that moment there was a sharp crack, like the sound of a single gunshot, followed immediately by the crashing and splintering of timber. He spun round and saw the shears smash down onto the *Weston*. The yawl was staved almost in two, with splintered timbers and planking thrown upward onto the rock and falling into the seas in the Gut in a shower of fragments, lying criss-cross on the water. There was a moment's stillness, the men frozen with disbelief and inertia.

Then all the company sprang forward to get down to the landing place, except Hawkins. He stood rooted to the stone stump of the tower, from where he could see John Trehearne lying unconscious and bloodied in the open hold beneath the fallen tackle. He saw that the other crewman was pinned under the timber shears and could hear him groaning. In the melee, no one noticed the mason who stood shaken and sickened at the sight.

A dazed Mr Richardson roused himself, issuing commands to clear the damage and to reach the stricken men. They saw the second yawl approaching, and it was not long before she was alongside the wreckage and the hands were passing over both men into her. Bowden and Jenkins were laid on the cargo of stones in the *Assistant*'s hold, and Sam Medling cast off again without delay and made straight for the land.

'Get them to a surgeon as soon as you can,' called out Richardson. They had done all they could but it looked bad, Trehearne appeared senseless and all but finished and Jenkins' legs were crushed under the huge weight and momentum of the falling timbers.

'There's nothing more we can do now but make safe the *Weston* and clear away the mess.' he told the dejected company gathered about him, and he pointed to the shears. 'Come on, lads, we have the small triangle with us; let's get this lot shifted and see to patching up Mr Bowden's boat where we can.'

Their mood was sombre, as they struggled to clear the tangle of ropes and timbers away, and to retrieve the parts of the shears that lay in the water. Joshua Hawkins felt a surge of relief spread through him. He became light-headed and had to bite his lip and stop himself from whistling. He had not been seen and it was over, it was done.

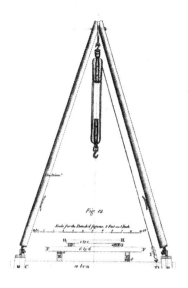

21

The dark reef

John Trehearne lay on the couch in the small wainscoted parlour of Breakstone Hall. He had been severely concussed and remembered nothing of the passage to Plymouth and the coach journey up to Dartmoor, with Alice at his side. They had brought him to her, and as soon as the doctor allowed she had taken him to the safety of her father's house in the shadow of the high tors. At the Hall, Alice could attend to his injuries and he would have all the rest and peaceful quiet he needed to recover. The accident had left him concussed and weak, with cuts and bruises, but thankfully no broken bones or permanent injury. When Squire Vasey heard of it, he had immediately sent for the local doctor, who prescribed plenty of rest and said he would call again to see him before his departure. Trehearne had been with them a week and he was much recovered, to the point where he was already thinking of returning to Millbay. Alice secretly hoped that he would stay a while longer. It was idyllic here at this time of year; with everyone so busy in the fields, they had the house to themselves. She sat by John's bedside, writing at a small portable desk. John watched her as she dipped the quill into its well and frowned in concentration. The nib scraped on the paper, and the ink flowed in sweeping loops as her hand travelled across the page.

'Tell Mr Jessop, I think soon I will be up and about, and hopefully able to rejoin the company in a week or so.'

She smiled at this.

'Not until that great swollen egg on your forehead diminishes. You may have lived, but you look a very poor, bruised and misshapen creature to my eyes.'

'But I must learn what happened to the others, and how the *Weston* fares. I hope they kept her afloat, and got her safely back.'

'Very well, then I shall ask him! You are not to worry yourself now until you are recovered. Here, listen, this is what I have written so far – now tell me if this is to your liking ...'

He listened impatiently, then interrupted, 'Very well, you've a gift with words, Alice, that will keep him laughing and in good spirits, I should say. But do not forget to write that I am intending to be back very soon, and what news is there of the yawl? Will she be seaworthy?' Trehearne put his hand to his head as the pain suddenly came back and stabbed at him.

'You shan't be going anywhere unless you rest now.' Alice rested a hand on his forehead. He was lucky to have escaped alive, she thought. For the past week, she had nursed him and been his only companion. The others were too busy, her father with his men at harvest, cutting the first stooks in the barley, and mother in the garden. Verity called in but had decided to go over to her friend's house. She took little interest in her sister's nursing, and they were often left most of the day to themselves. John entertained her with stories of their voyages to and from the Edystone, and his companions in the Edystone service. Though more than a year had passed since the event, he spoke vividly of his days spent locked up, a prisoner on board the HMS *Duke*, and of his release. The weather held fine for haymaking and the squire and his household were at full stretch, working long days out in the fields. The house was quiet and peaceful in the daytime, and in the next few days they enjoyed the privacy of the Hall and grounds together, only to be interrupted by Verity when she returned. Being in their company was heavenly, he thought.

256

Despite his injuries, he had never been so happy.

The fine weather held. The hot August days shimmered with a continual heat, and John and Alice passed hours in the cool shade of the gazebo. It stood in the corner of the terrace, from where they could see out across the fields and watch the distant figures of the men and women, bending to cut the sheaves of barley. A constant humming of bees and myriad insects filled the garden, now brimming with the scent and colour of roses and honeysuckles. The harvesting went on day after day, until suddenly the weather broke. Great grey clouds loomed large and heavy as the storm crept toward them. Thunder echoed in the distance. Lightning suddenly tore across an indigo sky, followed by a clap of ear-splitting thunder, then the rain burst from the heavens, turning the parched earth track to mud as they ran back to the house. They were soaking. Alice cast off her cloak and took John's waistcoat and hat and called for the housemaid, who bustled into the hall holding something in her outstretched hand.

'A letter here for you, Miss, delivered by messenger when you was out.' She offered it up. Alice took it graciously, then ran her finger inside the sealed stamp and unfolded the paper.

'It's from Plymouth, John, in Mr Smeaton's hand, I think.'

John followed her every move as she took the letter over to the light of a window. The maid returned with towels, and Alice picked up a hand towel to dry her long black hair. Then she began to read the letter aloud.

Millbay, 27th August 1758

My dear Mistress Appleford,

How glad I am to have received your letter, in which you say that Mr Bowden is much recovered and intends returning here soon. You can reassure him that we have done all we can to carry out the necessary repairs to his vessel and Mr Jessop tells me that she will be seaworthy in time for his rejoining us.

Jenkins is lucky to be alive and keen to come back; both myself and Jessop visited him at his home and we expect him to rejoin us in perhaps a few weeks time.

Since that unfortunate day I am happy to say that we have made good progress with the 'outwork'. We soon mended the shears and we have completed Courses XV to XX, though now the weather has turned and is suddenly against us again, but as I told the others, we will proceed till there is something to stop us, and I hope with every possible exertion to complete the Solid before the season's end.

I beg you not to be alarmed, but there is news that I should pass on to you before John Bowden's return to us. We have discovered that his was not an accident, due entirely to the perilous nature of the work upon the rock, but the outcome of a deliberate act. Mr Jessop found that the bolt (securing the rope from the head of the shears down to the rock – John can explain) was taken and it could mean only one thing: one of our own men caused the collapse of the shears!

At first we had no idea who the culprit was, but we had our suspicions. I thought it imperative that we apprehend the traitor in our midst, Jessop, Richardson and I each came to a similar conclusion. We decided to call in our man and give him a stiff interrogation. Well in short, he quickly buckled under our sustained fire, and confessed to committing this heinous act. I think he was almost relieved to have been discovered. It seems Joshua Hawkins was under continual pressure from his cousin, our old friend William Hill, who threatened him with violence should he not undertake to do the deed. But he would not say more! My guess is that Hill is acting on orders and puts me in mind to think that he is commissioned by John's enemies to do such work.

Though I was shocked at our findings, and regret the injuries caused to both Messrs Bowden and Jenkins, I am greatly pleased that they failed to inflict greater harm. It has led to their being brought into the light and we are determined to strike back – let us shine the light of Justice upon this dark evil. I am to approach the Admiralty Board regarding this matter. Our lives are at risk, and the task of building at sea is perilous enough without suffering further hindrance from these malefactors.

In the meantime I have prepared a plan, known only to Richardson, Jessop and myself. One day I will explain.

Yours very truly

John Smeaton

Towards the end of August John Trehearne had recovered sufficiently to return, and though Alice had hoped he might stay longer, he was impatient to be off. A few days afterward he found himself at the Stone. He was crouched low at the helm of the *Weston* in the teeth of a gale, heading out of the Gut. A strong ebb tide and stormy easterlies prevented their landing on the Rock and they could not get alongside the *Neptune* either. There was nothing for it but to ride out the storm in the dark.

'What shall we do, Master Bowden?' one of the men cried out.

'Nothing we can do, except get ourselves out of this damnable wind and rain.'

'Aye aye, sir.'

'Use the oars. The wind blows fresh at east; we'll go around to the west cliff and lie in the lee.'

No one said a word but there was a grim silence that spoke volumes. The oars dipped and swept through the calmer waters into the shadow of the west cliff. There they settled for the night, bringing her bow around to face the dark silhouette of the house, reaching up like a black stump against the night sky.

A voice called out, 'Don't just lie there, driftin' about on yer oars, come and get us off this bloody rock!' It sounded so near that it seemed to come from out of the darkness that surrounded them. It was quickly answered by another voice reprimanding the first.

'All right, that's enough of that. The *Weston* is staying with us and she'll take us off as soon as this gale abates. In the meantime, amuse yourself with your work – that will pass the time more quickly.'

A lantern appeared ahead of them on the rock, then another high up on the stump above them. The tapered column was now taking shape, approaching a third of its full height and affording them a reasonable shelter from the worst of the easterly gale.

'Is that you, Roger Cornthwaite?'

'It is, John – and glad to see you back, though you might have brought us better than this froward weather.'

'If I'd known we would be sitting out here all night, lying on the oars in the wet, I might have thought twice before leaving my warm bed!'

'Aye, more fool you, but I apologise for that young rascal down below, these tinners have no manners to bring out of Cornwall.'

'I know he can hear me. I can think of no better way to keep my watch, than to think of the hundred and one ways that I can teach him some in the morning!'

Roger's laughter bellowed out across the water. 'Well said, Master! I'll bid 'ee goodnight and God keep you from harm till morning breaks.'

'Thank ye, Roger.'

The men in the boat lay huddled upon the oars, their coats pulled up over their heads. The yawl rocked and rolled, rising and falling in the black waters. It was a dark, miserable night. The only lights to be seen were the flickering lanterns and candles of the marooned workmen on the House Rock who continued in their labours till dawn.

All night, in the wind and rain, to the leeward of the building: those upon the rock amused themselves with their work; which having their lanterns and candles, they were enabled to do. On the morning of the 31st the wind abated, and they got happily off without any further harm, than that there was not a dry thread amongst the whole company.

John Trehearne sailed into a serene Stonehouse Creek none the worse for his night's ordeal, except that he was, like the others, exhausted by a night in the open sea and relieved to return to dry land. He slept heavily the next night, and it was near midday on 1st September when he reached the workyard office, knocked at the door and entered. Smeaton looked up from the ink lines drying in the journal, took soft paper and laid it over the wet ink to take up the excess.

'Aha. Good day, Mr Bowden, did you sleep well?'

'Very well, sir. I feel refreshed, but I missed the tide this morning.'

'Never mind. We have things to discuss. There is news and I want you to hear this privately.'

Mr Harrison looked up and rose to leave the room. 'Excuse me, gentlemen, I must fetch the foremen's reports from Mr Richardson, for the accounts.'

'Very good, Mr Harrison.' Smeaton dropped his quill into the inkwell and stretched back, placing his hands behind his head. Once they were alone, he began to describe what had happened while John Bowden-Trehearne was recuperating with the Vaseys.

'After we deduced that the shears had been deliberately tampered with, an intolerable atmosphere of mistrust spread through both the companies. Jessop and I agreed that it was essential for the Service that we find the culprit.'

'And Hawkins was the one; he was put up to this?'

'Yes. William Hill paid him a sum of twenty guineas and he promised more upon your death.'

'But Hawkins is no ruffian; he must have been forced to it.'

'I agree. I have no doubt he is repentant, and terrified of being turned over to the civil authorities. Having committed such a serious offence he will most certainly hang.'

'The magistrates will send him straight to the gallows?'

'No doubt about it – unless we choose not to bring him before them.' Smeaton's shrewd gaze fell upon John as he explained further.

'I can spare him, though I have no choice but to dismiss him. The men expect justice for Jenkins' sake and your own. They are calling for an eye for an eye – but revenge will serve no one, in my opinion.'

'I have no wish to see his wife made a widow and his children go hungry because of it.' Trehearne spoke honestly.

'Very well! Tha's a noble sentiment. If *you* can find it in your heart to forgive, then so can the rest of us.'

'What has he told you?' Trehearne was intrigued to hear.

'William Hill is to land a prize from a homeward-bound man o' war. It seems they are still greedy to run stolen goods ashore.' Smeaton intended to see them caught and brought to justice.

'I have enlisted the aid of a close friend in the Customs House. Captain Reynolds will take us with his excise-men to Polparra tonight, under colour of searching for run liquors.' He paused, then added pointedly, 'Besides, I might learn the whereabouts of our great buoy. Most likely the Polparra fishermen took it off the *Neptune*'s mooring to use the cork therein for their net floats! Jessop tells me that now we shall have to drag for the mooring chains that have sunk to the bottom!'

'Am I to come with you?'

'If you feel strong enough, will you join us?' Trehearne-Bowden

261

nodded. 'Good, that's settled then. We leave tonight from the King's Docks aboard a vessel that will take us to Looe, from where we can ride along the coast road to Polparra.'

They sailed later that evening. From the tiny deck of a twelve-gun sloop used by the coastguard to patrol the shore, Smeaton looked hard in the direction of the dark reef and thought he saw the floating light. Then he looked up above him. A gentle breeze filled the sloop's ketch-rigged sails. With another month of good weather they might complete the first of the rooms, and he wondered if they could use this as accommodation for a temporary light – 'the lower store room,' he mused, 'with a temporary roof structure, sufficiently strong and weatherproof to protect the interior and its inhabitants … it would serve to exhibit a light in the coming winter.'

The night's foray to Polparra passed off safely. There was a skirmish, and amongst the men caught was William Hill. But though a party of excise-men scoured the nearby village and its harbour inlet, nothing was to be found of the great buoy. Returning, they reached Looe at first light and went on board the miniature man o' war. John Smeaton awoke later to find they had sailed with the tide and the sloop was making steady progress beating to windward in a choppy sea. He dressed, then bent low to open the small casement and leant out of the tiny sterncastle. The miniature warship was running close to the shore. He recognised the pyramid outline of Rame Head and the fishing village of Cawsand below it. They would soon reach the Sound. He had taken the captain's quarters, little more than a cupboard in size, but comfortable, furnished with a cot bed and a table and chairs. The captain's kind offer allowed him some degree of privacy and calm that he determined to make the best use of before they made landfall. He took up a quill pen and produced from his coat pocket a notebook containing some loose sheaves of paper. Composing his thoughts, he began to write a letter to the Elders of Trinity House requesting permission to exhibit a temporary light.

And in order to do so we shall make the store room completed, as it can certainly be effected within eight to ten days of working weather. The method I would propose for your approbation in providing this would be as follows; that besides making good the stone vaulted floor above the room, we lay a very strong platform of timber over it, covered with a tarpaulin, well lashed down.

Upon this Platform we can erect our Triangle, again having it well secured to the deck and suspended from this would be the Lantern that was made in Blackwall for the Neptune during the fitting out by yourselves for her employment as a Floating Light.

He finished the letter, then looked up from the table and saw the shoreline and the trees of Mount Edgecombe Park. Folding the paper neatly, he applied a drop of hot sealing wax to close it and placed it securely in his waistcoat pocket. The shore seemed very close through the open casement, and getting up he peered out. The woods clothed views of temples and summerhouses, as well as the occasional stone gun-tower overlooking the approaches to Cremyll Passage and the Hamoaze. The cannon within were hidden from sight behind the embrasures and ports, and these were disguised amid the great stands of mature oak and beech. The trees were thick and lush, forming a green canopy down to the water's edge, and then a vista appeared, cutting a swathe through the hanging woods. A broad grassy avenue led up the slopes to Mount Edgecombe House, its distinctive round turrets at the four corners surrounding a high square tower at the centre. He remembered his conversation with Lady Edgecombe and Sir Joshua at the Assembly Rooms last summer, and felt a stab of guilt that he had not yet honoured his promise to her to visit the Park. There was a knock at the cabin door.

'Come in.' He withdrew from the window to find Captain Reynolds ducking in through the tiny doorway.

'Have you slept at all, Smeaton?'

'I managed a couple of hours, Captain.'

'My redcoats have had to make do with the main deck, but they are used to these nighttime forays. They will have leave to rest ashore.'

'I was just taking in the prospect of Mount Edgecombe,' Smeaton observed.

'We will be back in the King's Dock within the hour,' the Captain replied. 'Will you be returning to London for the winter?'

'Yes, to my wife and child, I confess that I am aching to see them. I dearly wish to make amends in my duties as a father. Christmas will be merry, I promise thee. Perhaps you will come and stay with us in town? I owe you a great debt for your help.'

'That would be most agreeable. Are you leaving soon?'

'Not just yet; one goal remains. Our season's end is fast approaching, but if we can close in the first room of the house, I am determined we can effect a temporary light, as has been the custom of my forbears. Both Mr Winstanley and Mr Rudyerd lit the Edystone in the third season...'

'But your building is far from completed?' The captain drew a silver box from his coat pocket, opened it and took a pinch of snuff from it. He offered the box, but Smeaton declined. Captain Reynolds placed the powder on his cuff and, raising it to his face, snorted first in one nostril, then in the other. His eyes watered but he gestured for Smeaton to go on.

'Two of our hardiest men might lodge there, with well-stocked provisions, if I pay them enough. I have written here to Trinity House, proposing that we use the completed storeroom this winter to exhibit a light.'

'Perhaps you will be less troubled now?'

'Yes, I hope last night's foray will put an end to attempts to capture my men and hold up the work. What will you do with Hill, Captain?'

'Take him straight to a cell in the Citadel is what I have in mind, though I must act under orders from the commander. He will decide upon it. He will go to the assizes.'

'Hmm,' said Smeaton, 'he's nowt but a scoundrel.'

The men worked purposefully in the time remaining to them and the walls of the storeroom were raised remarkably quickly. It lifted their spirits to make such speedy progress, after the laborious task of constructing the solid. With the walls of the room completed by the end of September, Course XXIX (twenty-nine) was set, awaiting the first of the endless chains by the following day. It was a Sunday, and the sharp morning air reminded them that it was the first day of October. Richardson and his men had landed at dawn to lay the first chain. These were to be embedded into the walls at the level of each stone floor vault. Smeaton had slept aboard the *Buss* that night and was on hand early with Mr Richardson to observe and direct the work of 'leading in' the chains.

Endless chains in iron were to be incorporated in the bed joints of all the courses encircling the floors, based on the principle of Sir Christopher Wren's design for the cupola of St Paul's. Fascinated with the account of this in Wren's *Parenthalia*, Smeaton was yet unsure as to how Wren had actually achieved placing his chain in practice. Now the moment had come. The first of the endless chains arrived with the *Edystone Boat*. He stood motionless while the men raised up a mass of links, using the purchase tackle to bring them up onto the top of the circular wall. The chain had been oiled in the workyard before delivering to the rock and it glistened like wet seaweed. All hands were needed to unravel the pile and stretch it into position. Taut ropes drew it across the void until the great iron necklace was spread out and lay down upon the top of the stone perimeter. Then each forged link, about eighteen inches in length, was gently coaxed into the groove that ran along the centre of the wall. This groove or chase was cut some four inches square into the stones, the links fitting snug within. It was hot work and required a great exertion to complete. In the way that fitting a hoop or tyre becomes most difficult as the last part remains to be stretched over a rim, so the hardest part now came as the chain stretched taught. Using iron bars, Richardson's men strained, working the last of the links down into the chase, and there was a great cheer when the chain finally sat down into place within the stone channel.

They rested awhile as two iron kettles were set up below and preparations begun to smelt some six-hundredweight of lead in each. Richardson drew on a clay pipe and watched the flames from the faggots lick up skywards around the cauldrons. The heat was intense.

'Well done, Mr Richardson, tha made it look easy,' Smeaton applauded him.

'Well, to tell the truth, sir, I was worried we mightn't have enough muscle to bring the chain to a stretch, but I have to say she dropped in b'utiful.'

' Aye, tha knows – I dare say my tailor in Leeds could not have done better.' He saw Richardson's look of bemusement and added quickly, 'for fitting, I mean.' They laughed.

The smell of woodsmoke drifted across them, mingled with the acrid gaseous smoke from the cauldron. They tied wet handkerchiefs over their faces, following the workmen who were occupied in feeding the fires, attending to the kettles, and placing more and more lead into them with the iron tongs. Above them, a couple of men were puddling clay in a bucket. Smeaton climbed up aloft through the steam and smoke from the cauldrons and found them making their way around to each quarter of the circle, where they knelt and, scooping up the clay in their hands, proceeded to press it into the groove. Then they cupped their hands to shape the wet clay into dams rising out of the groove that would stop the flow of molten lead from one part to the next.

Richardson followed him up the ladder and stood, wreathed in smoke on top of the wall. He looked down. On one side was the small circular room, open to the sky, whilst on the other the wall fell away in a sweeping curve to the wave-washed rock far below. He saw the sea repeatedly breaking over all and then draining back into the gully. Standing on a wall a little over two feet wide, with the chain running at its centre, Richardson decided it was prudent to step down onto the wooden platform erected inside the room. Unperturbed by the situation and the drop behind him, Smeaton bent low, placing a hand on the inside face of the wall, which was cut in three grooves to receive the stone vault.

'Tha knows, Mr Richardson, that this chain is merely a precaution. Each dovetailed stone within the completed vault will ensure that there is no pushing out of force, to throw out the stonework in the walls.'

'So the chain need not be here?'

'Indeed! Unlike Mr Wren's great chain around the dome of St Paul's in London. His is very necessary to contain the great thrust of the stone structure within.'

'I don't wish to be meddlin', sir, but might I ask why are we going to this trouble?'

266

'You may. 'Tis a precaution that in the event of a stone breaking within the vault, then nothing can be displaced.'

'There's considerable extra cost in time and effort to achieve it.'

'Aye sir, I know it. But we serve the public and our mariners best if we can raise a house capable of standing beyond a mere age or two!'

'Begging your pardon, sir, but in Plymouth they think that your tower will be overset – just as Mr Winstanley's was by the great tempest.'

'Enough! I know, and it makes me apoplectic to hear it still ring in my ears. What do they know? Only hearsay and superstition mixed with a large helping of "general opinion". We must live with it until we prove them wrong!'

'They b'aint worth worryin' about – fools with too little brains in their heads to think for themselves. You'll prove how wrong they are. I see's it for myself – there's nothin' you haven't thought of.'

'Thanks be to God, for giving us all the strength to do it.'

'Amen.'

'Is the lead brought to a full red heat?' he called down to the men below. They were stripped to the waist, their backs running with sweat in attending to the boiling cauldrons.

'It is, Mr Smeaton, sir,' they cried. Shortly after they hooked up the kettle and stood away as the triangle and pulley began to lift and raise it up aloft. Three of the fittest, like lithe monkeys, ran up the wooden ladders and knelt on their haunches until the first kettle came toward them. Using boathooks, they drew in the cauldron with its viscous, smouldering contents and rested it on the wall edge. Two men below passed up long-handled iron ladles. They then proceeded swiftly, and yet with great care, to fill the ladles with the silvery grey liquid and start the pour. Clouds of steam rose from the chain bedded into its groove in the top of the course. The oil hissed and evaporated at the mere touch of running lead, the smell of it burning off, mingling with the woodsmoke wafting out from the fires inside the tower. Within the half hour enough lead had been poured in to reach the first of the clay dams and to immerse the chain forming a quarter segment of the circle. The molten lead ran freely, sufficient to fill the void and completely encase the great chain, before cooling and hardening. As soon as each quarter segment was filled and hardened Smeaton directed them to remove the clay dam to the next.

'Aye, Mr Smeaton, sir.' The man touched his forehead and bent down to knock out the heat-hardened clay, throwing it over the edge to drop, tumbling in pieces off the tower sides, into the seas below.

'And smear more oil on the chain there, the whole groove and chain must be coated!'

The new molten lead ran freely and conjoined with its solid counterpart. The heat passed through into the solid section, enough to re-melt it and cause a single seamless joint to be made. Sooner than expected they had completed the final quarter. The frantic hurry to work the hot lead ended, and calm descended. The smouldering fires were damped down and the ashes scooped up and thrown from the storeroom door opening. The empty iron kettles were lowered back down into the room.

'That was well done, Richardson.' Smeaton descended a ladder into the well to make for the boats. 'You can proceed with the shuttering as soon as it arrives tomorrow,' he added as he went down. Richardson followed, speaking as he felt for the rungs beneath him.

'Aye aye, sir. 'Tis simple enough to do; we can see from the saw-cut chases in the walls where the springing of the ceiling comes.'

Smeaton's voice echoed up to him.

'Indeed, but mind when you start that you set all the outward stones first to fully engage into them. I expect to be back, but the weather may not permit it. You must continue here while I put in hand the preparations for the light and the materials for our roof .'

'Very well, sir, we will do as we can, God willing.'

'That's the spirit, Richardson, though now you and I are in need of our supper, and a good night's sleep.' At the bottom Smeaton bent low to pass through the passage and clambered out onto a rope ladder that led to the rock path below. Richardson soon followed, emerging onto the ladder to the rock and down the slippery steps cut in the surface to the landing place. He climbed hand over hand down the wooden rungs in the fender pile into the waiting yawl and they cast off. With a line fixed to the Sugar Loaf the yawl shot clear of the Gut and soon they were out of danger, rowing toward the *Buss*.

On the following day the ribbed timber shuttering or 'centre' was landed and erected inside the walls. This supported the shallow domed vault of the floor stones. Once again the stones were shaped to interlock in a series of concentric rings. Their subtle geometric pattern would be completed with the insertion of the cruciform dovetailed centre stone, having a carved circular manhole within it. John Smeaton had sailed to Millbay, to prepare the temporary roof, but he did return on 5th October to supervise setting the first of the stones in the floor vault.

Two days later the *Edystone Boat* arrived, carrying the roof-platform components, and Jessop's company came to relieve Richardson. They landed and immediately went on with the outer ring of stones in the floor above them. They must complete the floor so that the timbers and tarpaulin roof cover could be fixed over it. But the weather grew worse.

October 7th 1758.

This afternoon we landed and went on with the setting of the outward circle of floor stones, made the holes in the wall for fixing the hinges of the Entry and Store room doors; and did not doubt but that one favourable day, would enable us to compleat this floor; and then we proposed to begin directly to lay on the platform roof; which would be perfected in two or three hours: and this being done would render the building watertight; we then intended to make a lodgement therein, and go on to the entire completion of this temporary part of the work; however, towards evening, a ground swell began to come on, and to such a degree as reminded us of the necessity of retiring, though two stones were wanted to complete the outward circle; and as the sky began to look foul-weather-like, I endeavoured to see every thing put into the best posture for receiving a storm.

'Bring the loose stones within the circumference of the wall, to be clear of the climbing waves!' Smeaton cried out, shouting to be heard above the rising gale. He felt the impact of a wave larger than before, hitting the rock and climbing up the sides of the column. The sun was gone, lost behind a column of rising water. It hung towering over them for a moment, then he could hardly speak through the weight of falling water.

'And hoist that last remaining stone upon the triangle. Its weight will keep it more secure, and less likely to be shifted.'

'We must go, sir,' Jessop called out through the drenching. He grasped a guide-rope with both hands to prevent himself being carried away with the flood into the well-hole. For a moment he was knee-deep in water until it drained away down the shaft in the centre of the floor.

'Right, that's as secure as we can manage. Everyone into the yawl quick as you can.' The company slithered and slid their way onto the ladder, and descended blindly into the well-hole before another wave struck.

Aboard the *Assistant*, Sam Medling did all he could to keep alongside the fender piles as the swell raised them upward, clearing the rock sides, and dropped them back down again. He looked anxiously to the entrance door, gushing seawater like a giant conduit. The falling water was the spent remains of a vast plume he saw explode upward in a huge white halo all around the half-built tower. When the first figure emerged from the doorway he gave a cry of relief. Soon the rest followed, slithering and scurrying down towards the boat.

'Come along, hurry! We cannot stay much longer.' Sam beckoned to them. They scrambled aboard, Smeaton and Jessop clambering in last, just as another mountainous wave ran up the sides of the empty tower. Another deep boom sounded and it was followed swiftly by the explosion of surf in an array of watery filaments, through which sunlight filtered. Rainbows appeared in an awesome light that encircled the stone shaft of the lighthouse.

'Cast off, Mr Medling, and bring us to the transport station. We will make the *Neptune* just ahead of the breaking storm. The *Edystone Boat* can ride at the moorings and we'll sleep on board the *Buss* tonight.'

They sailed homeward bound in the morning. Smeaton was anxious to return, though the storm continued unabated, to complete preparations for manning the house and bringing out the light. The gale grew worse into the evening. That night he could not sleep for the sound of the ships firing at sea; instead he sat at his desk and thought of the men he had left behind, now caught in a tempest. He lit a lamp and began an entry in his journal.

> *In the night the wind came to S.W. and S. and in the morning the swell was so great as to oblige the Edystone boat to quit her moorings: and as I wanted to be at Plymouth to expedite and finish our intended equipment and stores, which I had greatly at heart, and we were not likely to proceed soon with the business, I left orders with Mr Jessop for the compleating of the floor, and took my passage home in the boat. The evening of this day, Sunday October the 8th it blew a storm, the men of war in the Sound frequently firing guns of distress.*

In the morning Smeaton rose early and set off toward the Hoe with the telescope. The wind now suddenly veered to north-west but it still blew very hard. He made his way to the obelisk, where he would regularly erect the telescope, or sometimes just stand with a spyglass, for what might seem an age to anyone with him, and observe the men working on the house, fourteen miles out to sea. But today there was a sense of urgency. The storm continued, more severe than anyone had anticipated, and he was anxious to discover how they had fared. Standing, seemingly oblivious to the gale that tugged at his coat and the stinging driven rain that blew in his face, he put his eye to the telescope, focused the lens and saw the damage to the men o' war in the Sound. A dozen had lost their masts, cut away to save them from being driven ashore. He concentrated his attention further out and soon found the Edystone. His sense of impending danger and foreboding was borne out, for there was no sign of the *Neptune Buss*. Visibility was poor but he saw glimpses of the lighthouse with the sea continually breaking over it; at times entirely burying the half-completed column.

He felt sickened. He could hardly bring himself to believe that they might be lost! But as the skies cleared his worst fears were confirmed.

The sea was still breaking over the house, rising up in the form of a white pillar, considerably higher than the building, and of such magnitude as at times to intercept every part of it from view: but the air being more clear in the intervals of it's retreat, I could distinctly perceive the triangle standing upon the house, and the stone suspended thereon; but to my great mortification, found that the buss was really gone from her moorings and no where to be seen.

It was the worst of times. The reef had dealt a cruel blow. He thought how much he regretted leaving the *Neptune,* and he found himself thinking of Henry Winstanley, lost at sea with his company on the night of the great storm in November 1703. Had Mr Jessop, his foreman and good friend, succumbed to the same fate, he wondered. The loss of the *Neptune* was made the worse when, upon returning to the workyard, he received a communication from the Corporation of Trinity House. It ruled out his request to exhibit a light from the tower. He read aloud the contents of the letter to John Trehearne.

'They tell me *a light cannot be exhibited on the Edystone Rock until the lighthouse is "rebuilt"*. If only this had come a few days sooner. Jessop and company would be here now with us. Instead they have perished, all for my wanting to exhibit a light this year. I fear the blame is on my shoulders, I should have remained with them.'

Trehearne could find nothing in his heart to say. Instead he took a draught of ale and some bread and cheese and offered it to the engineer. He himself was troubled. Until today he had begun to think himself free of his pursuer. William Hill was behind bars – but somehow somebody had collared young William Jessop and passed a letter to him. William had no idea who the man was. The handwritten note had been addressed to 'John Bowden' but when he opened it he was chilled to read 'Trehearne – you have remained at liberty too long. I will have my prize.' There was no name.

Trehearne had intended showing this to Smeaton, but seeing John Smeaton's plight he felt pity and he put his own misfortune aside. He for one held out hope for the men at sea.

'Do not blame yourself, sir. What's done is done, and we must wait to see how they fare. We must not give up hope.' Trehearne placed the food and drink before him, but Smeaton stared into the dark and pushed it aside, dwelling in silence upon the loss of his men.

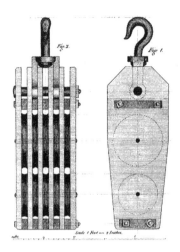

22

The hanging wave

In the early morning a rider came galloping into the works at Millbay, riding swiftly alongside the iron road, past the rows of stones and across the field to stop at the cooper's house. The door opened.

'They are safe and the *Buss* lies at anchor in Dartmouth harbour.'

Mr Harrison called for quiet from inside. 'What is it you say? Pray begin from the beginning.' The messenger dismounted and again told the news. A small crowd had quickly gathered, it seemed from nowhere, for the place had appeared deserted on his arrival. But the rider had been spotted on his approach from the shoreline.

Sam Medling and John Trehearne were busying themselves with 'worming' fresh cables for the outwork. Neither one spoke, nor wanted to; half the entire Service was lost at sea, Mr Jessop among them. Each was lost in his thoughts, wondering what had become of the company, and fearing the worst.

'It must be news of the others,' Sam said to John when he saw the workmen running from the shore up to the road, as the horseman galloped past the yard and on through the field. Dropping the cable and the thin hemp line they were using to bind it, they joined the rush of figures sprinting up from the shore and into the stubble cornfield above. They ran between a few remaining stooks of corn, and as they crossed the brook into the garden of the cooper's house, they heard a loud cheer erupt from the crowd already gathered there.

'They're safe!' and cries of 'thank the Lord!' followed. John bent double and put his hands on his knees to recover. His heart banged inside him but he felt a tremendous rush of joy as the messenger's words carried over the press of figures before him. He stood, placing one hand on Sam's shoulder and the other to his sides.

'... having got into Dartmouth road with the aid of a pilot they rode out the storm and warped into the harbour this morning. The sea-crew is to sail her home when weather and tide permit. The remaining company are coming home by land. Mr Jessop is due to arrive in Plymouth later this evening.'

'And all are well?' the voice of John Smeaton could be heard pressing the horseman for further information.

'I believe so, sir! Nothing more than torn yards and mainsails to put right. 'Tis thought very lucky that they got in. Your Mr Jessop being well acquainted with the coast knows well how the River Dart can afford shelter. The gale drove the *Neptune* too far ahead to make the Sound. Luckily Dartmouth proved easy enough to find – ours is an excellent harbour, though small to the casual eye.'

'Indeed, Mr Jessop told me a couple of years back, when first we undertook this task, that we run for Fowey if there is no way back in an easterly gale of wind, but I knew not where they would make for in this westerly. I thought this time they were lost. I cannot tell my joy in hearing you say they are safe in harbour. Thanks be to God! Here tonight you say? There'll be much rejoicing.' There was a hum of agreement around him.

'I believe we shall have to call a general holiday tomorrow morning – at least a half a day.' A further cheer erupted and then he continued.

'There is little we can do now before the next season. I have had reply from the Elder Brethren of the Trinity House, that it is their opinion a light cannot be exhibited until the tower is completed.'

The men let out a murmur of disapproval.

275

'I know, I know – tha's right to be put out. Ours was a very sound proposal to use the storeroom, and we had a lantern ready and at our disposal, that from the *Neptune Buss*. But theirs is the final word. It's but a small disappointment now that Jessop and his company are returned, and all are safe. I thank the Almighty, the loss of life I feared till now is no more.'

'I think that we have had so many scrapes, He is going out of his way to defend us,' Sam called out. Again a hum of good-humoured approval came from the others.

'I do not doubt it, Sam. I believe you to be right. There are indeed forces beyond our knowing.'

The Reverend Mudge had come into the yard and suddenly spoke very clearly.

'Except the Lord build the house, they labour in vain ...' He faltered, but Smeaton seized upon his words.

'The Rector of Lostwithiel quoted that same passage to me on my first journey hither... Which is it from the *Psalms*?'

Overjoyed to hear of their safe return, he had become suddenly exuberant, and his forthright manner and benevolence of spirit were redoubled. It was as if the stormy skies had suddenly lifted, now that the darkness was gone. With the news the men dispersed and made their way into the field, heading back toward the yard to tell the others. They laughed and jested in high spirits. Smeaton begged Trehearne to stay.

'John Bowden!' (Smeaton retained his pseudonym at all times). 'Have you seen the tower, besieged by the sea? We should have a good view of it this morning. The skies are clear after the rain and the gale is not blown over yet. I promise thee a sight, such as I have only seen myself this last two days for the first time.'

Smeaton would say no more. Instead they took up the telescope and set off toward the Hoe. Arriving at his favoured viewpoint, they stopped and proceeded to erect the tripod. Trehearne raised a hand to shield his eyes from the salt-laden wind and studied Smeaton's bent frame ahead of him. Then the engineer stood up from the telescope and beckoned him to take a look. A few moments elapsed while he adjusted the lens and steadied the heavy instrument. Smeaton became impatient.

'Does tha see the house?' he enquired.

Trehearne answered, 'Aye, now I see it,' and without breaking his gaze he turned the lens and sharpened the outline of the image. The stone shaft now stood at half its finished height, its swept sides rising almost to perpendicular, some thirty-five feet above the angled crown of the rock. He saw the pointed wooden tripod they had used to raise the stones through the well-hole of the stairs in completing the solid, still erected upon the top. A block of stone hung suspended from the tackle by a lewis. Open to the elements it swayed, eighteen inches above the storeroom floor.

'Good, keep a steady eye upon it. Tha sees the triangle and the stone we hung upon it like a pendulum?'

'Clear as day – the sea boils all around ...' Trehearne stopped and let out a low whistle of exclamation.

'Ah, now it happens,' Smeaton spoke quietly to himself.

John Trehearne saw the besieged tower become immersed in white water, the half-built lighthouse shrouded by the great white plume of a hanging wave. It climbed majestically upward and engulfed the entire structure, and continued rising to perhaps the same height again. For what seemed an age, the stone column disappeared, then suddenly it was there again, a tremendous and awe-inspiring sight.

Smeaton recalled how even Mr Jessop had met his ideas, at first, with disbelief. He leaned over so that he could be heard against the buffeting gale.

'When I first told Mr Jessop that it was my intention to build in stone, I remember the look on his face! He hardly needed to utter a word, his look was so black and contemptuous. But when he did speak, he told me that it could not possibly last! And now I see why! For Mr Rudyerd's wooden house was like a reed, bending to the stroke of just such heavy seas.'

Trehearne nodded. 'Aye, he likes nothing better than to tell of how the old house rocked back and forth on its timber legs – enough to throw the tankards from the dresser shelves, he says.'

'Not any more! We have devised means to build a tower as steadfast as the rock itself. See how it shrugs off the sea! Like a great spreading oak, resisting the force thrown up against it.'

'Solid as the rock itself.'

'I believe so. Not wanting weight and firmness, to withstand the sea and keep dry within.'

A drizzle set in and they decided to make their way back down the grassy slope to Millbay. As they walked, Smeaton gave John instructions that he was to set out with one of the seamen overland to Dartmouth, take charge of the *Buss* and sail her back to Plymouth as soon as the weather proved fair.

'I shall be leaving shortly for London, but Mr Jessop will keep me in touch with events going on here.' He smiled. 'But before I go I'd like thee to fetch that lass of yours. There's to be a small party at my lodging – Mr Cookworthy's house in Notte Street – this evening. I owe him a great debt for his advice to me in pursuing a successful water-cement. He takes great interest in our work. You've seen him often with me in the yard – the Quaker. He has even helped in measuring the stones, God bless him. And he is a great talker.'

That evening Smeaton told Mr Cookworthy and his guests that he would be returning to London. He had yet to see his newborn child and his work on the lighthouse would go on there. The designs for the iron railings to the balcony, the lantern glass and the copper work all called for his attention if these were to be got ready in the next season.

When Mr and Mrs Jessop joined them, Jessop drew Alice aside. Young William had told him of the stranger who had approached with the letter for Mr Bowden. It immediately alerted him to some further danger. He spoke of it with Trehearne, who had shown him the anonymous letter he had received.

It was no wonder that he had become so reticent, she thought. He was fearful of the threat that was now returned – that he would be captured and perhaps lose his life.

'Oh, Mr Jessop, what am I to do? John has told me nothing – I had even thought that perhaps I would lose him.'

'Now, Mistress Alice, you are not to worry yourself. I have already spoken of it with Mr Smeaton and the Master thinks there is a way we can end this … but first we must draw his enemy to us.'

Alice was anxious to hear more.

'Will there be violence? Must one of them die to end it?' she cried out.

Jessop took her arm, raising a hand to his lips, and appealed for calm. He reassured her that all would be well. He would send regular reports to Smeaton in London, he told her, and that a plan was devised to protect John Bowden-Trehearne. Though he did not divulge the details, Smeaton joined them and agreed that this had been put into effect.

'Ask for Jessop if the need arises. He knows what to do,' Smeaton said as he handed Jessop a large platter.

'Now I believe Mr Cookworthy is to tell us of his experiments in making porcelain.'

Almost two months had passed since John Trehearne sailed the *Neptune* home to Millbay and Mr Smeaton took his leave of Plymouth for London. Christmas was fast approaching, and now Alice was shocked to find her sister, soaking and bedraggled, standing on her doorstep. This was a complete surprise to her, and after ushering Verity inside and sending her straight upstairs to bathe and change, Alice sat her down and soon learnt what was the matter.

'Oh, Alice, I have run away. I told them I wish to marry my handsome beau – you remember? I met him at the Assembly Rooms, the young officer serving on the *Amazon* – but Mama and Papa won't hear of it!' She began to wail and fell into her sister's arms. Alice rocked her back and forth and signalled to the maid to pour the tea she had brought them.

'I came to Plymouth to join him, when I heard his ship was coming home. I went to the King's Docks and found him on the *Amazon*, but he has sent me away!' Verity sobbed loudly, tears streaming down her face.

Alice held her sister a long while until her tears subsided and she became still at last. She reached out for a teacup and put it in Verity's hands.

'Here, first you must drink this and then we will see what can be done.' Alice took a handkerchief and dried her sister's cheeks. She spoke firmly but with kindness. She felt for Verity but privately she sympathised with her young officer, and with her parents.

She suspected that Verity was both impatient and hard to please, and she supposed that even his best intentions were misunderstood.

She was so very young and headstrong, and perhaps it was that her young naval officer was not yet ready to take a wife, though Alice thought it best not to say so. Instead she thought of her own situation. John was in love with her, she felt certain of it, but something was holding him back. Was it the constant threat of being hunted down? Yes, it must be! More than two years had passed since they first met. She had dutifully mourned her husband's death and knew in her heart that he would wish her to be happy again. She sipped her tea thoughtfully until Verity interrupted her.

Alice put down her cup and asked, 'But did he give you no explanation?'

Verity sniffed. 'No. And he did not compliment me on my hair or my new dress ...'

Alice sighed and tried to change the subject.

'John tells me that the building work has gone well this season, despite the setbacks. Did you hear at home about ...'

'Oh, bother you and your lighthouse,' interrupted Verity. 'It's all you can talk about.'

Alice returned to her own thoughts. She had seen John more often these last few weeks and had hoped for some mention of their engagement, now that this season's outwork was ended. But nothing came, and although the Edystone service had afforded him the best protection he would not linger in the town. She pondered on this. Soon she would gain her twenty-fifth year and, although she was content, she hoped for more. Or was it all in her imagination? It seemed that he was unable to commit himself to her fully. Perhaps not until the work was finished and he had a chance to clear his name? Or was it the threat of capture, ever-present now, that prevented him from doing so? She thought of Smeaton's promise to help her. Could something be done? But how? She did not know, but it seemed to her more important now than ever before. She would write to him in London and ask him, for John Trehearne's sake and her own.

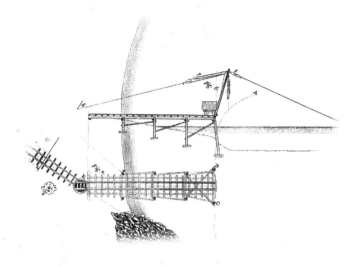

23

Mount Edgecombe

Spring 1759

John Smeaton is once again at his residence in London, attending to the business for completing the Edystone Lighthouse.

Mr Smeaton had not long returned from a visit downriver to Blackwall and he was still numb with cold. He warmed himself by the fire and took up a letter that he had received that morning. Jessop was as good as his word and had written regularly with accounts of the work being undertaken in the yard. Smeaton rested from working on his drawings to read the latest letter once more. Drafts for the design of the lantern cupola and sashes, and for the iron railings to encircle the balcony, lay before him. There were sketches of sash frames containing plate glass and cupola brackets in cast and wrought ironwork, as well as the copper-work of the cupola roof. Earlier he had been in Blackwall to see to the making of these at the foundry. On his return the river ferry had passed the infamous Tower of London. He studied the turrets on each corner of the White Tower. One bore a

281

very close resemblance to his design for the lantern roof. It had an ogee profile surmounted by a vane. However, the cupola for the lighthouse would be crowned with a golden orb. He saw in his mind's eye the smoke issuing from its crown.

'A concealed chimney flue contained within it,' he contemplated, 'to serve the iron stove below. The line of smoke would show from where the wind blows, for the lantern and the tower ports are aligned to the compass points.' This was very satisfying.

The lantern pieces were to be dispatched to Plymouth later in the year. It was already April, high time for him to return there. He held the letter at arm's length and sat by the mantel, where the fire burned brightly in the hearth. It was written just over a week ago, dated 27th March. In it Jessop told of their putting to sea on the 21st, this the first opportunity following a violent storm that had caused severe damage to shipping and houses in Plymouth. Voices came from downstairs, and he heard Anne talking to someone. But shutting out the intrusion, and frowning in concentration, he was relieved to read on in Jessop's account that the only 'derangement' to the work was that the sea had carried away the south fender pile from the rock, and also (from the top of the wall) one of three stones. Jessop had since taken down the triangle and stowed it away safely in the well-hole of the stairs.

Smeaton read on. 'The tower has withstood the test of winter storms, though the transport buoy is lost, and, with it the position of the moorings. I have put in hand the making of a new buoy and preparing the *Buss* to sweep for the mooring chains ...' – and Jessop concluded by saying that course 45 was now being worked upon the platform.

There was a knock at the door.

'Anne, is that you?' he called without looking up from the letter in his hand. She came in. He saw that she was genuinely upset.

'Then what is it, my dear?' He put down the letter and waited patiently whilst she regained her composure.

'I'm sorry, John. It's just that your being here has made these last weeks the most wonderful, and I know not what I shall do when you leave.'

'Now, my dear, we cannot allow this to happen. I have a few days remaining to me here before then. We shall dine with our friends tomorrow night. Mr Wilson is coming, and Joshua Reynolds. I met him in Plymouth – you'll like him, I reckon.'

'I suppose so,' she replied. Her eyes were drier and she smiled.

'Think, my dear, this is the last time I shall return to Plymouth, and then I promise I will stay at home. But now I must go as soon as my work here with the manufacturers is ended. London is the place for us for now, but I know your heart is in the north country. One day, I promise, I will take thee back there.'

'I know you will, John; you are very kind. What is your business tomorrow?'

'I am to go to the Admiralty building. I have a matter concerning one of my men. He has suffered continual hindrance and is pursued by his former naval commander, and fears for his life. I have made a promise to his friend – she is very much in love with him, I believe. I hope to convince the Navy to investigate the matter. A commission would perhaps bring some to justice.' There was an air of gravitas about him. It was bitterly cold outside and he wore his favourite housecoat, a fur-lined robe, to keep warm. They drew closer to the fire. Anne poured him some coffee. He sipped at it and began to tell her the story of the fugitive Trehearne, how he had come to them, what had happened to him, and how they had learned his true identity from Alice Appleford.

'Perhaps both Mr Trehearne and Alice's dead husband will be proven innocent.'

'I fear that may never happen, my dear. The Navy will keep its own counsel. But if they find out the truth of it, then I hope some action will be taken. Trehearne saved us from certain shipwreck, you know.'

Anne brightened and determined to be cheerful.

'Let's drink a health to John Trehearne, Master of the *Weston*, and to Justice.'

'To Justice!' – Smeaton raised his coffee cup. He had added to each a thimble of whisky; it went down well.

'That will defend us from the cold London air,' he gasped.

Anne felt a sense of warmth and protection.

'If at times I find myself alone and afraid I shall think of you in your tower, casting a light upon the waters of darkness.' She raised her cup to his and toasted 'the light that will never be extinguished'.

Early in July, John Smeaton's coach finally rolled into Plymouth and drew to a halt outside the house in Notte Street. He had been detained longer than he imagined in completing the details of the lantern and in staying long enough to see the new mooring chains made up for him in Blackwall. Anne was happy to see him stay a while longer but she knew that the time had come, if he was to finish his work in Plymouth this year.

'The earlier you go, the earlier you come back,' she told her husband as the day came to load up the coach. Once again a small army of servants and grooms was employed in carrying the array of items that he insisted on taking with him. They passed in a continual line along the short garden path that led out into the coach house in the mews. At last everything was stowed on board, not forgetting the pistol placed in a box beneath the seat. There was many a lonely stretch of road between London and Plymouth and he carried it as a precaution should the need arise.

Five days later he climbed out of the coach, to be greeted by a genial William Cookworthy, and soon after retired to his rooms for a decent night's rest. The journey had been slow and uneventful – not a brigand or highwayman in sight. That evening Mr Jessop called, enquiring after him and telling him that they had received delivery of the new length of chain from London. Smeaton was by now abed but he asked Jessop when would they sail, to reinstate the moorings on the Edystone.

'We have them neatly stowed ready aboard the *Neptune*. High tide will be four o'clock tomorrow morn.'

Smeaton groaned but replied soon after, 'Very well, see to it, and I will join you. The sooner we start the better.'

The passage was unremarkable. He took the opportunity to retire below for a few extra hours of sleep before the busy day ahead. A knock came at the cabin door and he awoke, just before eight in the morning. Jenkins entered, carrying a steaming pot of coffee, and placed it on the cabin table for Smeaton to help himself. Since the accident, he was no longer able to do the hard physical work of a seaman, so he was put in charge of the galley, where he proved himself quite handy. Opening the wooden port alongside the cot bed,

Smeaton saw the stone skirts of the tower, rising from the sloping shelf that was the House Rock, immediately ahead.

On Thursday 5th July 1759, work began again on the Rock. Smeaton came ashore with Mr Jessop and his company. He made a careful examination of the fabric of the tower, beginning with a close inspection of the stepped foundation where it joined the natural surface of the rock. The cement pointing had not only remained firm and intact in every joint, but was now so well weathered by the action of the wind and salt waves that he could barely tell moorstone from hardened cement. It had taken on a textured surface that he found most pleasing to the eye, and the whole was colonised with a coating of seaweed and barnacles that masked the joint between the stones and the rock. The column appeared to spring seamlessly from the rock it stood upon. Smeaton half closed his eyes, and again he imagined a vast and ancient oak rising from some mossy crag, with roots reaching down into the very rock. It was just so. Then, continuing his inspection, he found everything exactly as Jessop had described in his letters.

The men were setting up the shears and windlass and soon began to continue with the work they had abandoned in the eye of a storm the previous autumn. Setting the two remaining stones in the storeroom floor completed the first of the floor vaults. They put up a ladder, for Smeaton and Jessop to pass through and stand atop the half-built column. They were high enough now to feel safe from the sweeping waves below, but Smeaton reminded himself that it would not do to be so careless as to step off that perfectly flat disc of the vault, as he had done once before, lower down.

Thus began a tremendous period of building during which, from 5th July until 26th August 1759, the remaining twenty-three courses would be completed. Smeaton recorded it later as consisting of '*the greatest part of four vaulted floors, six circular chains, and in the whole 470 principal pieces.*'

'Well I'll be ...' Jessop snorted, you've a prince beating a path to your door, sir.' And so saying, he handed the notepaper back to John Smeaton, who sat in the shrouds and read the handwritten communication, speaking the words aloud. He folded the paper together again and saw that the stamp in the seal was that of Lord Edgecombe; the note had been written in his hand and signed 'Edgecombe'. The new lord had taken a great interest in the project ever since permission had been sought from his father to lease a couple of acres in the lower field at Millbay for Smeaton's works. Seeing the signature of 'Edgecombe' reminded Smeaton that he had missed his chance to make good his promise to visit the gardens there before the death of the old lord last winter. He recalled how Lady Edgecombe had told him of how they had created a 'wilderness' with an antique temple and a cell. Feeling doubly guilty, he read on:

'... that Prince Edward is desirous of seeing the model of the lighthouse and would it trouble you to call upon us this day, Tuesday the 17th July. Or if this is not convenient, then to do so at your earliest opportunity. The princes are remaining as my guests at Mount Edgecombe until the week's end.'

'Thou shall have to go!' Jessop saw that he didn't relish the idea.

'If only the *Edystone Boat* had stayed away!'

'It's a great honour, sir, to be called for! P'rhaps they have come especially to see it!'

'That's all very well, but there is so little time and we are making good progress here. I cannot leave the house until I can be sure that Mr Richardson's company have learnt the use of the new lifting tackle and completed a chain course.'

The stones for the next floor vault – course 33 – had been landed from the *Weston* with all hands working between three and four that morning.

'The *Weston* is still here with us, at the transport buoy – you can make swift passage with the next tide and be in time for dinner at Mount Edgecombe,' said Jessop.

'No, they will have to wait until I have seen the chains leaded in properly, then I shall go.'

'As you say. Though they won't like it if you keep 'em waiting too long.' Jessop made an expression as if to say 'have a care'. He took out a pipe and a leather pouch of dry tobacco and spent a few moments charging the bowl, then lighting it from a spill. The glow reflected in his weathered face and ruddy complexion. It told of years spent in the outdoors. He was subtly persuasive, and this was one issue on which Smeaton knew he would have to give way.

'You ought to accompany me, Josias. Lord knows you've spent long enough in making the models, building boats and doing my bidding since we began this.'

'Very kind of you to ask me, Mr Smeaton, but I believe the day is yours. I would that I am remembered as the surveyor to Mr Rudyerd's house, and I am glad to be of service now – but you are the author of this work. Why, I doubted it was even possible – it's taught me to keep an open mind. I expect the princes will be more acquainted than I in the sciences. You must show them the future!'

'Lord! You have a persuasive manner, Mr Jessop, when it's called for!' He paused 'Alright, I'll go – as soon as I see Richardson settled. But I insist you let me have William for the day. I need someone to help me carry the model and folio to the house.'

Jessop was speechless, and tears came welling unexpectedly in his eyes. 'Such an honour that'll be for the lad. I'll send a message to him to come to you first thing on the day. Though mind, I shall not tell him who he is to attend or he might take fright.'

'Aye, we'll keep it to ourselves, then he won't mind nor will his mother fuss over it.'

Smeaton took a passage on board the *Weston* the following day, and arrived in Plymouth in the evening, receiving an appointment to come to Mount Edgecombe the next morning. He breakfasted well and donned his best suit of fine cloth and satin, with a silk shirt. After breakfast he stood before the mirror and grimaced at having to wear a periwig once more. Then, collecting his drafts and the model in both arms, he went downstairs and into Mr Cookworthy's pharmacy, where William Jessop, now aged fifteen, sat awaiting him. The bespectacled William Cookworthy leant over the jars and phials; he looked up and smiled at Smeaton.

'Ah, here you are. William, here's Mr Smeaton come to fetch you.'

'Good morning, Mr Cookworthy, Master Jessop. Have tha breakfasted?'

'I have, sir. Mother gave me two eggs this morning for the journey.' William looked a little uncomfortable in his best clothes and leather clogs.

'Are you afraid, Will?'

'I am a little, sir. Mother never gives me two eggs without there being some reason for it. Last time I was sent to my aunt's for a week. And I've never had such a scrub and polish as last night and again this morning. What is to happen to me, sir?'

'Thou's not to worry thyself, Will. I need some help today with fetching and carrying, to oblige our visitors, 'tis all.'

'But why am I dressed up so?'

'Because your mother wants thee to mak' a good show. Look at me – I have to do the same. I'd much rather be attending to my work, 'specially now as the weather's so favourable. But no! We have been invited to Mount Edgecombe this morning. His Lordship has important guests.'

William's curiosity got the better of him, despite his apprehension. 'Who could it be?' he asked.

'Just friends of the new baron, but his friends are always very important and we must oblige them. Come on, lad, help me finish this toast and we'll get ourselves to Admiral's Hard. The coach awaits us.'

They set off for Admiral's Hard, the slip in Stonehouse Creek where a six-oared barge stood by to carry them across to Cremyll. It was a short crossing in good weather and not long until they saw the white towers of Mount Edgecombe coming into view above the shoreline, at the far end of the great tree-lined avenue that swept upward from the shore. The water was flat calm with hardly a ripple upon it. William trailed a hand over the side and eyed the bow wave spreading out like a fantail in their wake. The only sound was that of the oars as they dipped and rose, leaving spreading pools in the glassy surface. Cremyll Ferry lay ahead, a straggling row of cottages that began at the water's edge and lined the road leading up the hillside to Millbrook. The road skirted the estate and ran along the high ground above a sheltered inlet known as Millbrook Lake. The men o' war lay at anchor at the mouth of the inlet. Soon the masts and yards of their topsails disappeared behind the tree-lined foreshore, as it loomed larger. In a few minutes the barge touched the shingle and the foremost oarsmen hauled her up onto the beach, assisted by the ferrymen there. They stepped ashore.

© Plymouth City Museum and Art Gallery

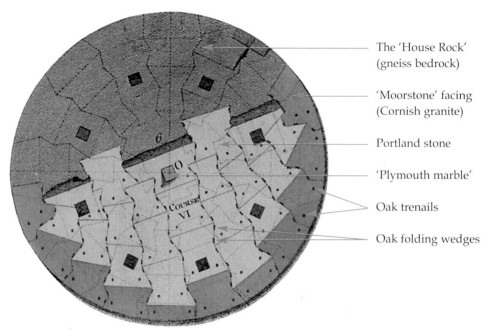

The 'House Rock' (gneiss bedrock)

'Moorstone' facing (Cornish granite)

Portland stone

'Plymouth marble'

Oak trenails

Oak folding wedges

9a. Cross-section of course VI, showing the four types of stone and the placing of trenails and wedges. Dotted lines indicate the positions of stones in the next course (VII) – the first completely above the bedrock.

© Plymouth City Museum and Art Gallery

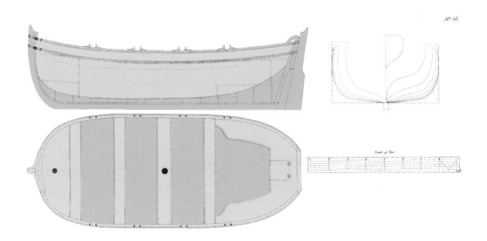

Nº 16.

Mʀ JESSOP'S DRAUGHT *by which the* YAWLS *were built, for the* EDYSTONE SERVICE.

J. Record Sculp 1786.

9b. Jessop's design for a yawl. *The principle of all our vessels, as far as they differed from common ones, was that they were considerably broader in proportion to their length, and remarkably full in the bows.*

© Plymouth City Museum and Art Gallery

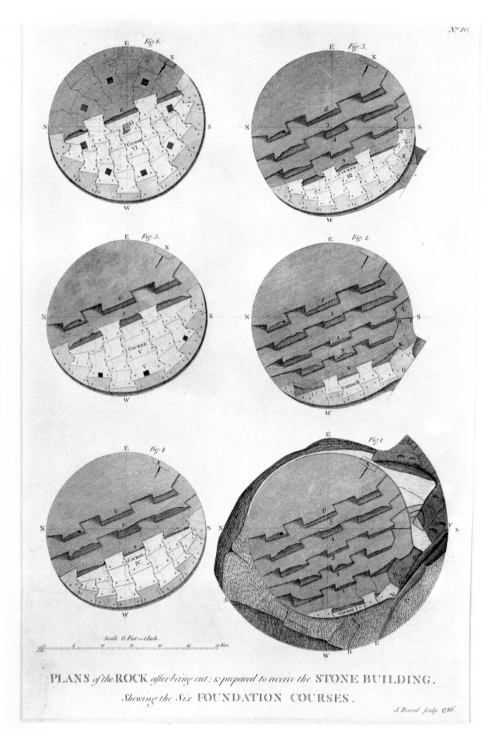

PLANS *of the* ROCK *after being cut; & prepared to receive the* STONE BUILDING.

Shewing the Six FOUNDATION COURSES.

J. Record sculp. 1786.

10. Sections across the foundation courses, showing how Smeaton's stonework was locked
into the sloping bedrock with steps and dovetails.

© Plymouth City Museum and Art Gallery

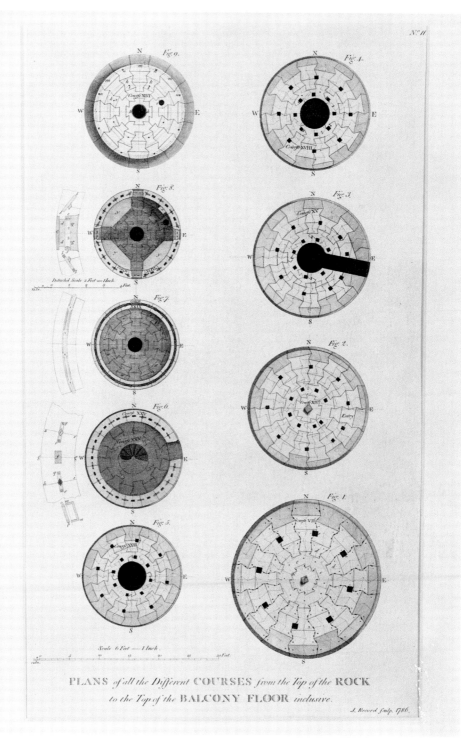

11. Sections across the higher courses of the tower.

© Plymouth City Museum and Art Gallery

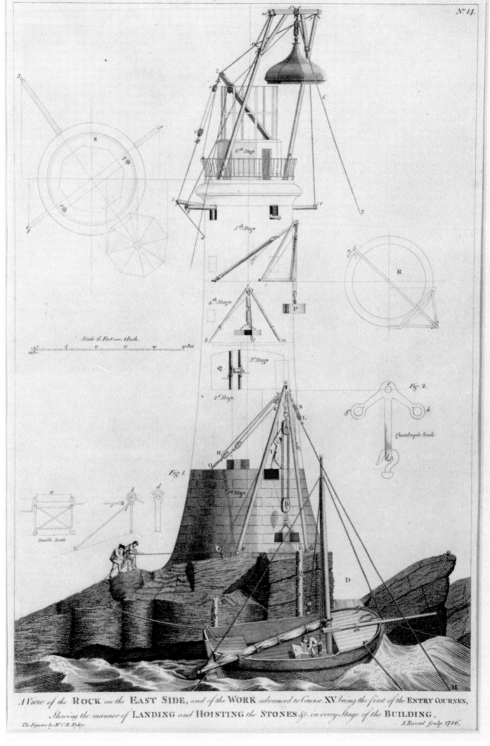

A View of the ROCK on the EAST SIDE, and of the WORK advanced to Course XV. being the first of the ENTRY COURSES, Shewing the manner of LANDING and HOISTING the STONES &c. in every Stage of the BUILDING.

The Figures by Mʳ C.R. Ryley.   J. Record Sculp. 1786.

12. Smeaton's illustration showing how stones were landed and hoisted, and how the cap of the lantern was finally swung into place.

© Plymouth City Museum and Art Gallery

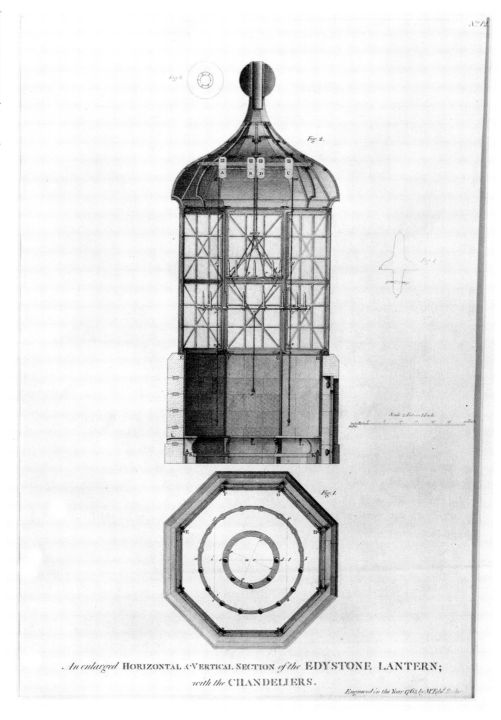

13. Cross-section of the lantern, showing the counterbalanced chandeliers.

© Plymouth City Museum and Art Gallery

South ELEVATION *of the* STONE LIGHTHOUSE *completed upon the* EDYSTONE *in 1759.*

Shewing the Prospect of the nearest Land, as it appears from the Rocks in a clear calm Day.

Engraved in the Year 1763, by Mr Edw.d Rooker. The figures by Mr Sam. Wale.

14. Smeaton's completed lighthouse, seen from the south on a calm day, with the Devon coast in the background.

15a. (Right) Visitors in the lantern of the rebuilt tower on Plymouth Hoe.

15b. (Above) The tower covered in scaffolding at the start of restoration work in 1999.

15c. (Left) A window in the lower store room, with the shutter closed against the weather.

16. Smeaton's tower as it is today, restored.

Suddenly William gave a start and almost dropped the precious model of the lighthouse that he was holding into the water.

'Whoa, have a care, lad!' Smeaton cried out. 'What ails thee?'

'I'm sorry, sir, it's nothing – I slipped.' William was visibly shaken.

'No matter – there's nothing broken,' said Smeaton as he looked the model over in William's hands and took up the drawings from the boat. 'I expect you are as full of fright as I am to have to come here.'

William said nothing, but he had seen a face leering at him – one of the ferrymen who had taken hold of the gunwale to haul their boat ashore – and he instantly recognised him as the same man who had pinned him to the wall and thrust the letter for John Bowden into his hands.

Smeaton felt himself a little nervous in having to fulfil this engagement, but he enjoyed Will's company and decided they should walk up to the house. Carrying the model and rolled drafts, they entered through the park gates onto the wide greensward that led up to the house. Once they had entered the confines of the park William told John Smeaton what he had seen on the shore and the reason for his fright.

'And he said nothing to you?'

'Aye, sir, he just grinned – but it was him, I'm certain of it.'

'I believe you, William. Don't worry, we will see to it that Mr Bowden comes to no harm. The Admiralty know of the threats. I have their word they will investigate the matter and deal with the culprits.'

They fell silent, but he was grateful to William for alerting him to the present danger.

Smeaton raised his hat to a line of gardeners that spread right across the width of the huge clearing, swinging their scythes back and forth and inching their way down toward them. They parted to let them through. At the top of the avenue, they climbed a flight of stone steps that lead up onto the terrace. William had never seen Mount Edgecombe close up before; it was like a fairy castle, he thought. There were four great octagonal towers, one at each corner, and in the middle, a large square tower like a keep that rose up above the rest. The crenellated walls were nothing like as thick and solid as those of the Citadel in Plymouth. Instead the walls were of smooth white limewashed stucco, pierced with pointed windows that threw the mansion into stark relief against the green landscape, and gave it an ethereal quality. It had always been there, splendid and unattainable; he could hardly believe he stood before it now.

They had been seen, and were met by a clutch of servants.

'Very sorry, sirs, but we was expectin' you to come by coach along the drive. You tricked us into thinkin' you was the gardeners.'

'Quite alright, we understand – but now we need to get these things indoors. Take William's folio, would you? And here, my arms can hardly stand the weight of this much longer.' Smeaton thrust the Edystone model into the arms of the head manservant. Another relieved William of the drawings and followed him as they entered inside and were ushered through into a spacious hall that lay at the centre of the house. Here they sat and waited.

This was, William thought, the grandest room he had ever set eyes upon. It appeared almost to be as high as it was long. A fire burned in the great marble fireplace that stood alongside the entrance passage through which they had entered. Giant black marble columns and pilasters ran around the walls at each storey, the lower supporting a frieze and galleries at either end. Firelight danced upon their veined surfaces, while above them shafts of daylight streamed in across the dusky ochre wall panels from windows set high in the upper storey of the hall. They waited.

'We shall have a chandelier in the lighthouse,' Smeaton said in a whisper and pointed at the elegant chandelier. It was suspended from a single chain three times its own length, perhaps thirty-five feet in its entirety. This was the centrepiece of the hall, hung from an oval panel in the centre of the ceiling and directly above an oval-shaped star of marble inlaid in the floor.

'Ours shall be in hoops of iron,' he spoke softly, 'less decorative I grant you but fit for its purpose. We shall have two rings, one great, the other small, with the smaller in double the thickness so that they are of equal weight and one shall balance the other'

'Why, sir?'

'The candles will need regular trimming. It will hang so that the whole can be let down to the floor. Since both hoops shall be equal in their weight, so one shall assist the other as they pass inside and out, going up or down.' William had a puzzled look, so Smeaton added, 'no matter, you will see, it's quite simple.'

He pointed to the elaborate pendant chandelier above them. 'This has lamps of oil, a very modern fitting – but it must still be lowered to replenish the fuel and to trim wicks and to light the lamps and so on.'

They heard the sound of footfalls and voices coming toward them. Smeaton stood, and through the open doorway centred in the far wall he saw figures striding toward them. William began assembling the model and arranging the drawings for viewing on the table beside him. Two dogs entered the room, wandered about, and settled by the fire – and were soon followed by the gentlemen. Lord Edgecombe came first and, stepping boldly forward, he shook Smeaton's hand and turned to introduce Smeaton to his houseguest. He spoke with great gravitas.

'Your Royal Highness, may I present John Smeaton, our esteemed engineer. Mr Smeaton – His Royal Highness Prince Edward.'

John Smeaton bowed low and looked at William to do likewise. William stopped fidgeting with his hat and bent himself low.

The Prince was very pleased to meet them, and expressed his great satisfaction at seeing they had brought the models of the new lighthouse to show the scheme. Smeaton nudged William to raise himself and motioned to him to attend the Prince, who was already looking in through one of the tiny window ports of the model tower. He turned to Sir Richard. Baron Edgecombe had recently inherited, following the death of his father. He was a man in his early forties and was himself a keen patron of the arts.

'My Lord,' said Smeaton, 'may I say how saddened I was to learn of your father's death during my time in the capital. I am but recently returned here or I should have made my condolences personally.'

'Thank you. Yes, it was quite unexpected, but his was a long and fulfilled life. I would be happy to accomplish half as much in my own. He spoke very well of you, you know.'

'I am honoured, my Lord.'

'Come, the Prince awaits us with the others. I am delighted you could join us. They are all very keen to meet you and see your work. It has been talked about in London. I can vouch for it, for when I was at

Mr Walpole's Strawberry Hill in Twickenham they all wanted to hear an account of your progress. Quite caught the imagination!'

The guests had gathered about the Prince, surrounding the table, and were engrossed in the model lighthouse. Smeaton introduced himself to each, shook hands, and then began to describe to his audience the work currently being undertaken and the principles of his interlocking masonry. He opened up the model to show them in intricate detail how each course of stones was joined together with cubes of 'Plymouth marble'.

'My Lords, whilst the lower part, now built, consists of one massive and fundamental solid, the rooms above have walls of single blocks in thickness which present their outer face to the elements and their inner to the interior. I realised early on that having mortar joints running straight through from one side to another presents a weakness in our design, for the seas are driven with such force upon the walls that the damp may eventually penetrate the entire mortar in the joint, all be it some twenty-six inches in depth.'

'Are you saying that it will leak, sir?' asked the Prince. Some in his entourage smirked. It brought a mixed reaction of concern and suppressed amusement from the others.

'They say it will do more than leak,' came another unkind observation.

'Now that will do,' Lord Edgecombe intervened, 'my brother George is an admiral in the fleet and he for one has every faith in Mr Smeaton's project. The Royal Society has given us their best man for the job! I know that he has had to endure every obstacle and opinion in the course of his work. Pray go on, sir.'

Smeaton pressed on doggedly.

'Therefore in devising the construction I have been most concerned to defend the interior and its occupants from the ravages of seawater. The cubes, or "joggles" as I call them, are sunk in mortises in the top and middle of the stones, and combine with marble "rhomboids" – these diamond-shaped stones here in the white wood.' He opened the model to reveal a course of stonework, sixteen dark wood blocks of 'stone' with delicate white inserts in the joints.

'These insert into the perpendicular joints of the next course above. The joints are made fast by leading in iron cramps over the top of each joint. By this combination I hope to create a completely watertight construction.' He signalled to William, who promptly removed the top half of the model and showed the interior of the living room. Again the walls were modelled in the blocks of a dark red wood, each having a small white wooden cube inset on top; Smeaton took up a spill from the holder and pointed it to the V-shaped grooves in the ends of each wooden block that when placed in the circular wall formed a diamond-shaped (or rhomboid) void with its opposite number. He continued.

'A finely cut rhomboid stone of impervious marble is placed in this cavity at each vertical joint between two stones, the "rhomb" is inserted by the masons once the stones are set.' He saw that they were now quite engrossed in his methods, and went on to explain how delicate this operation could be.

'We have found in building the first storeroom that extreme care is needed to tamp them into place without causing a force that will break the hardened mortar in the surrounding bed joints.'

Smeaton began to draw on a loose sheaf of paper as he continued describing the build-up of the watertight joint. 'The rhomb locates in a socket in the joggle stone below and acts as a seal or water-bar against the seas that will break over the wall joints. Finally, the whole circular course is brought as tight together as possible, by fixing great iron cramps into the recesses and sockets above each rhomb, in the top surface of the stones. This lies flush to receive the bed joint of mortar for the next course of stones, and so on.'

'Fascinating, and how is it that these are fixed, Mr Smeaton?' the Prince enquired, noticeably more respectful now. William continued to open up and reveal more and more of the building's interior secrets, until the table was covered with circular model segments.

'The iron cramps are brought to a dull red heat and let in on a bed of oil that is displaced when we pour the molten lead. As the cramps cool there is a tendency to pull the stones tight together, thus giving the greatest possible strength and water resistance to the tower.'

A bell sounded, and Lord Edgecombe clapped his hands.

'How quickly the time has flown! It must be due entirely to our accomplished speaker; but come along, everyone, dinner is served in the dining room.'

William was excused. He ate with the head servants, and afterwards was taken by them to meet some of the young men working on the estate. Smeaton continued to answer the questions of Lord Edgecombe and his guests, and to tell them how he had succeeded in carrying on the work of building a lighthouse in stone.

'Our military engineers in the dockyard tell me that you have developed a "water-cement" in your building that is far superior to any other.' Lord Edgecombe steered the conversation back to the Edystone as his guests finished another course and took wine. Smeaton obliged.

'Indeed, my Lord, our success depends upon it. During my studies, I made a tour of the Low Countries and it was there that I first saw how waterworks and sea defences rely upon a similar mortar in their composition if they are to last.'

'Pray tell us how you came to yours, Mr Smeaton.'

'I set about finding a composition for making such water-cements. Mr Cookworthy has a great expertise in chemistry and advised me to examine every mix of lime and sand and plaster that I could possibly imagine, with every kind of lime from here to Lincolnshire! I made an experiment of each and settled on what has proved to be a most efficacious mortar consisting of one part of blue lyas lime from Watchet in Somerset to one part of puzzolan, a lava rock found at Civita Vecchia in Italy.'

'Then there is no sand?' the Prince interrupted.

'None at all, sir.'

'By Jove, that's novel.'

'I agree, it most certainly is. Were it not for reading Belidor and Vitruvius, and the chance discovery of a ship's cargo of the stuff lying at anchor in this coast, then I might not have had the opportunity to try it.'

'The fates were smiling upon you, sir,' laughed the Prince.

'It is said that the ancient baths and waterworks of Rome were built of this kind of mortar, and their duration has perhaps proved the validity of the composition.'

'Look to Antiquity, Mr Smeaton.'

'Indeed, sir, but unless I am mistaken and they have the lyas limestone in Italy, I believe it is reserved to our work on the Edystone to have the two materials effectively combined. The perfect water-cement: a proper mixture. It has proved by far the most suitable, setting very quickly and achieving a hardness and imperviousness approaching that of the surrounding stones within a season.'

Applause followed and signalled the end of the talk. A sorbet was served, then a further course, but thankfully Lord Edgecombe and his guests seemed fully satisfied with the presentation and the talk turned to other issues – the war, events in Plymouth, the news of a great victory for his Majesty's navy against the French at Quiberon Bay. Then Lord Edgecombe mentioned a local scandal.

'I know it to be of some concern to the Admiralty. They have sent a commission to Plymouth to investigate these allegations.'

'I have heard likewise,' said another.

'And what is it that is causing such rumours?' The Prince enjoyed local gossip.

'I am told that it has to do with smuggling prizes held aboard his Majesty's ships.'

'This will not do. What incentive would there be for our fellows to risk all in battle, engaging our enemies, were it not for the reward to be had? Why, my own brother has himself amassed a not inconsiderable fortune from spoils of war.'

Smeaton kept his own counsel on the subject, but it had not escaped him that it might be that his complaint to the Admiralty was now bearing fruit.

Later that evening they crossed the water to visit the works at Millbay. Smeaton saw William home and returned to attend the Prince and his party on their arrival. Courses 45 and 46, comprising the cove and cornice, and two courses of the octagonal lantern murette, stood erected upon the platform.

One of the Prince's party climbed a ladder and heaved himself up onto the stones. He was clearly impressed with their sheer size and magnitude.

'Here is a great strength and solidity that cannot be appreciated, even from your excellent models and descriptions, Mr Smeaton.'

'Aye, sir, thou has to see it in the flesh, so to speak.' He was suddenly struck by this lord's own largeness and excess of flesh, but kept a serious demeanour about him. 'I believe there are none greater than these stone blocks for size in any work in England. We have manufactured our own lifting gear. See the purchase tackle there, 'tis capable of raising any stone in this yard.'

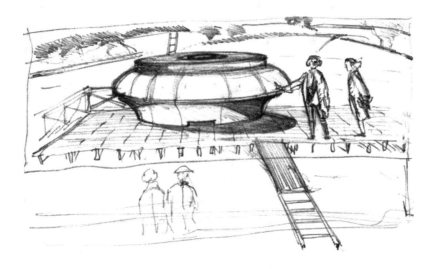

'Marvellous, marvellous invention.'

'Simple mechanics, my Lord. Once understood, we can harness our own puny manpower to achieve what seems the impossible. But the real task lies out there!' He pointed seaward toward the setting sun, toward the Edystone.

'Everything we do, we must do here first! For it is my experience that if something is not first tried and doubly tested here, then it shall not fit there. So we rehearse and rehearse, like players, until it seems that the whole runs smoothly and easily together.'

'Tell me, Mr Smeaton, what will you do next, when this is completed?'

'I have not thought of it much. Though I have my mind made up for me, for the work is begun on my designs for the Calder Navigation. It will take me back into the north country.'

'Back onto familiar ground, eh?'

'Happen yes, that's a truthful observation, Lord Edgecombe.'

'Maybe, but a shrewder one might be that you can never go back after something of this magnitude. Not every man has his moment so

296

clearly written. Tell me, what power will the light have?'

'Much as before, sir, twenty-four candles held in a chandelier, though I believe our lantern will be far superior in its clarity and transparency, over that of Mr Rudyerd's with its wooden sashes.'

'I hope to see it,' said Edgecombe.

'I think from Rame you will, sir. I believe as much.'

Mr Jessop had organised a demonstration of the working machinery within the yard. The party enjoyed watching men rolling the carriage, carrying a stone destined for the outwork from the platform to the pier. They expertly turned the carriage on the turntable junction and allowed it to roll freely down the track running at right angles toward the shore. Then they took their leave shortly after. Lord Edgecombe had a building project of his own in Stonehouse that he wished to show the Prince, and Smeaton was anxious to return to the Edystone. He wondered how Richardson's company were getting on in constructing the second floor-vault. The water remained flat calm, and he gave instructions that the six-oared barge stand by, to row him to the lighthouse later that evening. They departed on the tide at half past two in the morning, landing upon the rock at six.

24

The rainbow

Two days later, Smeaton awoke in the early hours. Already there was the sound of men working up above. He reminded himself that today was Saturday, and that since Richardson and company had now finished the second floor, he might take the opportunity to rest a while longer. He felt the gentle motion of the *Buss* riding to and fro at the mooring, and reached out to the cabin window, fumbling to open the sash. It swung inward, and he slid free the iron barrel bolt of the wooden port. With a thrust of his hand he sent the shutter out around its hinges to slam back against the planking. Shafts of dawn light reached in through the square aperture, casting a dim light into the dark recesses of the tiny cabin. He lay motionless in the cot bed and heard the company go off in the yawl to begin their day's work upon the Rock. It was still some while before sunrise.

'Jenkins! Bring me a pot of coffee, will you?' Smeaton called out toward the murky quarters beyond the cabin door. Since the 'accident' when the shears fell last summer, Jenkins could no longer work aloft, but he had instead turned his hand to ship's cook, proving a good one. He had produced some memorable stews from his tiny galley.

Jenkins' lameness meant Smeaton could tell his whereabouts this morning, by the shuffle and thud of his movements above him on the deck of the *Buss*. It came back louder in a few minutes, and the delicious aroma of fresh coffee reached him before Jenkins had opened the door.

'Thank ye, Mr Jenkins. Would tha leave it there on the table?'

'Aye, Mr Smeaton, sir. Hope 'ee doesn't mind my interruptin' before breakfast, sir, but there's the carpenter up on deck just come back over from the house, sir; says he would speak with 'ee right away.'

'Very well, if he must, send him down to me.' He voiced his thoughts aloud, 'I wonder what it is that warrants my attention so early, that Mr Richardson cannot settle.'

Jenkins touched his cap and spun about deftly on his good leg, then he stepped forward, swinging the other around in an arc, and with a lurching gait he left the cabin. Once again Smeaton heard the dragging sound of the leg as Jenkins pulled himself up the stairs onto the open deck. Smeaton poured the rich, exotic liquor from a tarnished pot and raised the hot porcelain cup to his lips. The black brew had a strong bitter taste to it that he craved; it was his one luxury on his visits to the outwork, when he lodged aboard the *Buss*. Soon he heard the sound of approaching footfalls on the creaking timbers, then a knock again at the cabin door.

'Come in.' It was the carpenter. He was a tall fellow with large hands and the bony knuckles so often found in a skilled artisan. He wore the frock coat and breeches of a landsman. Smeaton perused first the hands, then the face, from behind his raised cup and asked what was the matter. The carpenter looked at him a little awkwardly.

''Tis the lead 'malgam, sir. I've fitted the ironwork and straps to the entry and storeroom doors. As ye know they come out yesterday on the *Weston* and I set about to fit and hang the doors straight away,' he paused, 'but now I comes to the work of leading in the door hooks into the jambs I find that the tin you ordered has been left ashore.' The engineer burnt his lip on the hot china rim of the cup and dropped it down onto the saucer he held.

'Forgot? But I told Mr Cornthwaite only yesterday, to remind Sam to bring it out with the port-lids.' Smeaton blew a long blast of air as if to empty his frustration physically from within. 'This is a blow!'

'Shall I continue with just the lead, sir?'

'No, sir, you shall not!' Smeaton exclaimed, a look of anger and exasperation on his face. 'The tin is to be smelted into the lead, for the purpose of giving it a proper hardness, otherwise the hooks will undoubtedly shake loose.' The carpenter heard the annoyance in his voice. 'The purpose of my coming out here is to see this is done in the right manner.'

'I'm very sorry, sir. We asked for it, but it was forgotten by the men ashore.'

An idea suddenly came to Smeaton.

'Go to the cook.'

The carpenter stood bemused.

'Have him fetch all the plates and trenchers he can muster and bring them to me. Do it straight away, sir!' The carpenter touched his hat and went to find Jenkins. Smeaton finished dressing, sank the remainder of his coffee and followed him up on deck. A few minutes later, the carpenter presented him with a sackful of pewter plates and tankards. There was enough for their immediate need, he thought. They carried the sack of goods between them to the galley, where Smeaton removed his jacket and, rolling his sleeves to his elbows, set about stoking up the fire in the stove. Soon the heat was building in the ironclad room.

'Mak' way, Mr Jenkins, we have need of your stove.'

'What is it, Mr Smeaton? Was there something amiss with your breakfast; was the coffee brew not to your liking, sir?'

Jenkins' look of bewilderment turned to anguish as he saw them put the ship's pewter plates and jugs into the firebox furnace until they glowed red-hot.

'Lay some sand ballast on the deck here. We need not set the *Neptune* alight.'

They poured sand on the deck about them, while Smeaton fanned the fire to a bright blue flame.

'Set to with the bellows,' he urged the carpenter, who began working the bellows furiously over the coals. In less than an hour they had succeeded in smelting down the plates. They then added the lead, producing a coarse amalgam ...

... to make according to Mr Rudyerd, a coarse kind of pewter; it answered my purpose; and the fixing of four hooks was accordingly accomplished.

The composition I afterwards used for leading those in, was one pound of block tin to three pounds of lead. The hooks were let in Lewis or dovetail fashion, and were keyed in hot; and, like the cramps and chains, run in with oil; and while hot, the external part of the iron was tarred over.

Austhorpe Lodge, October 1792

William Jessop recalled the sight, sound and smell of molten lead running and of red-hot iron being forged in Mr Smeaton's yard, all those years ago when, as a boy of fifteen, he began his working life. William ran messages, but once helped to cast the iron cramps used in the walls of the lighthouse. Now, thirty-three years later, he was himself a renowned engineer, held in high regard in his own right, and an ironmaster. His Butterley ironworks in Derbyshire, founded just two years before with Mr Outram, was thriving, producing shaped cast-iron rails to his new design.

His training had been second to none, for in those days there were few if any who would call themselves a 'civil engineer' as John Smeaton did. Even now it was extraordinary how many of the new engineers revered the older man sitting before him. William had never ceased to be grateful that 'Father' Smeaton had chosen to be his guardian and teacher, when his own father died. Now the old man looked frail and weak in body, William thought, and he knew he might not have this opportunity to speak with him again.

After dinner the old man retired with his guests to the parlour, where they entertained themselves at cards and talked late into the night.

'I was just musing, William. Did your father ever tell you of the rainbow?'

'Perhaps, but I do not recall it.'

'It was such a sight as I had never seen before or since. I wrote of it as a "phenomenon new to my observation". I was reading its description this afternoon, here in the *Narrative*. My sight fails me though. Here – you take the book, perhaps then you can read the passage.'

William took up the heavy leather-bound volume and turned the handmade pages, scanning the print till he found the description.

[Wednesday, 8th August 1759]

This day I was presented during a considerable part of it, with a Phenomenon new to my observation: we had light breezes at the west, and frequently drifts of thick fog, which, as the sun shone out, presented to us upon the top of the building, a rainbow making an entire Circle, except where cut off below us by the shaft of the column.

'Drifting fog banks sailed in below us and hid the outlying rocks from our sight, and then the whole began to change as the sun shone through the veils of mist. I can see it in my mind's eye as though it happened only yesterday, William. As though it were all a few hours ago.'

The elderly man had closed his eyes to listen, and then he smiled.

'We stood atop the near-completed cornice looking down upon a rainbow that seemed to pass right through our work! It reached out far into the horizon, lost in the mists beyond. Your father thought it an act of God; the men took it to be an omen,' he paused, 'but thought it

a very good one. I knew there to be a scientific explanation, and it was no less wondrous for it. A circular rainbow like a huge disc between us and the sea!'

'Extraordinary – but I cannot recall Father telling us of it.'

'It had such an awesome beauty, William. Such a thing your father believed the work of the Creator, as do I. He had a deep sense of the Almighty in all things. If there were any thing unexplained, then it had its source in Scripture. He would often quote me the Flood to be the cause of it.'

William laughed, but with great sympathy and respect for his father, who had died thirty-one years earlier. The old man continued to speak his thoughts.

'Until that morning I believed a rainbow's qualities lay in its sudden appearance – spanning the heavens from hill to hill or shore to shore, created in the form of an arch, with a beginning and an end. Imagine then how astounded I was to see with my own eyes, beneath us, a great disc, with no beginning or end. Why, it seemed to gird the reef together, as firmly as the endless chains we had just laid.'

'Will you be leaving us tomorrow, Mr Jessop?' asked Mary. She knew William almost as a brother but always spoke politely, especially since he had himself become an engineer, eminent in his profession.

'Yes, I'm afraid I have to travel. I am expected back in Derbyshire.'

'The affairs of the world will not wait. We quite understand, William.'

He felt the old man's hand rest lightly on his shoulder. 'Though I confess it has been a great pleasure to me to see you again, and time passes too fleetingly while you are here. I hope you may have occasion to come and see us again before long.'

'I am sure I will, sir,' said William. For a few moments the elderly engineer seemed far away in his thoughts. He was – he thought once more of Josias and found himself again on the Edystone Rock during August 1759.

The Edystone Reef, August 1759

In the fine weather that followed the sighting of the rainbow, great progress was made to complete the stone column. Mr Richardson returned with his company on the 13th to shift that of Jessop, and John Smeaton arrived from the shore. A few days later, the elliptical stone vault that enclosed the bedroom and formed the platform of the lantern floor and the outside balcony around it was finished, and Smeaton gave the instruction to strike the wooden formwork from underneath.

'Well done, sir, to you and your company. I believe that you could not have done better in capping off the column. This is a vault worthy of St Paul's, Mr Richardson. Have your men dismantle and take down the shears into the well.'

Richardson flushed with pride. 'Aye, sir. Will we be needing them again?' he enquired. He never failed to be impressed by the Master's meticulous attention to detail. He had devised every means by which the stones were to be raised up from the Gut below. There was to be another change now. During a long pause, the engineer looked about him and over the edge of the 'corona'. He seemed not to have noticed.

Perhaps he had not heard him, Richardson wondered. Then Smeaton's gaze fixed upon him.

'Nay, now that the corona is set, we have no further need of them; they can be got up and sent home.'

'Very well, sir.' Richardson touched his hat in acknowledgement.

'We shall instead erect the small triangle, and bring the remaining courses for the building of the lantern murette up through the middle.'

'Inside the house?' asked Richardson.

'Indeed, Mr Richardson. It will be much more convenient. The stones that make up the murette are all of an equal size and shape, are they not? I'm sure your men are capable of nursing 'em through the manholes in the floors.'

'I will see to it they take great care not to knock the arrises. They should pass through if lifted head first, by the dogleg.'

'Aye, thou knows how moorstone is the hardest kind of stone, and yet it bruises easily!'

'Yes sir.'

Richardson called for the shears to be carefully taken down and went on to set up the triangle. They made the alterations to the tackle and hoisting gear to haul the smaller stones for the lantern murette up through the internal manholes. This took a great deal of time, but in any case the plinth stones for beginning the octagonal murette had not yet arrived. The *Weston* would be delivering them on the next sailing from Millbay.

On Friday 17th August, the main column was made complete. That evening, Smeaton called together the men of Richardson's company. He had got Jenkins to send over a cask of rum and now he presided over it, issuing each man with a beaker full of strong liquor. They crowded into the newly closed bedroom at the top. He was in a great good humour and made a speech in which he apologised for taking their pewterware and forcing them to drink out of wooden cups. A cheer went up. A fiddler began to play in the room below. The plaintive notes of the instrument encouraged their grog-fuelled throats into a tuneful harmony that resounded within the tiny chamber.

'See to it that the men do not drink to inebriate themselves, Mr Richardson,' Smeaton cried out above the din. 'I am mindful that throughout our time here we have not suffered more than broken bones and a sore thumb. I do not wish to see that changed now.'

'Aye, Mr Smeaton, I will keep an eye on 'em till we get back to the *Neptune*.'

It was strangely quiet on board the *Buss* in the morning as Smeaton went over the side down into a waiting yawl. Jenkins, the only hand to be seen and at his duties, had served him breakfast, and offered to row him across. He swung himself over the gunwale and, in spite of his lameness, dropped down with remarkable agility into the small boat alongside. Smeaton followed more cautiously, carrying a loose coil of fine rope with a large, pointed lead weight attached to the end. He placed the coiled rope over his shoulder to free his hands, and descending the ladder slowly.

The lighthouse was deserted and silent. He thought how it suited him very well, for he could begin his survey of the house without any hindrance. He began his preparations for measuring the column, to record its dimensions and perpendicularity. Any deviation from perpendicular could only be determined with any degree of accuracy by measuring in all four directions from a true pendant at the exact centre of the tower. Suspending the line and hanging pendulum weight from a pair of timbers down into the dark of the storeroom, he secured it to a timber frame on the bedroom floor. The frame was made of two timbers, having a simple half-lapped joint between them to make a cross. By carefully adjusting and calibrating the cross he was able to determine the centre of the bedroom floor. The lead-weight plumb line was lowered further through the manholes to within a few inches of the floor at the bottom of the well-hole (the spiral stairs had not yet been constructed). It measured a height of forty-nine and a half feet. He measured and re-measured to the cardinal points in the lower storeroom. With slow deliberation he checked and rechecked the dimensions to the centre, until he finally concluded that the column leant to the east not more than one quarter of an inch from plumb.

Later that morning Richardson led in the company to take up their work. Smeaton carried on, now taking vertical dimensions from the base upward, assisted by Richardson. Together they worked their way up in stages, from the foundation stone at sea level (low tide) up to the balcony floor. At length he deduced the perpendicular height of the column to be seventy feet exactly in total. Whilst the two men completed the survey, the company carried on with the numerous items of work remaining to be done. They sought to take advantage of the continuing fine weather and complete the outer structure and weatherproofing of the house. After a late start they soon got themselves settled and the sounds of industry reverberated loudly from high within the stone column. The *Weston* and the *Assistant* arrived at the House Rock both together, Masters Bowden and Medling vying with each other to tack and come into the reef soonest and to have first call in landing their cargoes. Bowden gave way and common sense prevailed; there was always danger lurking below the waterline even when the sea's mood was tame and flat calm. Sam Medling had brought the iron rails for fitting around the corona, to guard the balcony. Made up in eight equal sections in wrought iron, each having a curved handrail and toe rail, with eight sturdy balusters spaced evenly between.

Medling looked on as the iron railings were hoisted up one by one from the yawl. His thoughts turned to an incident that had occurred during their preparation in the yard, but which he had hardly had time to ponder upon until now. A week ago he had spent a good deal of the day assisting the blacksmith and two hands in preparing them to go to sea. It was stifling hot and thirsty work, for each section of railing had to be brought to a 'blue' heat before they could brush the linseed coating onto it. He noticed a disturbance across the bay at the jetty. A naval cutter had sailed into the channel and come alongside the wooden pier. He could hear what sounded like raised voices drifting across the shoreline.

'The iron is ready, Sam,' the blacksmith said gruffly, demanding his attention to the task.

'Very well, Mr Hodges, take this section from the fire and start another.' He turned to the others. 'Right, lads, the Master wants it brushed all over with the raw linseed oil, *all* over, mind.' They acknowledged his instruction and took up their brushes. There was a heady smell of burning linseed that hissed and smoked from the blue metalwork, running swiftly into every joint, crevice and flaw in the iron.

'See how it sets like varnish. The Master says it will stop any rust forming before we can paint 'em.' No sooner had the hardened linseed set over the blue ironwork than he heard a voice calling his name repeatedly. It was Mr Harrison, the clerk. He came running toward them, his hands waving to gain their attention. Laying down the curved railing, Sam turned in the direction of the approaching Harrison.

'What is the matter?' Medling called out. Harrison stopped running and gulped a few breaths of air in between his words, so that it took him a while to break the news.

'It's Mr Bowden, Sam, impress officers have come to take him.'

'But he has his medal?'

'Aye, he has, but there is a lieutenant here who says that it offers him no protection, since he is a fugitive whom the Navy will bring to justice.'

'The Navy should have settled this or forgotten him long ago. What of John Bowden?'

'He is safe. We have hid him beneath the platform. They will not find him there unless they choose to remove thirty tons of the lantern murette first.'

'Hah. I think, Mr Harrison, that Mr Bowden owes his life to your quick thinking.'

'Do you really think it?'

'I do. This lieutenant wants the Master of the *Weston* put out of harm's way.'

'What do you mean, Sam?'

'Put plainly, he wants him dead!'

'Dear Lord God Almighty, then how can we help him?'

'Well, one thing is certain, he must not fall into his hands!'

John Smeaton heard the news and came rushing up to hear what had happened. He spoke Sam's thoughts.

'Aye, they will certainly be back, and very soon, I believe. And we must be ready. I intend returning to the house as soon as this piece of work is completed. Before I go, I would have you and Mr Harrison join me and Mr Jessop tonight. We must decide exactly what is to be done when they come for him.'

'But what can we do?'

We must deny them – and to do it, they must believe he is already gone to his maker. Mr Harrison, you have heard of how we saw a full rainbow encircle us, at the outwork?'

'Yes, sir, I have. And I believe such things as we do not understand can happen.'

'They can, especially in such places. We must mak' something extraordinary occur before their eyes. Seeing is believing, is it not?'

Smeaton brought his mind to bear upon the present. He too was uneasy but there was far too much to consider to be allowed time to dwell on this. All about him were numerous tasks that called for his attention. Richardson's men were erecting and leading in the balcony railings; the joiners inside the house were assembling the cot beds. He could hear the sound of masons driving the holes into the stone jambs of the openings and the hammering of the carpenters, busy hanging the shutters in the ports and putting in the miniature-paned sash windows, set behind the granite rebates of the port openings.

'Lend a hand here, Mr Cornthwaite ... Nay – tha does see right! It's a halved barrel.'

Smeaton had brought up a short circular tub, about a foot high, with which to plug the topmost manhole. This was to be a simple and temporary means of closing the bedroom interior from the elements. With Cornthwaite's skill and strength, the tub was driven into the manhole, forming a tight fit and leaving an upstand of about eight inches. They placed a larger inverted tub over it.

'There, that should suffice to keep inside dry at night, least until the lantern is complete. 'Tis easy to fit and all.' Richardson agreed.

'Now I must get hence, I'll see thee in a few days if all goes well.'

He made his way down the wooden ladders, passing the workmen below, until he reached the well-hole, and finally the rope ladder that hung from the entrance to the rock below. Word had come that the long-awaited components of the bronze lantern had arrived from London and the pieces were delivered at last to Millbay. This was good news, for the haulier had managed to leave the greater part of them in Bristol, where they had lain for some weeks until a new team of oxen could carry them the rest of the way to Plymouth.

That night he made passage aboard the *Edystone Boat* to Plymouth.

The following evening found Smeaton examining the lantern sashes in the workyard at Millbay. He had learnt that the haulier had left the iron components of the lantern behind, adding a further week's delay. Furthermore, they had been loaded in a careless fashion, causing two of the bronze sash frames to break during the journey. There was no time to lose. The carts were unloaded and work got under way upon the platform to assemble course fifty-two, the topmost, and then to fit the iron sills of the lantern frame. Smeaton inspected each piece and, deciding that the sashes might be easily repaired in the yard, he headed up the hill toward the office.

It was time, he thought, to write to Trinity House notifying them of his intended date for the 'exhibition of a light in the house'. He sat down in the dusky gloaming. Outside, the evening sky deepened to indigo. A calm silence descended, broken only by the sound of moths striking the windowpane, attracted to the lamplight, and the lapping waters of the shoreline below. Voices and movements seemed clearer and louder in the still evening. He heard the last of the men working to complete the lantern frame, picked up his quill and began to scratch the words neatly and meticulously onto the paper:

The Corporation of Trinity House, Bethnal Green, London

Dear Sirs,

I think it now proper to write, to acquaint your Brethren with the state of the building, and therein to express my hopes that the Lantern will soon be completed and, if the weather continues moderate, we will soon be capable of exhibiting a Light in its proper place; and the house made completely habitable, and proof against wind and weather, without the aid of any temporary contrivance...

He signed and sealed the letter with wax, and sent Harrison to fetch William Jessop, their messenger, to carry it to Plymouth. Shortly afterward the boy came. Smeaton extinguished the lamp and closed the door behind him. Then they set off through the yard together in the gathering darkness. The rows that had held the stones stood empty now. How many times had they carried the rough-hewn stone blocks to and fro, assembled course upon course on the platform before shipping them out to the Edystone? He mused as they walked along.

'Tha'd best mak' sure to place that into the London mailbag yourself, Will, first thing in the morning. The coach leaves at seven. I shall be expecting to hear soon from Mr Shuttlewood, the Secretary of the Trinity House Corporation, with his reply.'

He bade goodbye to William, who went off into the darkness whistling cheerfully to himself, the letter placed securely in his satchel. Smeaton turned about and saw in the last remaining light from the west the iron skeleton of the cupola. The cupola ribs and lantern top sill stood erected upon the platform. He climbed up onto the wooden deck and spent the few remaining minutes of daylight carefully examining the framework. Somehow a means for fixing the heavy copper sheet roof to the shaped iron ribs had to be found.

'Still here, Master?' someone called out. Smeaton saw his round face in the light of a lantern he held aloft. It was the coppersmith.

'Aye, Mr Lamb. How now, will you be going home tonight? It's long past suppertime, is it not?'

'Missus Lamb don't mind, sir; she knows how it is when there be a job to finish on time.'

'Well, don't let me keep thee unduly. I have yet to decide how we must fix your work to the ribs, in a manner that is both simple and weathertight.'

'I have the sheets here, sir, made ready to the pattern, but by God they are heavy and too thick to form a lap for a seam or roll.'

'I know, Mr Lamb – I ordered the heaviest gauge – three and a quarter pound to the square foot. Since we have no timber to support it, the sheet must be capable of making its own rigid shell.'

'There is a way we would do it in the dockyard, sir. When we are making up a boiler. We bring the pieces together and rivet the seams. Perhaps we can do it here?'

'But the joints are not flush, Mr Lamb. How can we make a seam over the rib to join the sheets at the mitre? The angle creates a ridge.'

'How I would have it done, Master, is to mitre the sheets so they butt together. Then cover the joint with a strip of copper, say about three inches broad – a saddle piece I calls it – and fix it with two rows of copper nails all riveted together.'

'Thus making easy what would otherwise be very difficult! I thank thee, Mr Lamb. We'll try it tomorrow.'

'Very well, Master; good night to 'ee.' The coppersmith laid down the last of his cut sheets and, taking up the lamp, headed off in the direction of the entrance gates. The night air was so still that Smeaton heard him say 'goodnight' to the night watch upon the Stonehouse road.

That same evening, at dusk, John Trehearne found himself staring into the troubled waters that ran, even in fine weather, over the ragged rocks beneath the *Neptune Buss*. It seemed akin to his own life. While all seemed well on the surface, beneath ran the dangerous tides and currents he feared, and over which he had no control. He thought Alice more beautiful now than when he first met her, three years before, and he was certain of her feelings for him ... But there was no reason he could give her for his slow response. How could he expect her to understand?

He looked up to view the tower, silhouetted against the last of the light. It stood now seventy feet high above the House Rock, its sides tapering to a cylindrical column that ended at the 'cove', the smooth curved cornice that was intended to throw off the climbing surf beneath the balcony. The pink streaks in the sky sank lower on the horizon. Soon the lantern would complete the house and their work here be ended.

And what then? Surely his enemy would come before the end? Were these to be his last weeks of freedom?

The truth of it was that since the accident he had feared to think of the future – but he knew now that he must ask for Alice's hand or risk losing her. He would do it.

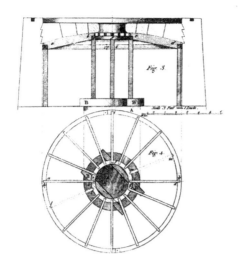

25

The inner room

Squire Vasey and his daughter Verity were seated in the study when Josias Jessop entered the room with Alice.

'This is Mr Jessop, Father.' Alice introduced him to the others. 'My father, Squire Vasey – and Verity, my sister.'

'Very pleased to make your acquaintance, sir, and yourself, young lady.' Jessop bowed to them both, holding his hat to his chest. 'Are you in Plymouth awhile?' he asked politely.

'Just a few days, Mr Jessop. Mrs Vasey has gone to her sister in Taunton so we thought we might come to Alice in the meantime. We have just heard that Alice is to be engaged to one of your men. I must say this has come as quite a shock to us, my dear. Your mother didn't know whether to laugh or cry upon reading it in your letter, which came only last week. But I understand you wish to marry very soon?'

'We do, Father, but I want you to be happy for us and to give your consent to it!' begged Alice.

'Well, you can do as you please, my dear! I for one found your Mr Bowden a splendid fellow. It's your mother, you know. He's not known to us in the county and she had hopes you would look closer to home – to one of our local landed gentlemen. And I hear that your Mr Bowden is really a Trehearne from Cornwall? What am I to make of it and what shall I tell your mother? You know she very much wants you to marry again, but not to a fugitive! What shall I tell her? She has insisted I come here to take up some references. Perhaps the esteemed John Smeaton will be able to oblige us?'

'I'm certain of it, sir,' replied Jessop. 'He is away upon the "stone" at present, but we expect him back soon.' He turned to Alice; he was beaming at her.

'Congratulations, my dear, this is good news. Mrs Jessop will be pleased. She sends her regards to you. She will want to know all. When will the wedding be?'

'Thank you, Mr Jessop. This month, we hope. 'Tis quite sudden, but we thought it timely. Now that the house is soon to be completed, and with the situation here coming to an end.'

'I dare say. Can it really be more than three years since we began this enterprise? It seemed then we had a mountain to climb, and I was far from certain that it could ever be done, you know. Now here we are on the highest part, almost reached the peak.'

Verity stepped forward and took her sister's hands, then kissed her on the cheek.

She wasn't much interested in lighthouses and could contain herself no longer.

'Sister, am I to be your bridesmaid?'

'Of course you are, Verity! Now that you are here you must help me decide on what I shall wear.' Verity spun round laughing, her red hair flying out.

'We shall have gowns in finest silk – will it be a grand affair? Can I ask my young gentleman, he is promoted to Lieutenant aboard *Hercules* – I have been writing to him you know – he is to return this month.'

'Of course, but I would keep discretion, for fear of attracting the wrong sort. Mr Trehearne's life has been put in enough danger.'

Alice saw her father's look of bemusement and decided she must tell him everything. She took a deep breath and proceeded to speak the truth of what had happened.

She had confided in Verity, whom she had sworn to keep silent, but Verity, always excitable, broke in with her own version of the truth about John Trehearne – how he had sailed with Robert Appleford and fought to save him on the deck of the HMS *Dart*, how he had jumped overboard to escape Lieutenant Colquhoun, and how Colquhoun had thought him dead.

'Verity, stop!' cried Alice, alarmed that she would only succeed in muddling the facts. She reminded Verity of the subsequent events of the past two years – of Trehearne's being recognised when the ships met at sea, his imprisonment on the gunship and, later, the attempt on his life. 'Do you not remember? That is why we brought him to the Hall, to mend in safety, away from his pursuers.'

'Well, my dear, what are we to make of it all?' said her father, concerned as ever about the practicalities. 'As I say, your mother hopes you will marry again – but that you would find a gentleman, perhaps a farmer who might help run the estate. I'm not getting any younger, you know.'

'Yes, Father, I know – John may very well wish to turn his hand to it. A seaman's life is hard.'

'Hmm,' the squire opened his mouth to speak but she got in quickly with the advantage –

'He has done well to rise in the Edystone service and become Master of the *Weston*. I know he has put aside a regular income.'

'But what of the Navy?' The Squire was troubled. Mr Jessop thought it timely to allay the old man's fears.

'We have news from a reliable source that the Admiralty commission is making headway investigating the HMS *Dart*. It's said the loss of the French gold is proved, and customs men have raided the houses of fishermen in Polparra to arrest the men involved. William Hill was among those taken, and he has been in gaol these past six months. He has confessed to save himself from the gallows.'

'Then Trehearne is likely to be pardoned for his desertion?' asked the squire.

'I believe so, squire. In any event the Admiralty will most likely drop any charges held against him. I am sure they will hinder him no further. He jumped from the ship to save his life.'

'Then all is well?'

'It will be, sir, as soon as the Lieutenant and his associates are shut up – they're dangerous fellows, an insult to his Majesty's service. They will stop at nothing to save themselves, and not even the Edystone medal can give immunity against such evil.' There was a silence. Verity felt her heart racing with fear and excitement.

'I will marry him, Father,' Alice insisted.

'Now then, child, let's not be hasty. I want you to be happy, but I cannot countenance putting you in harm's way!' the squire pleaded.

'Poor Alice.' Verity put her arms around her and then turned to Mr Jessop.

'There must be something we can do – go to the magistrates or the Commissioner of the King's Docks for help in this matter.' She took his hand and looked at him searchingly. Jessop collected his thoughts and spoke them, quietly and deliberately.

'Well, my dears, of course your father is right. How can he possibly consent to Alice's betrothal in such circumstances? Colquhoun will stop at nothing. A most despicable and cowardly man! If we are proven right then Lieutenant Colquhoun will risk all to take John Trehearne before long.'

Mr Jessop took out his long clay pipe and asked for permission to smoke it.

'Yes of course you may, Mr Jessop, but tell us – what is your plan and what is it you would have us do to help!'

'Miss Alice, I am sworn to secrecy,' he calmly replied.

Thursday 23rd August 1759

'So, Josias, tha's to have the honour of laying the last stone with Mr Richardson.'

'A great honour it is, sir. Spent all those years in patching and repairing Mr Rudyerd's wooden house, and now this. I never expected such a thing. It used to try my brain, how we could keep the place from decay and storm damage. I thought it would be my lot until old age handed it to another.'

'Have you all you need?'

'Everything is stowed on board. Mr Smart says we make sail in an hour.'

'Quite so. Watch out for any sign of our enemy, and I do not speak of the French, Josias. I feel it in my bones that he will be drawn before we end our task.'

'I dare say, but everyone is prepared, sir. Trehearne has instructions to head for the house if he has need.'

They looked on as the lintel-stone was lowered into the *Edystone Boat*.

'The last stone to complete the lantern walls. We should be ready for the interior steps from tomorrow, if all goes well.'

'Well done, Josias – well done indeed, all of you.'

A group of stonemasons stood with Smeaton on the jetty, waving and cheering the men aboard the *Edystone Boat*, as she slipped away from the wooden pier into the bay. The masons' work was done, and this would be the last time they saw off the outward-bound company as employees of the Edystone service. Close friendships had been made during the three years that had elapsed, and there was a sense of pride tinged with sadness, now that their part was come to an end. A good number were taking passage from Plymouth to return to Portland within the week. Each in turn received his pay from the clerk and handed him the valuable silver medal that had offered them such effective protection from the marauding press gangs. (Though one man had been taken for not having his medal with him when a gang landed upon the rock.)

It was strangely empty in the workyard, but there were still signs of activity, and new trades had come in. The coppersmiths worked at their forge to complete the cladding of the lantern cupola, whilst the blacksmith next door hammered out the forged rings of the great chandelier. Their best shipwright carpenters had turned to making joinery and furniture for the interior fittings of the house, and the painters were busy grinding and preparing the lead and other ingredients they needed to make up paint. The master gilder had decorated the ball finial that was to crown the lighthouse. He had burnished the layers of gold leaf and sealed them with varnish, until it seemed to glow dark gold in hue.

Whilst Jessop and Richardson were completing the masonry work at sea, Smeaton contented himself with attending to the finer details that remained. Entering the forge, he found two of the coppersmiths struck down with sickness. Without a moment's hesitation and to avoid any further delay, he soon was removing his jacket and assisting Mr Lamb at the bellows, and soon took up the hammer himself.

'You seem very handy with the tools, Master,' said Lamb as he held steady the copper sheet and placed another rivet for John Smeaton to hammer home.

'Never tak' a file to where a hammer can go, Mr Lamb! That's the secret of good workmanship in metal.'

'Couldn't agree more, sir, but 'tis most unusual to find a gentleman such as yerself, and a man of learning, to be familiar with artisans' methods.' Smeaton paused, holding the hammer aloft, whilst he replied.

'Ah, well – I would not wish to propose anything that proves impossible in the making.'

He brought the hammer down with a well-timed blow onto the rivet and spoke in between the swinging of the hammer.

'Ever since I were a lad I would go to my workshop (bang), and mak' all kinds of things that took my fancy (bang). I built a lathe (bang), and taught myself to turn a screw (bang) before Father sent me away to be a lawyer.'

'Didn't care for the law then, sir?' Lamb asked him between the ringing sounds of the hammer blows.

'Heavens no, I tried to stick at it for Father's sake but I was miserable; went down to London (bang), but I couldn't wait to come home and get back to my mechanical experiments (bang). Ever since the day I saw the workmen come to Temple Newsam to build an engine there (bang), I was smitten. It was one of Mr Trevithick's beam engines.'

'Like those in the tin mines, Master Smeaton?'

'Aye, the same – but in those days there was little more than waterwheels to see about Leeds. That engine changed the course of my life. I showed no aptitude for anything else (bang). Father knew it.'

'He must have been disappointed.'

'Aye, but not for long (bang) – he saw my mechanical leanings – though he never guessed of my becoming a *civil engineer*, it being such a new thing.' (Bang, bang, bang.)

'There, that's the last of the roof sheets fixed to the ribs. Now we can start on the saddle pieces over the joints. 'Tis an elegant piece of work, Mr Smeaton.'

'First it must be practical, but I confess it does move me to see it tak' shape. I see now your idea for the saddle pieces over the seams to be the right answer for a waterproof joint. I think I could take a bath in this if we turned it t'other way up – it wouldn't leak a drop.'

The engineer ran his hand over one of the eight mitre joints that curved down from the small neck at the top to the wide octagonal sill piece at the bottom.

'Now we only need to fit the ball for it to look complete, sir.' From a workbench in the far corner of the workshop Lamb had fetched the golden orb that would fit on top of the lantern cupola.

He held it out for Smeaton to place atop the slender ogee neck of the cupola roof. He measured it.

'Two foot two inches in diameter.'

The ball concealed the flue-pipe outlet of the stove's chimney, combining functional utility with symbolic imagery. It was made of a copper sheet, decorated in layer upon layer of gold leaf, burnished to a golden brilliance, and protected by layers of varnish set hard as amber. Smeaton imagined the blazing sunset setting alight the antique gold of the ball so that it shone as clearly as the light itself. But how to fix it? It was too precious to place on the cupola until it was fixed in place.

'It will need a collar, Mr Lamb, forged by thee, that we can screw securely to the cupola neck.'

'I'll see to it, Master.'

Smeaton passed it down to him and took his leave. As he walked across the Hoe, he saw in his mind's eye shafts of sunlight against a darkening stormy sky. The ball of shining gold atop a completed lighthouse with its cupola painted a lead-grey, its white lantern sashes, and a white murette crowning the great pillar of moorstone. As was his custom, he stopped for a moment to draw his telescope and scan the Sound in the direction of the Edystone rocks, and then continued on his way to his lodging at Mr Cookworthy's house in Notte Street.

That evening, John Smeaton sat in his rooms in Notte Street and took out his journal. He thought awhile of the image that had come to him earlier. Then he went downstairs and joined the household for dinner. Mr Cookworthy was some years his senior but they had become great friends. Cookworthy enquired as to progress on the tower, and when he heard that the last stone was to be laid, it was he who suggested they should make passage to the house and give thanks to God. Smeaton thought this a most excellent idea and agreed to call upon the Reverend Mudge to accompany them. His relative, Dr Mudge dined with them that evening, and he too offered to accompany them in a 'hymn of praise' as Cookworthy called it. There was a great sense of relief and thanksgiving, and goodwill, amongst them that evening. So great was the pervading atmosphere of uplifting happiness, that it inspired Smeaton to celebrate the completing of the lantern walls. He determined that on his return to the lighthouse he would carve the inscription and date upon the lintel stone:

LAUS DEO 24th August, 1759

The inner room

Monday the 27th Mr Richardson and Company arrived from the Edystone, and gave account that they had lived in the House ever since the 23rd instant, and found it very warm and comfortable; much more so than the Buss's hold and cabin. That he set the last stone of the Lantern, being that making the door head, on Friday the 24th; and then a part of his hands were employed in fixing and completing the fixture of the iron work of the window Ports, while the other part was setting the stone stairs; and lastly, that they had put on the cap stone of the stair head and finished everything belonging to the masonry on Sunday evening, the 26th of August.

By mid September, the octagonal lantern was fitted. At last, the extraordinary sight of the lantern cupola strapped onto the deck of the *Weston* signalled the last phase of the operations to complete the new lighthouse. It was to be carried out to the house and lifted entire, by means of a crane that Smeaton had devised.

'Saturday, September the 15th between three and four in the morning, the Weston was got into the Gut, and delivered of her cargo, consisting of the pillars, sashes, and framework of the Lantern ... I gave my principal attention to establishing the frame of the lantern upon a bed of lead, and the screwing of it carefully together; seeing that every joint was filled, and screw covered with white lead and oil, ground up thick for paint; and every crevice so full, that the bringing the screws home made the white lead matter to ooze from every juncture; thereby to exclude all wet and moisture, and so as to prevent the iron-work from rusting.

The attention of Mr Jessop was chiefly confined to the other artificers: and the rooms being so much encumbered with materials and stores, that there was scarcely room for the workmen.

On Sunday all was made ready, though the weather had suddenly turned stormy.

All that night Smeaton lay fitful. To carry the structure complete and hoist it more than seventy feet up from the seas was perhaps their boldest operation yet. Would it prove impossible? The following morning, to his relief, dawned calm and settled. The conditions were perfect for the raising of the cupola. The *Weston* sailed in a calm sea and Smeaton followed aboard the *Edystone Boat* while Sam Medling brought every conceivable article necessary to them aboard the *Assistant*.

The lifting-tackle was erected and declared ready by noon, when Mr Jessop gave the signal for the *Weston* to come into the Gut. Smeaton directed a couple of the men to make ready to go on top of the cupola with staves to fend off against the tower walls should any breeze catch it and cause it to swing, but it remained so still that this was deemed unlikely. Instead the lift went swiftly and smoothly, without incident, and within half an hour the cupola was raised and resting on the lantern frame, undamaged and ready to be fixed down. By the evening, with sufficient fixings in place, they cast off the tackle. Soon afterward the wind blew up fresh at east. Now the silhouette of the tower appeared against the evening sky with only the ball remaining to complete it.

By Friday 28th September 1759 the work to complete the house was well advanced and the date now set for advertising the lighting of the permanent light. From his quarterdeck aboard the *Dart*, Lieutenant Colquhoun saw for the first time a completed lighthouse away on the horizon as he sailed in towards Plymouth past the floating light around the Edystone reef. He trained his spyglass upon it and saw the small yawls and a sloop, each bearing the mark of the lighthouse painted in black upon the mainsail.

'There they all are, like moths round a lamp,' he thought, 'and Trehearne there amongst them.'

The moment he had waited for was fast approaching. All these months away – as far as the Guinea coast – he had thought of little except how he might take his revenge, and now there was another reason to do so swiftly. Whilst at sea he had received a communication ordering him to attend an Admiralty commission to answer allegations that he knew were true. But there was only one man who could prove it – there on that damned rock.

His orders were to return to Plymouth, to present himself before this accursed commission. He had almost panicked and thought of running – but there would be no coming back, and it would stamp him a criminal. No! There was still hope, but it lay in his silencing the one man who could prove his guilt.

When word reached John Smeaton that the *Dart* was returned to Plymouth and lay at anchor in the Hamoaze he was in his tower. When the light-keepers failed to arrive, he took up residence in the lighthouse, determined to stay on to make a trial of lighting the light. For now the date was set for the light to be exhibited. Smeaton had dispatched an express communication to the Corporation of Trinity House, Deptford Strond *'giving notice for Tuesday the 16th of that month as the day of lighting the House'*. At the same time a yawl carried the communication to Captain Symonds aboard the floating light. The two light-keepers had indeed come out, but one of them, walking on deck, had fallen and dislocated his shoulder during rough weather aboard the *Buss*.

'What news of the keepers?' asked Smeaton when Sam Medling made landfall with more of the winter stores intended for the lighthouse.

'The injured man is carried home aboard the *Edystone Boat* and the other will not come into the house alone.'

'Then I will stay on as their replacement until they do come. Take this letter to the master of the floating light, and then make all speed for Millbay. I want you to bring out John Bowden on your return.'

'To fetch Mr Trehearne here, sir?' Sam Medling enquired.

'Indeed, if that is his real name then it is imperative that he is seen to come here. And make sure those aboard the *Dart* see him come.'

'Let's see if we can draw him to us, is it, sir?'

'Exactly, Sam. I believe it to be now or never!'

A knock came on the drawing-room door where Alice sat playing at cards with her sister Verity.

'Mistress Alice, there is a Mister Sam Medling in the hall; he says he must speak with you.'

'I am coming down, Mary,' and she rose straight away, with a look at Verity.

'Verity, call Mr Trehearne, will you?'

'Is it time?' Verity flushed with excitement.

'I think so,' Alice replied as she headed off downstairs. Within a few minutes John Trehearne met them in the hall. 'Sam, what brings you here?'

'Master wants you to come out to the Edystone; I am come to fetch you, John. Hurry now, the *Weston* waits upon us.'

'Very well; what is the matter?'

'Don't you know? The *Dart* dropped anchor in the Sound yesterday, you're to come straight away.'

'Are you certain?'

'All I know is the Master and Mr Jessop have some kind of plan to release you. Now can we go?'

Alice stepped forward and kissed him, then pushed him away. 'Go now, God be with you.'

Then they were gone. The *Weston* sailed on the tide, but their mainsail did not go unnoticed.

Given news of Trehearne's sailing, Lieutenant Colquhoun seized his chance. He barked an order to his midshipman, Baines, to make ready the ship's launch. Within the half hour he was standing in the stern and giving the order to cast off. The men lowered the oars and within a few strokes they were rowing with taught precision, away toward the Sound. Propelled by the powerful, steady rhythm of the oars, the launch sliced through the swell. They came around in the lee of the *Duke*, at her moorings in the Sound. The ship's side afforded them a smoother passage, until they set course beyond her, heading out with the tide and the breeze to their aid. Less than fourteen miles to row! The Lieutenant stood erect in the stern. Opening his spyglass, he scanned the seas ahead of him, in the direction of the Edystone. He picked out the newly completed profile of the tower on the horizon. Then his lips parted in a thin smile of satisfaction, as his eye discovered the sail of a small vessel. The sail carried the unmistakeable emblem of the tower painted in a black silhouette onto the sailcloth.

'There's nothing more we can do yet awhile, Mr Richardson, we can but wait and see,' said Smeaton as he stood on the bench running round the lantern walls and opened his small telescope to scan the coastline.

'Come, let us make a trial of lighting the candles. Perhaps it will lift their spirits aboard the *Weston*.' He got down from the bench and reached for the chandelier ropes. Unhitching the twin ropes of the smaller upper ring he pulled on them gently, and down it came, passing through the outer ring that floated up past it into the top of the lantern. They lit the eight tall, tallow candles slowly and deliberately, one by one, before raising high the small ring back up into the lantern. At the same time the great ring descended. They lit the sixteen candles upon it. Each ring counterbalanced the other, the smaller having double the thickness of forged iron to make up for its disparity in size. Gently Smeaton raised up the second lighted ring, and brought the lights in both rings closer together in the middle third of the lantern.

'Have one of your men keep watch up here, Mr Richardson.' he ordered.

'He's coming, I see him, he's coming! There – on the horizon – a sail showing the Edystone mark!'

Smeaton rushed up into the lantern, followed by the others from below. All watched in silence as two small boats appeared, heading towards them across the water. The men in the first boat, an Edystone yawl, pulled frantically on the oars to keep their lead.

'Pull, men, pull!' The oarsmen responded to the call by straining at the wood to force her through the water. Closing behind them, a Navy launch was gaining inexorably. The officer in charge crouched forward, his pale gaze never leaving his anticipated quarry. Soon the two boats were within a few lengths of each other, pitching and rolling through the 'hollow seas' besetting the reef.

The watchers in the lighthouse leant out over the newly fixed iron balustrade that encircled the lantern balcony and watched the drama unfold. They peered through the veils of rain that drove toward them across the open sea. It smattered in silence on the windward sashes of the lantern, running down the panes and beading upon the fresh lead paint that was just barely dry. Wet glistened on the freshly oiled lead sheet of the balcony and the cove, and darkened the granite faces of the octagonal lantern wall to windward.

In the yawl, the oarsmen heaved and sweat ran down them, despite the chill rain that soaked their backs. No sound breaking their labours except the sound of their gasping breath and the oars turning, and in their wake, the commotion of the midshipman barking at his men to increase the stroke. His lieutenant maintained a stony silence.

The crews eyed each other through the driving rain, the boats now separated by a single wave's length, and as one rose to the crest, so the other pitched into the trough between. Sam Medling, having left the casks of lime lashed to the shrouds to act as ballast, now drew his sword and cut them away. They dropped beneath the water, and then came to the surface, thumping into the prow of the launch and fouling the oars. For a few vital moments the launch lost its power as the oars clashed long enough for Sam to gain a few strokes that carried the yawl across the last remaining fathoms into the reef. One of the casks was broken open and its contents spilled into the water, turning it a milky white. Colquhoun, armed with sword and pistols, looked hard at Trehearne, but by the time the launch got under way once more the yawl was at the landing place. Trehearne leapt onto the rock. He clung on and found the steps cut in the rock face. A pistol shot rang out and the ball flew past him against the rock. Climbing up to the massive stone base of the solid, he laid hold of the rope ladder and pulled himself up toward the entry into the house.

Another shot narrowly missed him, striking the curved walls.

He saw his pursuers gain the reef and row the last few fathoms into the Gut. Trehearne reached up to the entry door. A hand held out and pulled him inside, leaving the heavy door open, flung back on its hinges against the solid walls

In the launch, the Lieutenant saw his quarry gain the rock, climb up and enter the lighthouse. It galvanised him into action. Approaching the landing place, he yelled at his men to stow the oars and come alongside, and risking life and limb he leapt from the rocking boat, scrambling to gain a purchase on the slippery stone. He favoured his left arm, nursing the old injury in his right shoulder. The massive stones in the solid foundation glistened with the constant sea spray as the waves thundered on the Edystone reef below. Making his precarious way towards the ladder still hanging from the open door, and using his good arm to pull himself up, he forced himself up and scrambled inside. Without pausing to draw breath he cast about him and felt his way along the low passage until his eyes became accustomed to the dark. He stood in the well and drew his pistol. Slowly he climbed the winding stone staircase towards the dim light from the room above. He could hear the voices of the landing party outside and called back to them 'not to leave a stone unturned' in their search. Voices carried faintly down from above, whilst he came up into the first small chamber. A lantern upon an iron hook cast low light over the room. Searching hurriedly amongst the stores and provisions stacked about the stairwell and piled almost to the vaulted stone ceiling, and satisfied that no one could be concealed in such a small space, he climbed upward once more. A wooden ladder led up to the next room, passing through a circular stone manhole in the floor vault above his head. Leading with his pistol held high, he emerged into a second storeroom. It was a little taller than the first and furnished with a single square window. He flung open the wooden shutter without, and read in the dim light the inscription carved in Roman capitals around the low granite frieze.

'Except the Lord build the House they labour in vain that build it.'

Colquhoun prodded the bundles and sacks that were piled up until he was satisfied that there was no hiding place. Then he was already heading upward to the next level. Throwing off the wooden manhole cover he emerged with his pistol ready to shoot. This room, by comparison, was well lit, having four sash windows all with their outer wooden shutters thrown open. He addressed the two men who were sitting there at a small table.

'Where is he? Where is that man who entered here but a few minutes past?' The men looked tense. Colquhoun stood opposite, the circular stone manhole between them, and they eyed each other. All was quiet except for the distant thunder of the seas breaking below and the steady ticking of a timepiece somewhere up above. At last one of the two men replied.

'Tha must be mistaken, sir, for no one has come up here nor passed by us, to our knowledge. Are you sure he entered the house in t' first place?'

'Of course I am sure. I saw him, but ten minutes ago, enter in through the stone portal. It seemed there was someone came to his aid.' The Lieutenant was livid, his face ashen, with pale eyes staring. Each recognised the other but made no acknowledgement of it, except for the Lieutenant's cutting remarks.

'If only I had known that day I found you, stranded helpless in your boat at sea. I could have blown you out of the water. I should have boarded you and taken him then. It would have saved me time and trouble. But I have no quarrel with the Edystone service. Hand him over to me now and we can part amicably.'

329

'If it is Mr Trehearne you speak of, the man we know as John Bowden, where is he? You may take him from us – but let me remind you he carries the Edystone medal.'

'He has need of far greater authority than an Admiralty protection where I am about to send him,' the Lieutenant spoke softly. 'He is mine.'

Even though the coals burned red in the iron grate, a chill descended that permeated the whole room. The Lieutenant called down through the manhole in the stone floor to his midshipman.

'Secure the door, there is to be no way out. He will not slip away from me again.'

And seeing there was nowhere in such a tiny living room to hide, he began to climb up the next ladder into the room above. The bedchamber was directly beneath the lantern. Colquhoun saw a high vaulted ceiling that sprang seamlessly out of the walls in a perfectly formed ellipse, curving up to yet another manhole above him. Three identical wooden cabins fitted snugly against the circular walls, their fronts forming three sides of a square.

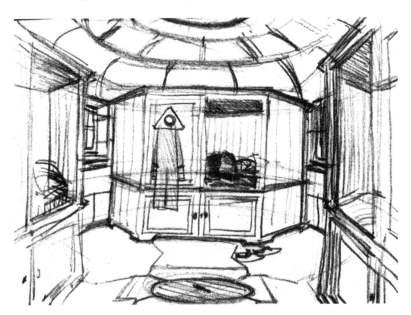

Kicking the manhole cover back into the floor opening. He threw open the door of each cot bed and the cupboards beneath, but found nothing. He looked out through the four sash windows in between. 'But these are impossibly small for a man to climb through,' he thought, 'and the curved outer walls are too smooth to scale without a rope.'

Colquhoun believed there could be only one way out. He looked up through the last manhole into the lantern cupola. Climbing carefully and looking all about him, he emerged onto the lantern floor. Above him hung the great chandelier in the still silence of another empty room. The candles burnt cleanly, their steady flame oblivious to the elements without. Only the patter of rain against the sash panes and the tick of the timepiece disturbed the silence. Colquhoun climbed onto the octagonal bench and looked out through the bottom sash panes, then dropped down to the door that led outside onto the balcony. He reached carefully for the handle.

'Ah, now I have you at last – you shan't escape me again. There is nowhere left to run, Mr Trehearne.' He smiled to himself and gently slid back the great bolt of the door. Slowly, he eased it open. The sixteen flames of the candles in the greater ring flickered, pulled by the sudden draught of air. Ducking his thin frame, he stepped out through the doorway. He noticed on the stone lintel above him the Latin words

LAUS DEO

And a recent date:

24TH AUGUST, 1759

The wind and rain caught him. Pressing himself to the wall he cocked the hammer on his pistol, and began inching his way round the eight outer faces of the lantern walls. At each corner he passed the inscriptions of the compass points, carved upon the sill above: SE, S, SW, W, NW, N, NE, E – but no one was there. He was back at the door. He darted inside then went out and round again, quickly this time, the opposite way. He leant out to look over the balcony rail, making certain that there was no means of climbing down or hanging beneath the coved cornice. At last the midshipman led his men up into the lantern and out onto the balcony. The workmen followed the sailors, crowding onto the circular balcony walkway. They were joined by John Smeaton and Josias Jessop, who strained to hear the Lieutenant's words above the wind.

'Anything, Mr Baines?' The midshipman shook his head.

'Not a sight nor sound, sir. We've been all over – inside and out. The men think he may have jumped.'

'Would you?' whispered the Lieutenant in a silent rage. 'Tell me, could you jump from this and hope to live?' Baines leaned out over the railing, his eyes searching the sea and rocks below.

'Perhaps he swam from the Rock, sir. He may be hiding somewhere in those rocks out there.'

'But I swear I saw him enter in here. He cannot simply vanish.'

The men looked awkwardly at each other. The colour drained from the Lieutenant's face; his voice cracked.

'He cannot simply disappear!'

'Get inside!' Richardson beckoned a startled John Trehearne to lie down and enter a space not much larger than a coffin.

''Tis better that they search the house and find you gone,' he said as Trehearne slid into the hole feet first. Then Richardson passed him a sack, before sliding the stone back into the wall. A tiny vent admitted air into the chamber within the massive stone solid. He lay silent, entombed in a space twenty-four inches high, a void within the interlocking shapes of the surrounding stones. Trehearne gasped for breath – he could barely breathe, and could see only the chiselled stone of his hiding place. Out in the passage, he heard muffled sounds as Richardson quickly brushed away the loose sand, before standing and inspecting his work. Satisfied at the perfect fit of the stone, he climbed the steps to join the others. Smeaton and Jessop, having taken up and set working the new timepiece, sat at the table brought up into the living room. They spoke in hushed tones, and Richardson heard their voices drifting down from above as he wound his way up the spiral treads. And now he heard the sound of footfalls in the entrance passage below him.

'Good luck, John Trehearne,' he said softly to himself.

In the waiting moments there was nothing more that could be done. Smeaton sat with Jessop beside the stove in the tiny living room. They talked of how to fix the copper 'conductor' and Smeaton told of his visit to see the lightning-struck tower of Lostwithiel Church. But each concealed fears that perhaps the hiding-place was about to be discovered and their well-laid plans would go awry. A man's life was at risk.

'Yes, I saw it myself,' said Smeaton. 'The rector did invite me to come and observe the damage – I met him once on my first journey to Plymouth, a keen astronomer. He showed me the lightning strike. The masonry was shattered in a very surprising manner and I thought the damage rendered by some kind of elastic vapour, bursting forth to liberate itself from the confines of the spire. Yet I found this was not so. At the ground I saw a hole had pierced the structure through a buttress some eight feet in thickness!'

A sound came from below, and he paused. There was a palpable silence, until a sound of something grating on a hard surface echoed up through the well and the storerooms above it. They heard it again, and then Richardson's footfalls on the steps coming up the well.

'There, 'tis done.'

'Done well, I hope … It must be done perfectly to hide him from such a determined enemy.' At this the bald head of Mr Richardson appeared in the manhole. They saw beads of sweat running from his brow and down his face. He jerked his head without speaking and they realised he was not alone. Smeaton switched his topic of conversation to continue as before.

'I therefore concluded that there could be no certainty of making a wall so thick as to resist the action of lightning, and its effect.' He paused and raised his cup. Josias improvised with a question.

'Does Dr Franklin say how tall buildings can be saved from lightning by such a conductor?' It sounded plausible, to his relief.

'He does. Though there are as many of my Fellows in the Society that think this to be an abominable danger.'

'P'rhaps they think it might attract lightning bolts to strike over and over?'

'Aye, perhaps they do, Josias. But I am of the opinion to put Dr Franklin's method into practice here.'

They watched as the barrel of a pistol appeared in the manhole in the centre of the floor. It was cocked and held high above the head of Lieutenant Colquhoun. Richardson got as far out of the way as he could in a circular room that was no more than eleven feet in diameter. He sat himself on a stool by the stove, transfixed by the Lieutenant's pallid stare. It scanned the room, resting on the men, searching amongst the equipment and supplies for any clue that would lead him to Trehearne. He recognised the faces of Jessop and Smeaton. They exchanged words in an atmosphere suddenly so charged, Jessop thought, that it too required a conductor to dispel it before it burst in a sudden clap. Richardson wished he were somewhere else; cold sweat poured from him. His back pressed so firmly to the curved wall that he felt a sensible movement as the sou'westerly wind sent waves thundering over the rock foundation far below. It was a strange sensation that only added to his discomfort – as if the heavy seas displaced the very rock on which the house stood.

Then Colquhoun looked upward through the manhole above him, and he motioned with the pistol for Richardson to set the ladder up into it, that he might climb higher. The midshipman came next, following close on the heels of his lieutenant, pushing aside any that got in his path, and racing upwards to the next level. Up through the low entrance room, into the storeroom, the living room, the bedroom, and at last into the lantern octagon at the top.

The fugitive had flown. Searching the sides of the smooth stone column beneath them, they could find no sign of his escape. No rope, nor any grappling iron for him to have scaled the outside face. Speculation reigned. Did he jump? Could he have lived if he did? Surely he would have struck himself upon the great spreading girth of stone? Colquhoun had to admit he was baffled.

'Sir!' Midshipman Baines cried out for his attention.

'This workman says he saw a man in the water!' He pointed to rocks in the reef yonder and Colquhoun snapped open a small telescope.

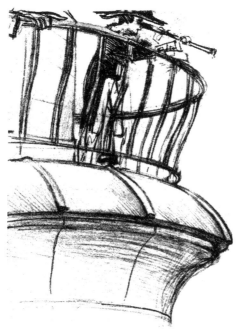

It was true, there appeared to be something in the water – but could it be him? How could anyone fall from this height and not be smashed to pieces on the rocks below? But some thought it was him. Trehearne was known to be an excellent swimmer.

'Could he swim to the floating light from here, in these seas?'

'If any one can, 'tis him. Done it before, didn't he?' said one of the many workmen who had come up into the lantern room immediately after the navy men – sent on up by Smeaton to add to the general confusion and distraction.

'Silence!' roared Colquhoun as he rounded on the unfortunate fellow (a glazier) who had spoken out.

. 'What's it to be, landsman, a turn in his Majesty's service for your insolent tongue?' Colquhoun's pallor had left him; his face burned crimson with rage as he glared at him then trained his spyglass on the waters, but saw nothing more.

'If it was him, it surely must have been his body,' he thought aloud. 'Trehearne knew himself to be a dead man and jumped rather than be taken … to deny me.' he thought. But it did not make sense.

'Why come here?' Colquhoun was baffled and his mind raced as he stood there, looking down onto an empty reef. 'Unless he wished us to think it? But he cannot disappear without trace.'

But that is exactly what did happen. And although there were others who believed John Trehearne had jumped, perhaps to his death, in the seas about the Edystone, no body was ever found. Some thought he survived. They said he swam to the floating light – though nothing of fact supported this, except that he was a very good swimmer. Perhaps a Cawsand fisherman pulled him from the water, for were they not renowned for their skill in fishing the reef at low tide?

Lieutenant Colquhoun could not explain it. Instead, he grudgingly convinced himself that Trehearne had indeed perished upon the Rock that day, and told himself that now at last his secret was safe. Indeed it was, for there was not enough conviction to seek any further evidence following the news of John Trehearne's disappearance. But Colquhoun was tainted with dishonour, even if it was nothing more than rumour and idle talk. He was never to make the rank of Post Captain. In a few years he would give up the Navy, and was never seen in Plymouth afterward. But wherever he went doubts plagued him, and more than once he dreamt how the fugitive had escaped him that day. How had he disappeared? Sometimes in his dreams and innermost thoughts he saw Trehearne alive. Could it be that he had not perished that day, and that the mystery of his disappearance was but a very well-kept secret?

Richardson told no one. The whole company, even the crew of the *Buss* and the other seamen, believed him when he told them that John Trehearne was lost in the sea, attempting to swim toward the floating light.

After three days of storms the dawn was foggy, calm and still. Alice felt the moist, cold air in her face, but as she walked the mist that screened the estuary began to disappear. The sun climbed higher into the morning sky, and in the sunlight shining on Millbay she saw the ghostly outline of a seventy-four-gunner, grounded, lying on her side and surrounded by vessels. She watched the preparations under way to tow the man o' war off the mud on the next approaching tide. It was the *Duke.*

'The gales in the night must have driven her, dragging the heavy anchors until she ran aground,' she thought. The guardship's masts and square rigging came sharper into view in the strengthening sunlight. By the time Alice reached the workyard, the mists were gone from the mudbanks. Ahead of her, two of the Edystone boats stood ready to sail from the jetty. The figure of Smeaton beckoned to her to come aboard. There was hardly a breath of wind. They set forth, following the thin navigation channel dredged out from the pier to the main river channel. Using the oars, they slipped past the *Duke,* well clear of the stranded leviathan, and headed out into the Sound.

'What news is there of John Trehearne, Mr Smeaton?'

'None as yet, my dear.'

She sank at this. 'If he lives, will I see him again?'

'Of course you will. There is every hope. Some say they saw him swim out toward the floating light.' Smeaton felt he could tell her no more. But he could not leave her without hope. It would not be long now, he thought to himself.

'Meanwhile we have our finishing to attend to. I did not let the painters fix the golden ball, for fear that they may do it casually. I must do it myself. I sent for you because I believe that if there is news of him it will come first to the house.'

'Then I will accompany you,' said Alice with great determination.

'Very well, my dear.'

Further out a stiff breeze sprang up; Sam Medling gave the order to bend the sail, and with the mainsail hoisted they made good progress.

'Expect to arrive at the *Buss* before four o'clock this afternoon, sir.'

'Very well, Sam, then there should be time enough for us to visit the house before dark, God willing.'

Unable to go into the Gut to land their cargoes, due to a stiff easterly wind, they tied up alongside the *Neptune*. Later, Smeaton and Alice were rowed across in the yawl to land on the rock, and to enter the house alone.

26

A star of the fourth magnitude

Austhorpe Lodge, October 1792

Alice returned to that day in October 1759 when she accompanied John Smeaton into the tower.

'Do you remember, Mr Smeaton, the inner room? I will never forget. I watched you place an iron (I believe it is called a lewis) into the stone wall in that tiny entrance passage, and turn it one quarter turn, then you withdrew the stone. It slid open as easily as any door.'

'Yes indeed, but when I peered inside there was no one there! We saw an empty chamber, holding nowt but a thin line of damp where seawater had penetrated through.' Smeaton nodded sagely and added, 'It took great courage and strength of mind, to enter in there and be shut away, not knowing when you would see daylight again, John – but I had fully expected you to be there when I returned!'

Trehearne recalled the feeling of incarceration, not knowing how long it was he had lain within the stone 'solid'.

'I lay therein two days, I discovered later – in pitch dark, when my candle burnt out, damp and cold and afraid.'

William Jessop, who had joined them for a last view of Austhorpe before leaving, looked puzzled.

'Let me enlighten you, William,' said Smeaton. 'It happened that some time before, and soon after the attempt to wreck our boat, I hit upon an idea with your father. I determined that by taking away two of the locking dovetail stones in the solid we gained a space large enough for a man to lie in. It happened then that our work had reached the entrance to the house – course number fifteen. I saw before me that we had two such stones, there in the pattern that I had just chalked out. The stones abutted the void to be formed where the entrance passage would be. It was easy enough to do, but we would have to work in great secrecy. For which I would give the company a day's leave. Then, when course fifteen was all laid and closed, we remained behind and immediately set about removing the two stones we had chosen, before the bed was sufficiently hardened. I had seen to it that our most trusted mason, Roger Cornthwaite, was the only one who knew of our plan, and with his help we lifted out the stones and covered the void with timbers and some barrels of lime to conceal it. A thin slab was laid facing the passage. This concealed the room from the entry passage. The sixteenth course above it was laid like all the others, from the four great hook-scarfed stones that surrounded the well in the centre, then working outward. When it came to the part above the void, we shifted the barrels and placed the stones over the void as soon as possible, and once again this was done in secret with only Roger Cornthwaite with us. Your father, Richardson, myself and Roger were the only ones to know of it.'

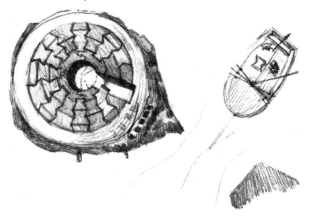

'So it was *that* which my father called the secret of the stones?'

'Indeed, William, that was the secret,' answered Trehearne. 'Your father it was who released me from my cave, and I returned in secret with him to Plymouth. There I stayed until the others returned. We knew nothing then of your coming to fetch me, sir.'

Alice remembered vividly how bad weather and the race to finish the house kept her in the lighthouse with Smeaton, unaware of Trehearne's fate.

'Do you remember, Mr Smeaton, how terribly unhappy I was then? There was nothing could console me, even your showing me how John had been secreted away into the very stones of the house. When you found him gone, I knew without asking that you thought John had been betrayed. And there was nothing could be done about it. It was days before news came and I had no choice but to remain with you on the Edystone, anxious and unknowing, until the ball was fixed.'

'I had no choice but to finish the house in time, lass. I had agreed the date for a light to be exhibited. It was less than a fortnight away

341

and much remained to be done to complete the tower without any further hindrance.'

'You were so concerned with that ball, that it was properly fitted and such.'

'I know you thought me foolish, but I was nimble in those days and capable. The gilded ball was too precious to allow it to be fixed with undue care. I wanted to be certain it was secure, to withstand the elements and last as long as possible.'

'You almost fell off in doing it!'

'And I was determined to remain in the house and keep the light till proper persons were engaged and sent off,' the old man replied.

'The weather worsened,' said Alice, 'and I found myself marooned with you in the confines of the lighthouse. Still there was no news of John, and I could do nothing – I could not leave the place. At last, the *Edystone Boat* arrived, but they were unable to come in to us so they filled a keg and cast it into the sea to be drawn up into the house. A letter was delivered amongst the goods by means of the keg. It was addressed to me ...'

The Edystone Lighthouse, October 1759

'Is it bad news?' Smeaton asked her.

'No not at all, sir, it is very good. John is alive! ... He writes to ask what keeps us.'

Smeaton smiled broadly and held out his arms to her. She flung herself against him and then cried uncontrollably, burying her face in his waistcoat.

'Praise God, all is well then. It's not been easy. I thought that perhaps John's enemies had returned and found him here. But I see I need not have worried. Will you write him in reply?' Alice withdrew and drew a deep breath to calm herself.

'I shall! I am overflowing with joy and happiness. I want to send it forth in every direction.' She pressed his hand in both of hers.

'Like the light we shall exhibit here to the four points of the compass. What say you that we make passage home as soon as the *Neptune* can raise anchor?'

'That would be most agreeable to me, sir. I am not suited to the confines of the lighthouse. I wish more than anything to go home.'

'That's settled, then. We deserve to rest from our labours – I feel heavy with fatigue. We might then return refreshed for the first lighting. All is in place; the keepers are to come in tonight.'

The next day came and still the new keepers held off. Smeaton gave instructions that Henry Edwards and John Michell, his two remaining tinners, should instead take his place for the lighting and keeping of the light.

> *Those ... being persons upon whom I could depend: and who had seen and assisted in the lighting of the house in the day time, in the 1st instant, I could have no doubt but that ... my directions would be punctually observed, and the house lighted according to it's destination the 16th instant, in case I could not myself be present.*

It was time to leave. At four o'clock in the afternoon of Tuesday 9th October, Alice, Smeaton and the remaining company boarded the *Buss* for the last time, leaving the two tinners behind with the one keeper who had come out. A storm was blowing up and despite their haste to get under way it took an age to raise the chains. Link by link, the moorings and the bridle were heaved up. Smeaton was shown a link close to breaking.

'One more hard gale of wind would have broke us adrift, sir. 'Tis more than half worn through. The iron is bright from chafing 'pon the rock.'

'Lucky for us our time here is at an end. Why, the last time we pondered over chains we almost never got back,' said Smeaton, remembering the near-fatal night passage to Fowey almost three years earlier. At last the chains were raised.

'Take us home, William Smart!' Smeaton cried out to the master. Hoisting sail and with the wind at south-west driving them landward, they made Plymouth Harbour in less than three hours – a record for the *Neptune Buss*.

The tower was complete.

> *To the great joy and satisfaction of all concerned. And thus, after innumerable difficulties and dangers, was a happy period put to this undertaking, without loss of life or limb, to any one concerned in it.*

Plymouth Hoe, Tuesday 16th October 1759

As dusk approached, John Smeaton was heading up toward the Hoe to view the lighthouse. He was nervous and excited at the anticipated lighting of the light. Alice and John too were making their way through the crowds to gain a good vantage point. It seemed the whole town had come out for the occasion. The lighthouse stood fourteen miles away to the south-west, and although it could be seen by day in calm clear weather, a tiny finger upon the horizon, the light had always remained invisible by night. Nevertheless a good crowd had gathered, thronging about the obelisk. A stiff wind blew from the south-west. Poor weather had prevented Smeaton sailing back to the Rock, and so he had come here instead. Seeing John and Alice, he waved and beckoned them to come and look through the eyepiece of the telescope. The light fell away swiftly as dusk came on.

'Aha – tha's just in time, I think, for soon the light will be lit. I wonder whether it will be visible in these conditions to the naked eye.' Smeaton did nothing to disguise his excitement. He motioned for Alice to take his place at the telescope, and read aloud a passage from Henry Winstanley's account of the seas breaking over *his* building, the first Edystone Lighthouse:

> *finding in ye Winter the effects the sea had on this House and Burying the Lanthorn at times altho' more than sixty foot High. I raised it 40 foot higher than it was at first, and made it as it now appears, and yet the Sea in time of Storms flies in appearance, 100 foot above ye Vane and at times doth cover half the side of the House and the Lanthorn as if it were under Water.*

'I see now that he was not exaggerating. It is truly *sublime*, Mr Smeaton.'

'Is there any sign of the light, Alice?' he asked anxiously.

Alice watched the lighthouse disappear as another wave broke on the rock. It rose majestically in a column, shooting up and over the cove and blanking out the filigree lantern.

'No, I think not as yet, though I can hardly see for the seas breaking there! I never saw such a fearful sight. John, come and see.'

344

Alice stood away to let John Trehearne look into the eyepiece. Still they waited. Smeaton gestured towards the gathering crowds about them.

'Mr Jessop is hereabouts. I saw him earlier, just returned on the *Edystone Boat*. He saw the floating light leaving her moorings today. Said she sailed very close by the house and as she passed, her crew did raise their hats and give "three cheers". Jessop told of a hearty return from the balcony, where the keepers threw up their hats in reply.'

'I see something – the light, I think.' Trehearne stepped back to allow Smeaton to see for himself, but then the view closed as another wave broke and the tower was once more engulfed in a vast climbing column of white water.

'There it is! I see it!' he cried out loud. Turning to the others, etiquette forgotten, he embraced them both in turn and threw his arms aloft. A permanent light was clearly exhibited once more upon the Edystone.

'*Edystone resurgit.*' He breathed out the words and filled his lungs with the fresh night air. Above them the stars were coming out, and around them a strange murmuring grew louder. People were pointing toward a finger of light glimmering faintly but visibly on the horizon. It was the Edystone. For the first time, they could see the light here in Plymouth. It was a momentous feeling. Great cheers rose up from the people.

'I would say it's like a star of the fourth magnitude,' said Smeaton, enthralled by the sight.

''Tis a wondrous thing!' said Alice. 'Come, let us celebrate your achievements at my house this evening. I am growing cold stood here.' They packed away the telescope, as the crowd began to melt away. Soon it had dispersed and they followed, back across the Hoe. Smeaton dwelt upon the surprising phenomenon they had witnessed. The light, a mere twenty-four candles, was seen by all gathered there that evening, some fourteen miles from the source.

'A star of the fourth magnitude,' he repeated.

That evening they enjoyed a fine meal together. Verity had come up from the country and joined them at the dinner table.

'What a pity you arrived too late to come with us up to the Hoe, sister.'

'Yes, I should have loved to join you. It must have been very exciting, seeing so many there. I passed the crowds returning on my way here, and heard it said that the Edystone Light had never been seen in Plymouth before!' said Verity. She paused, then asked Smeaton a question.

'Tell me, sir, will you be taking your leave of us, now that the house is complete?' Verity spoke aloud what Alice and John were thinking.

'Yes, I have a family to go to. Anne has been very patient, but she must think at times that she is married to a reluctant husband who puts his work upon a rock at sea before his home and family.'

'I do not believe so, Mr Smeaton. Your wife sounds the most charming person. I'm sure she is both patient and understanding.'

'Thank you, Alice. I must say I am very much looking to the day when I will see her and the children again; drawing nearer now.'

Alice could not let him go without making an announcement.

'It's a pity you are to leave so soon, for John and I are to be married.'

'I know, my dear,' replied Smeaton, 'your father has asked for my recommendation. And I told him you shall not find a better man – nor a better sailor should you have need for one – and a true and loyal friend.'

Alice closed her eyes as Smeaton took her hand and kissed her on the cheek. He turned to John Trehearne to congratulate him. Verity swept across to her sister and gave her an affectionate embrace.

'It will be a lovely spring wedding, Mr Smeaton, at our family church. Will you come?'

'I should like nothing more, Verity, but I have other work to carry on, far from here.'

'And what will you do now?' Alice asked him.

'There's my proposed scheme to improve navigation upon the River Calder. I have been working upon designs for it for some time. Perhaps we will remove to Leeds to be near the work. I would welcome a scheme that is near at hand, both less remote and less physically demanding than the Edystone.'

'I dare say you will have any number of callings upon you by men up and down the country, once news of the lighthouse has reached them, sir.'

'Thank you, John, it will do no harm, I think. But what of you? Where will you go? Have you any plans?'

'I should like to think that we will settle at the Hall where I can try farming and assist in the affairs of Squire Vasey's estate.'

'Well, tha has chosen the pick of the crop in Alice,' said Smeaton.

Alice smiled. She was very happy – and even a little embarrassed – by Mr Smeaton's obvious affection for her. He was a handsome man and such an accomplished, clever fellow. His humility and caring took her by surprise. 'It's just as well that he is married,' she thought, 'or else I might be torn between the two of them, heaven forbid!'

'This is excellent news, John. Let us drink to a happy future ahead of you, and to us all.' Smeaton took up his glass and toasted them. 'Here's to us and to all who served upon the Edystone – *in salutem omnium.*'

The three men in the lighthouse awaited the approaching yawl. They looked down from the balcony as the yawl rowed into the landing place, and Smeaton, Jessop and another man climbed the steps to reach the entry. Inside, John Michell, the tinner who had stood in for the third light-keeper, busied himself preparing tea on the hot stove for the visitors.

As they came up into the living room, Smeaton immediately enquired of them, 'How fare you all?'

He was pleased to hear 'All well'.

He and Jessop had brought with them John Hatherley, the new keeper who was to relieve Michell. Over tea, Henry Edwards gave a detailed account of how they had weathered the storm, carried out their duties and lit the light for the first time, and how the candles burned steadily despite the raging gale outside.

'The broken seas were passing in great quantities over the ball itself, sirs.' Edwards paused to let his words sink in, and raised his finger aloft. He then pointed to the shutters. 'We packed oakum caulking in around the port shutters to windward.'

'Go on,' Smeaton urged him.

'It was a tremendous roaring and soaking we had all night, but here inside stayed both warm and dry throughout.'

'Is there any damage, have you found anything broken?' he enquired of Edwards.

'We've a few minor remedies, making good and such like, but nothing untoward to attend to.'

'We've brought thee the last of the coal, water and stores for winter provisions.' The store was intended to last six months. Smeaton would bring to an end the 'bad old days' and the shocking reports of keepers being reduced to eating the candles, when their supplies were exhausted. He explained the system put in place.

'You are to provide for yourselves as ye wish, the *Edystone Boat* being at your service, but this store of "sea provisions" provided by the Proprietors is for use in emergencies. At this season's end, you will only be accountable for what has been taken out.'

The men listened attentively. The daylight was fast fading, and through the small square sash in the western quarter of the room they saw the sun set. The timepiece chimed. It was time to light the candles. The new man went up into the lantern with Edwards, and Smeaton and Jessop bade them farewell. It was time for them to return if they were to make Plymouth by midnight. Smeaton took a last lingering look up through the vault and saw candlelight casting tall shadows high inside the cupola ceiling. Then he went down the ladders and out onto the rock, where the *Edystone Boat* awaited them for the final journey home.

Within a few days, the workyard in Millbay was cleared, equipment dismantled, and the remaining stores and equipment sold off or decommissioned. Mr Harrison's ledgers and accounts were bound up and dispatched to London, completing more than three years' work. Once the last of the men remaining in the Service had been paid off, Mr Harrison closed the door of his office for the last time. He saw the yawl arriving at the wooden pier, and made his way down to bid them farewell. Smeaton climbed up from the boat, insisting that he must visit him in London, 'on account of a new venture that may interest you.'

'I will, sir. I promise to call upon you once you are returned to town.'

'Very good, Harrison. Take care and God speed you on your way.' Seeing Harrison standing alone in the empty yard, he knew they were free to cast off and leave the distant tower in the hands of its new inhabitants, the light-keepers.

'Thank God it has all ended well, Mr Harrison! Would you have William Smart and the *Edystone Boat* carry you to Exeter?'

'Thank you for the offer, sir, but no! I have a place on the mail coach express. I prefer to go by dry land – I really am no good on water.'

They shook hands, and Smeaton watched him head off with a bag in each hand in the direction of the road toward Stonehouse.

That evening Smeaton was the guest of Mr Cookworthy in the house in Notte Street, where a surprise dinner party was given in his honour. The Quaker had taken to this young man from the north and wanted to ensure that his achievement was celebrated in the town. His guests that evening came from all over Plymouth. William Cookworthy had proved himself a great friend and the Cookworthy household had become Smeaton's 'Plymouth family'. He was, furthermore, a brilliant conversationalist and a great if somewhat eccentric wit. Laughter and applause followed and could be heard in the street outside the impressive mansion house. That evening they enjoyed a meal that was simple and yet delicious, the cook serving them pigeon pie. John Smeaton savoured the satisfyingly plain Quaker fare that had sustained him after many a soaking-wet return from the Edystone.

Austhorpe Lodge, October 1792

'I see you make no reference to the "loss" of Mr Trehearne in your book, Mr Smeaton,' said Alice.

'Indeed not, for in my mind this would only draw attention to our story. I thought it best not to.'

'And my disappearance remains a mystery to this day,' Squire Trehearne concluded. 'When Richardson's company returned, there were some, I learnt, who swore they could see a man swimming away in the water.'

'There you have it, William, how it was that we concealed a secret within the stones. Of course, being concerned that the tower should have no point of weakness, I arranged with your father to fill the hiding-place with the two missing stones (by inserting them in cut portions) as soon as possible afterward.'

350

The old man shook William Jessop's hand, and William suddenly felt this was to be their last meeting.

'God be with you, William.'

'And you, sir.' William embraced his guardian. He kissed Mary Smeaton on the cheek and embraced her affectionately. It was time for his departure. The groom led his horse from the stable out into the courtyard.

'What became of the Lieutenant?' William asked Alice while he adjusted the stirrups of his saddle.

'The ship's company was so much improved in morale that they signed a petition against him, and presented it to the Port Admiral to deal with him as he saw fit. He left Plymouth soon after and was sent out to the West Indies. The commission absolved both my former husband, Robert Appleford, and Mr Trehearne of any guilt.'

William shook the squire's hand, then climbed up into the saddle.

'As for my father, he kept your secret to the end. We never had any knowledge of it – yet I remember how he would sit and keep us amused for hours with stories of building the Edystone.'

'Well, I dare say there was many a tale he could tell to keep a young lad enthralled, without touching upon my own,' the squire answered.

'But I think yours has been the most extraordinary, Mr Trehearne.'

'And there is not a day when I fail to remind myself of it. But it's time for you to make your way now – fare thee well, William. Come to see us when you are next in Devonshire.'

'I will.' William Jessop urged his horse to lead on and set off toward the lodge gate and out onto the road to Leeds. They watched him turn into the road beyond the gate and disappear from view.

Later that day, the elderly John Smeaton walked with the Trehearnes on a tour of the flower garden. The afternoon sun sent golden rays slanting across the lawns and through the trees, soaking into the south and west walls of the house. Smeaton's other tower, his 'sanctum', stood bathed in a light as rich as the amber varnish of the golden ball upon the Edystone. They walked in the late-autumn sunshine, along stone-flagged paths through the flower garden. Trehearne appreciated how, in old age, the engineer retained his air of calm dignity, and his

351

benevolence towards him. Theirs was a friendship at the deepest level.

When they went back indoors, Smeaton's manservant was returning the volume of the *Narrative* to its place on the study table. He bowed and left the room. Smeaton picked up a letter from the table that he had kept all these years and he read a little.

'Hmm, a pity. I left this out deliberately to show William.'

'What is it, Father?' asked Mary.

'A letter from Dr Mudge, dated 15th January 1762. After Josias's death Richardson was appointed Surveyor for the Edystone, but he was never a writer and so, if there was need of a communication, Dr Mudge wrote to me on his behalf. Needless to say, I did not receive written news as a matter of course, as I had done before from Josias. You can imagine my concern when it arrived here that winter. Had some tragedy occurred?'

'But by then the lighthouse had proved itself durable and completely safe, had it not?' said Mary.

'Of course, lass, but there were still those who held doggedly to the opinion that *nothing but Wood could resist the sea upon the Edystone.*'

'It's as if they wanted to see it fall, just to say "I told thee"!'

'Aye. They insisted that if such a storm as destroyed Winstanley's lighthouse should happen again, mine must share the same fate.'

He steadied his hand and passed the letter over to Mary. It told of the terrifying storm that had swept the coast early in the new year of 1762. She read aloud:

> I could not but feel the utmost anxiety for the fate of the Edystone: and I believe poor Richardson was not a little uneasy, – several times in the day, I swept with my telescope from the Garrison, as near as I could imagine the line of the horizon; but it was so extremely black, fretful and hazy, that nothing could be seen; and I was obliged to go to bed that night, with a mortifying uncertainty. But the next morning early I had the great joy to see, that the Gilded Ball had triumphed over the fury of the Storm.

The old man's eyes twinkled and he went on.

'One of those who had been used to predicting its downfall said afterward "if the Edystone Lighthouse is now standing, it will stand till the day of Judgement".'

The year was nearly over, and it would soon be November. Some days after the departure of William Jessop, Squire Trehearne and his wife waved a last goodbye to the elderly man who stood at the door of Austhorpe Lodge in the early-morning sunshine. They agreed that the journey had been worth the effort to see their esteemed friend once more, and perhaps for the last time. John Trehearne felt it was time to look forward.

'You know, we must call upon Verity one day soon, when we are home. Plymouth is not too far by comparison.'

'Yes, we will. But not before we have made sure that all has gone well with the apple harvest,' Alice replied.

'Indeed, not before then.'

The old man sat in his garden. It was going to be another fine day. He closed his eyes and listened and felt himself drifting ... The voices of Mary and the servants, and the steady fall of Waddington's hammer, grew faint. He remembered everything. In his mind's eye he was once again far away from the house and his 'sanctum'. He fancied he could see the tower on the Edystone Rock, fourteen miles out to sea. It was time to snuff the candles. The great iron chandelier came silently down, and then rose effortlessly back, up into the lantern. He saw a light ahead of him, dispelling the dark. The light of twenty-four candles shone forth from within the glass and iron octagon, casting a glow upon the troubled waters down below. It grew stronger, but this time it was not a phenomenon that he could in any way explain. It was like looking at the stars and wondering what lay beyond. The light was so intense ...

John Smeaton: a biographical note

John Smeaton was born on 8th June 1724 at Austhorpe in the village of Whitkirk, a small country hamlet on the outskirts of Leeds. His father was a successful attorney and John grew up in comfortable circumstances and received a sound education at the local grammar school in the nearby town.

From his early years he displayed an aptitude for mechanical pursuits, and later spent hours at work in his workshop developing hands-on skills in metalworking, casting and forging, making his own tools and designs. When a gang of men arrived to construct a steam-powered water pump in the nearby coalmines, he studied their work and set about building his own, which he set to work before the colliery engine was completed. So successful was his own pump that it drained his father's fish pond – killing the fish, much to his father's annoyance.

His father expected him to follow him in the legal profession and at sixteen he began his training to be a lawyer. But it was no use. Whilst studying in London he wrote to his father, who reluctantly agreed to finance his starting up as a mathematical instrument maker. At the age of seventeen he had met a brilliant if eccentric clock maker, Henry Hindley, in York, and this influenced his decision to pursue his new career. Smeaton returned home but following a love affair and proposal of marriage to a young lady in Leeds, his disapproving parents threatened to disinherit him and the affair ended with his return to London in 1748, where he started a small instrument workshop.

Now in his mid-twenties, Smeaton engaged on a number of new scientific appliances, including a vacuum pump and a mechanical ship's log (a water turbine). He soon began to extend his studies into the design of watermills and canals, and regularly attended the meetings of the Royal Society. Elected a Fellow of the Society in 1753, he contributed several papers to the Society's *Transactions* and read a paper on 'the Natural Power of Wind and Water Mills' in 1754, for which he received their Gold Medal. That same year he went on a tour of the Low Countries to further his interest and understanding of the engineering of canals and harbours.

Then came his great challenge. Late in 1755 the wooden lighthouse upon the Eddystone rock was completely destroyed by a fire that had ignited and taken hold in the lantern. Robert Weston, the principal shareholder, appealed to the President of the Royal Society to recommend 'a man of genius' to undertake the task of rebuilding the house. Lord Macclesfield thought of Smeaton, who was told in a letter that 'thou art the man'.

During the following three years Smeaton and his men of the 'Edystone service' would survive storms and near-shipwreck, press-ganging and innumerable perils in completing the tower. Smeaton led the way, following his maxim 'to proceed until there is something to stop us'. He made the fourteen-mile sea-passage to the rock many times, and from his early observations and survey soon decided that he should build a tower of stone. This was unheard of, but ignoring the prevailing criticism he set about designing a structure that would resist the tremendous and immeasurable force of the sea, using an ingenious method of interlocking stonework, in combination with a hard-setting 'water cement' previously unknown. His proposals were meticulously presented and found acceptable by the Eddystone Proprietors and the Elder Brethren of Trinity House.

It was in the midst of his designing and making preparations to begin the construction work at sea that Smeaton returned briefly to London. There he married Anne Jenkinson in 1756, but he was to spend the greater part of the next three years away in Plymouth supervising the work.

After the completion of the tower in 1759 Smeaton returned to his native Yorkshire. On inheriting the family estate in 1758 he made Austhorpe his family home and professional headquarters. The first person to call himself a 'civil engineer', he consulted on a wide range of projects throughout the length and breadth of the country and established himself as an engineer of outstanding ability.

In 1771 Smeaton became a co-founder of the Institute of Civil Engineers, a meeting place where members of the new profession could gather to discuss informally their common interests. Following his death in 1792, the society was renamed the Smeatonian Society of Civil Engineers in his memory, and from it in 1818 would emerge the Institution of Civil Engineers.

But it was the Eddystone Lighthouse for which he was best remembered. In later years he turned to writing following a bout of illness in 1783. This, and the death of his wife Anne, prevented him from accepting any further commissions. Thirty years of intense industry had taken its toll, and he decided that he would publish a textbook of engineering. He began by writing his account of building the Eddystone Lighthouse.

The *Narrative of the Building and a Description of the Construction of the Edystone Lighthouse with Stone* took him several years to complete. He said he found it more arduous than the task of building the lighthouse itself. At length, the book was published in 1791. After his death, Smeaton's other written works, his manuscript papers and reports were published by the Society of Civil Engineers. The Royal Society produced a volume of his papers, which appeared originally in the *Philosophical Transactions*.

In his later years there were many who clamoured for Smeaton's services. To discourage them and buy time for his other interests, he raised his fees to 50 guineas a week. He had once been courted by a Russian princess to work abroad for vast sums, but instead chose to remain at home. This approach allowed him to continue his interests in other fields of science, particularly astronomy. Even so, his industry was staggering, considering the volume of consultancies he was engaged upon and the sheer difficulties of travelling in the latter half of the eighteenth century.

John Smeaton died at Austhorpe on 28th October 1792.

With his passing came the end of an era. A new generation of engineers was emerging. These were no longer self-educated pioneers who studied engineering from first principles in a combined philosophical and scientific approach. They were the specialists now required in the increasing pace of industrial development to build the new canals, and later the railways.

However, it was Smeaton's interest in scientific method and the articulate lucidity of his written work that distinguished him from his engineering contemporaries, and these qualities lay at the very foundation of the engineering profession. A great and lasting testament to him was made by James Watt, who called him 'Father Smeaton' and said that 'Smeaton's precepts and his example have made engineers of us all'.

Smeaton's Tower, 1756–2005

1756 Smeaton is commissioned to build a new lighthouse on the Eddystone Rock.

1759 Smeaton's lighthouse is completed. A light is first exhibited on 16th October (20–67 candlepower).

1807 Captain Lovett's lease, taken out in 1705, expires and ownership of the Eddystone Light reverts to Trinity House.

1810 The candlelit source is replaced by new state-of-the-art illumination with oil-fired catoptric reflectors (1,000 candlepower).

1818 A report by Robert Stevenson, the Scottish lighthouse engineer, expresses concern that the House Rock and the cave beneath the tower are a potential hazard to the building's continued safety.

1838 Further modifications and upgrading of the tower structure. The interior is strengthened with iron straps and ties built in to the stonework extending down through the rooms. Outside, Smeaton's curved cornice is cut away in an effort to reduce the shock of waves striking the column.

1845 The original iron lantern is replaced with a larger bronze version, containing a trimming gallery. The light source is again modified, now to a French-designed (Fresnel) revolving dioptric lens (3,216 candlepower).

1859 Centenary celebrations include the reproduction of the lighthouse alongside 'Britannia' on pennies minted in 1860.

1861 The exterior of the tower is painted for the first time, all in white, following parliamentary legislation concerning sea marks.(Subsequently painted in the red and white banded livery in1875.)

1877 A decision is taken to replace Smeaton's Tower with a new (fourth) Eddystone Lighthouse. This follows increasing concern that the cave in the rock beneath the lighthouse is undermining the tower's stability.

1878 Building of the new lighthouse, designed by James Douglass, starts with the preparation of the chosen site, a bed of gneiss rock which is only exposed at low water, forty metres south-east from the House Rock on which Smeaton's Tower stands.

1879 The Duke of Edinburgh lays the foundation stone in a ceremony on 19th June.

1882 Douglass's lighthouse is completed. It is more than 150 feet high from the rock bed, almost twice as tall as Smeaton's Tower.

1882 Smeaton's Tower is discontinued, becoming dark on 3rd February. The tower is decommissioned and dismantled. The first twenty-four courses (Smeaton's 'solid') are left in place on the rock. Smeaton's Tower is carefully dismantled, and returned to Plymouth.

1884 Smeaton's Tower is rebuilt on Plymouth Hoe on a new replica base, on the site of Drake's beacon, paid for with funds raised by public subscription. The tower becomes a public attraction. However, the rebuilt structure lacks the integrity of Smeaton's original construction. Voids remain where the internal joggle stones and weather bars have been omitted in the reconstruction. This, and some haphazard replacement of loose iron cramps, creates the possibility of damp and damage occurring inside the walls.

1999 Restoration of the tower begins.

2001 Restoration completed for re-opening to the public at Easter.

Notes on the restoration, 1999–2001

Following investigatory work, the tower was cocooned within a surrounding scaffolding giving access to the exterior surfaces. The hard non-porous Portland cement used in the tower's nineteenth-century reconstruction was cut out of all the internal and external stone joints to a depth of 2 inches (5 cm). The modern exterior and interior paint finishes were removed by a non-abrasive steam method. Older oil paints on the interior surfaces were lifted off by poulticing. Historic paints, graffiti and painted signs were protected and conserved. Stone arrises originally damaged in the dismantling and re-erection, and subsequently filled with Portland cement patches, were repaired using a combination of stone-dust mortar mixes. The stonework was repointed with a breathing hydraulic-lime mortar mix, to encourage the interior to dry out.

The Smeaton coved cornice profile was reinstated, along with a new weathering of leadwork to the balcony based upon Smeaton's original. The balcony railings were dismantled and adapted to modern safety regulations without the need for previous unsightly mesh cladding. The lantern fabric in bronze was stripped and repainted in traditional lead paint (being beyond the reach of children). The golden ball vent and vane was repaired and re-gilded in layers of burnished gold leaf. Smeaton's original features – the outer doors and shutters – were reinstated, the windows replaced with replica nineteenth-century four-pane wooden sashes.

Internally a core-drilled duct allowed modern electrical power and services to be routed discreetly up the tower. A replica of Smeaton's chandelier was installed within the lantern (though reduced in size to fit within the nineteenth-century trimming gallery). The house was part-furnished with replica nineteenth-century furniture, including the storeroom dresser cupboard, a second box bed in the bedroom and a stove and lead-lined sink in the kitchen. (The restricted size for public access has limited the extent of furnishing and equipping.) Interiors were painted in coloured limewashes, assuming this to be most likely in the years spent on the rock.

Externally the tower was repainted (though the option was presented to keep the exterior in natural stone) using Keim paint in red and white banding using tones that closely matched the lead white and red oxide oil paint colours of the nineteenth century.

Glossary

arris: the sharp tooled edge of a finished masonry block

baluster / balustrade: vertical railings between a handrail and floor to provide guarding

beat (*nautical*): to sail to windward; to keep close-hauled on a wind

bolster: a bricklayer's or mason's wide chisel

chase: a groove or channel sunk into the surface of a stone

corona: Smeaton's name for the lighthouse's coved cornice at the top of the column

cupola: a small roof dome

cutter: a small boat belonging to a man o' war; sloop-rigged, with a deep keel

davit: a hoist for raising the ship's anchor or moorings

dovetail: a carpentry joint of interlocking fan-shaped tenons, employed by Smeaton in the shape of the stones to lock them together

fetch (*nautical*): to reach an objective to windward without having to tack

grout: slurry mix of wet mortar to pour into and fill small joints and voids in masonry walls

gunwale: the rail or upper edge of a ship's sides

header: a brick or stone laid lengthways across or into a wall or pavement to bond the stones together

heel (*nautical*): to list or lean over

joggle: small stone used to key together larger blocks; Smeaton used cubes of Plymouth marble set in pockets in the larger stones

jumper: a tool for hand-drilling holes in stone

kettle: a large iron cauldron

lantern: the glazed structure at the top of the lighthouse containing the light source

363

lapped / half-lapped: a timber joint, where two pieces of the same cross-section are notched to half the depth to fit flush together, forming a cross

league: a measurement of distance in common use in Smeaton's time; a league measures approximately three land miles

lewis: a hoisting mechanism using pincers or a bar fitted to corresponding holes in the stone; self-tightening when raised

mile: one nautical mile = 1.152 statute (land) miles; the distance from Plymouth to the Eddystone is fourteen land miles (twelve nautical miles)

mitre: an angled joint; here between metal sheets of similar thickness

moorstone: granite, referred to colloquially as *moorstone* by the inhabitants of Devon and Cornwall in Smeaton's time

mortise: the hole cut into stone or timber to receive a projecting tenon

murette: the octagonal wall supporting the lighthouse lantern

ogee: an S-shaped profile, having a double curvature

painter: a small boat's mooring rope attached to the bow

pennant: a long narrow flag flown from ships' masts

pewter: an amalgam of 'block tin' and lead, used for fixing the iron crooks of the door and window shutter hinges into the stone jambs of the tower

plug stone: the rectangular stone set at the beginning of each new course, in the centre of the lighthouse *solid*; the stones were made of Plymouth marble, and formed a continuous column around which the hollow centre stones of each course fitted

Portland stone: a durable white limestone used in building, especially popular during and since the eighteenth century; sourced from quarries on the Isle of Portland, or Portland Bill, in Dorset

press gang: gangs of naval ratings led by an officer to *impress* or forcibly induct civilian men into the Royal Navy

puddling: kneading raw clay to a workable, plastic and watertight consistency

purchase block: the massive tackle block designed by Smeaton for lifting the heaviest stones

puzzolana / pozzuolana (referred to as *puzzolan* and *puzzylan*): volcanic rock found at Civita Vecchia in Italy, employed by the Romans in making cement and, for the first time by Smeaton, mixed with lime to make *water cement*; this was a hydraulic lime mortar capable of setting in sea-washed conditions and increasing to the hardness and consistency of the surrounding stone (or modern concrete made from Portland cement).

Quaker: a member of the Society of Friends, a non-conformist religious group well established throughout the West Country

quoin: a large stone set in the corner of a wall

scappel: an historic term meaning to rough-cut masonry to an approximate size and shape, for finishing afterward

scarf: a carpentry joint that joins the ends of two timbers to make one continuous member; *hook scarfed* is the term Smeaton uses for an intricate scarf joint in the stones around the stairwell to lock them together in a continuous ring

sconce: an ornamental candlestick fixed to wall

shears (shear-legs): the hoisting apparatus consisting of two inclined wooden masts forming an A frame, with pulley blocks at the apex and the legs pin-jointed at the foot; used to lift the stone blocks, and similar to others found in dockyards in the eighteenth century

sheet (*nautical*): a rope used to control the shape of a sail

shroud (*nautical*): stay-ropes from the masthead to the ship's sides

sloop: a sailing vessel, rigged with a single mast, fixed bowsprit and jibbed stay

snatch block: the pulley block fixed to the rock between the shears and windlass, as part of the winding apparatus for the shears

spall: to break off small pieces of stone, causing damage to the facing surfaces in masonry work, either by natural weathering (frost action) or by striking a blow

streake/strake: lines of planking on a wooden ship's sides (the modern spelling is *strake*; the eighteenth-century spelling may derive from the appearance of lines or stripes, sometimes painted in contrasting colours)

stretcher: a brick or stone laid lengthways

tack (*nautical*): to turn a boat (generally when sailing to windward) by bringing the bow through the wind

tenon / loose tenon: a projection on a timber that is inserted into a mortise, to join two pieces together, or a loose block connecting two mortised or grooved timbers; Smeaton's interlocking masonry employs joints in stone analogous to those used in traditional carpentry

theodolite: a surveying instrument for measuring angles and levels from a stationary point; invented in the sixteenth century, and an essential surveying tool in the eighteenth; Smeaton based his 'definitor' for mapping the rock on Alberti's description of instruments used by renaissance sculptors to measure their work

tinner: a Cornish labourer, commonly known as *tinners* due to their common employment in tin-mining

trenail: an oak needle or nail, commonly used in eighteenth-century ship construction. tapered, square in section and about 24 inches in length; Smeaton used these, driven into preformed holes, to mechanically fix the freshly laid stones to the course beneath

triangle: Smeaton's tripod apparatus for hoisting and setting the stones

windlass: a hand–operated winch for hoisting the stones

Worming: Smeaton's description for the practice of binding rope cables with a small diameter rope to form a flexible protective sheathing

yawl: a small wooden vessel or ship's boat that can be rowed or sailed; the Eddystone yawls designed by Josias Jessop were single-masted and built to a unique design, having a blunt D-shaped bow, which improved their stability and seaworthiness in the 'rough hollow seas' about the Eddystone reef

366

Bibliography

John Smeaton. *A Narrative of the Building and a Description of the Construction of the Edystone Lighthouse with Stone.* G. Nicol, London, 1791.

Edwin Mitchell. John Smeaton: thou art the man. *Leeds and West Riding Topic,* September 1974.

Mike Palmer. *Eddystone: the Finger of Light.* 2nd edition. Seafarer Books, Rendlesham, 2005.

N. A. M. Rodger. *The Wooden World : an Anatomy of the Georgian Navy.* Collins, London, 1986.

Jason Semmens. *Eddystone: 300 years.* Cornwall, 1998.

Samuel Smiles. *Lives of the Engineers. Vol. 2. Harbours, lighthouses and bridges; Smeaton, Rennie.* John Murray, London, 1874.

Trevor Turner. John Smeaton FRS. *Endeavour,* vol. 33, January 1974. ICI publication.

Epilogue

Frans Nicholas

This book tells the human story of a remarkable building. Even today, rising safely from the green sward of Plymouth Hoe, Smeaton's Tower will generously confide something of its salt-stained story to any man or woman willing to listen imaginatively to muffled sea sounds and past voices, welling up within round, once wave-washed walls.

This book, however, is not only informed in full measure by the spirit of place that abides in the tower today, but also by the fuller story that the tower graciously revealed when we came to repair it: one which so bore out the veracity and accuracy of Smeaton's *Narrative*, that a sea-girt patch of the eighteenth century became suddenly so clearly illuminated, that fiction and fact relating to it could be robustly woven together with confidence.

Christopher Severn came to know this lighthouse intimately, and the story its repair revealed, while working for our architectural practice on the conservation of the tower. His was the intimate knowledge of one who skilfully envisaged and drew many parts of it, basing his drawings largely on those of its remarkable designer: indeed, a large part of our initial work consisted of poring over Smeaton's consummate drawings and exemplary prose, to understand the full significance of what we were repairing. No doubt Chris, like myself, was exposed to the tower's presence in a more personal and emotive way when, at the end of those long days we would find ourselves alone in the tower when everyone else had gone, still measuring and deducing. Then, with an architect's ability to imagine away the institutional finishes the tower by then carried, from a century of public visiting through turnstiles, we could, if we let go, feel ourselves out at sea.

Our practice became connected with the tower at the invitation of Plymouth City Council's Museum Service, at first by writing a Conservation Plan for them. I had become involved with lighthouse conservation some ten years earlier, and the practice had, by then, already surveyed several historic lighthouses for the National Trust.

(Since then, we have also worked as conservation architects for Trinity House Lighthouse Service.) We were then instrumental in English Heritage's decision to review the Smeaton's Tower grading, ending with it being re-graded from Grade II* to Grade I. This was important to Plymouth later obtaining Historic Building Grant and Heritage Lottery Fund Grant to repair and re-present the tower: work in which the author of this book played a significant role.

The conservation problems of the tower, when we first encountered it, were mostly the legacy of its rebuilding on the Hoe in 1884, when Smeaton's pioneering interlocking of masonry was not fully recreated. A century had then passed with it as a tourist attraction, with a presentation that was becoming increasingly tired and anecdotal, and less and less authentic to its time on the rock. A full account of these problems must await publication elsewhere. Some remain ongoing, for good conservation seeks the least drastic intervention wherever possible to buy more time, and several issues await the conclusion of further monitoring over the years to come.

One thing, however, must be explained to the reader who visits the tower, after having read the book. They will wonder why we have not restored it fully to Smeaton's original design, especially as we now know that it so accurately bears out his *Narrative*. They will, if they know something of conservation issues, want to say 'we understand caution when a lack of knowledge means that any restoration must be conjectural (with the implicit risk that it may then be wrong): but here Smeaton has offered, on a plate, the information you need for an almost perfect restoration of his design.'

There are a number of reasons why, after considerable debate between ourselves, Plymouth's museum service and conservation officers, and English Heritage, the tower was conserved, not to the 1750s, but to a date in the mid 1870s: a date just after the tower was first painted in red and white stripes; just before the cornice was cut back; and not many years before the tower was replaced by the present, larger Eddystone Lighthouse, and subsequently partially dismantled and rebuilt on the Hoe.

Firstly, the greatest significance of Smeaton's Eddystone lighthouse, from an international pharological perspective, is that it was the world's first truly successful wave-washed tower, pioneering the principle of interlocking masonry that was to be the basis for successfully constructing most of the world's great lighthouses of later years. Truly successful, because it stood the test of time, and was in useful service for 125 years.

Secondly, these years spanned a crucial period in the rapidly developing technology of navigation light propagation, and changes in light generation meant adaptations to the building itself: adaptations that, to use William Morris's phrase, 'left history in the gap, and (were) alive with the spirit of the deeds done midst its fashioning'. The greatest alteration, perhaps, is the installation of the present bronze lantern, which only dates from the 1840s, and replaced Smeaton's. But this lantern is now itself over a 150 years old, and its design, even at that early date, paid homage to Smeaton, copying many of the features of the original, while offering more space in which to accommodate a state-of-the-art optic of that time. This lantern thus has gained a historic significance of its own, and one must hesitate before considering jettisoning it to make way for a mere replica of Smeaton's lantern, even if it can be an exact copy. A counter-argument can also be mounted: if the original design intentions of Smeaton are, in the end, the paramount thing to celebrate, then they are already so well documented and presented in his *Narrative*, that the creation of a full-sized replica to achieve this is not strictly necessary.

Finally, we cannot ignore the later history that brought the top two thirds of the tower to the Hoe. The author of this book, in particular, mourned the difficult decision made to repaint the bare granite tower again after the paint had been removed, a decision that moved the outward presentation of the Tower, at a stroke, from Smeaton, the eighteenth century, and an age of sail, to the late nineteenth, and the age of steamships. But, by 1884, the very legend of the tower had begat yet more history, and it was rebuilt (in the painted form by which it was universally known and loved by that time) in an extraordinary gesture by proud Plymothians: and proud of it they remain today, for its silhouette and striped form is now a symbol, and unofficial logo, of a great city.

We did, nevertheless, do so much to reinstate Smeaton's design within the conservation discipline we had set ourselves: in particular, we recreated much of its original silhouette by re-constructing the elegant shape of Smeaton's lead-covered cornice, which had, in its last years on the Rock, been cut back to reduce the tower's resistance to the sea. We also added back Smeaton's shutters (and had to invent a way of closing them from within, one of the few details where the *Narrative* was silent). We even broke away from the agreed conservation date of the mid 1870s once, to accurately rebuild Smeaton's chandelier, including reintroducing the ingenious system of pulleys that allowed the light-keeper to pull down first one ring, then the other, balanced against each other, to light the twenty-four candles.

If you want to visualise, even more completely, Smeaton's Tower as it would have been in its early years, then you should look to Smeaton's *Narrative*; then to the tower itself as it stands today; and then you could do no better than turn to this book, and convincingly people a scene of great human endeavour you will by then have illuminated before you.

Finally, if you want to begin to take part in this story yourself, you could always take your chances, and make your way steadfastly out to sea for fourteen miles, where the lowest third of the third Eddystone Lighthouse by John Smeaton still stands untouched: still defying the sea, still not toppled by the cave in the Rock.

The author

Christopher Severn was born in North Wales in 1959, but moved to Oxfordshire at the age of seven, where he spent much of his childhood. Due to his father's serving in the RAF, the family travelled overseas to Holland and Germany. On returning to England he gained a degree in architecture and then a postgraduate diploma at the Architectural Association. Here, he tutored for some years whilst working in London architectural practices, returning to Wales in 1989.

He met and married his wife in Pembrokeshire, where they now live with their two daughters aged nine and twelve, two Staffordshire bull terriers, and other assorted small animals in an equally small cottage.

Christopher first became involved with Smeaton's Tower in 1999 when he began work on the proposed conservation of the Lighthouse with Frans Nicholas Architects. The tower, which stands today on Plymouth Hoe, is a Grade 1 listed monument. Seeing the stones stripped of their paintwork, and reading Smeaton's diaries and *Narrative*, brought the remarkable story of the lighthouse's construction at sea to life. He was intrigued and resolved to write this book, bringing to light the story of Smeaton's Tower for a new and wider audience.

His other interests include traditional field archery, gardening, divining and dowsing, reiki healing, investigating crop circles and playing banjo.